CONTEMPORARY
BUDDHIST ETHICS

General Editors:
Charles S. Prebish and Damien Keown

The Curzon Critical Studies in Buddhism Series is a comprehensive study of the Buddhist tradition. The series explores this complex and extensive tradition from a variety of perspectives, using a range of different methodologies.

The Series is diverse in its focus, including historical studies, textual translations and commentaries, sociological investigations, bibliographic studies, and considerations of religious practice as an expression of Buddhism's integral religiosity. It also presents materials on modern intellectual historical studies, including the role of Buddhist thought and scholarship in a contemporary, critical context and in the light of current social issues. The series is expansive and imaginative in scope, spanning more than two and a half millennia of Buddhist history. It is receptive to all research works that inform and advance our knowledge and understanding of the Buddhist tradition. The series maintains the highest standards of scholarship and promotes the application of innovative methodologies and research methods.

CONTEMPORARY BUDDHIST ETHICS

Edited by

Damien Keown

CURZON

First Published in 2000
by Curzon Press
Richmond, Surrey
http://www.curzonpress.co.uk

Editorial Matter © 2000 Damien Keown
Typeset in Sabon by LaserScript Ltd, Mitcham, Surrey
Printed and bound in Great Britain by
TJ International, Padstow, Cornwall

British Library Cataloguing in Publication Data
A catalogue record of this book is available from the British Library

Library of Congress Cataloguing in Publication Data
A catalogue record for this book has been requested

ISBN 0–7007–1278–X (Hbk)
ISBN 0–7007–1313–1 (Pbk)

For Silvia

Contents

Acknowledgements

Two of the chapters in this book have been published before. The first chapter, 'Buddhism and the Virtues' by James Whitehill, was first published electronically in the *Journal of Buddhist Ethics*, volume 1 1994:1-22. The third chapter, by the editor, first appeared under the title 'Are there "Human Rights" in Buddhism?' also in the *Journal of Buddhist Ethics*, volume 2 1995:3-27, and subsequently in *Buddhism and Human Rights* edited by Damien V. Keown, Charles S. Prebish, and Wayne R. Husted (Curzon Press, 1995). Portions of chapter two by Charles Prebish appeared earlier in 'Text and Tradition in the Study of Buddhist Ethics,' *Pacific World*, NS 9 1993:49-68. The editor is grateful for the permission of the respective publishers to reproduce this material here. Thanks are also due to Curzon Press for the careful and speedy production of the volume.

Contributors

James Whitehill is a Professor of Religion at Stephens College in Columbia, Missouri. He currently chairs the Program in Philosophy, Law and Rhetoric, while also directing Japan Programs. A founder and director of the Columbia Zen Center, he has published articles on Buddhist ethics and related subjects over the years. His most recent article, 'My Dharma Teacher Died Too Soon,' is a meditation on his late wife, Hiroko, and on her shaping of their marriage as a 'Buddha field' in which he was her student.

Charles Prebish is Professor of Religious Studies at the Pennsylvania State University. He is the author of eleven books and more than fifty articles and chapters. Most recently he has published *Luminous Passage: The Practice and Study of Buddhism in America* (1999), *The Faces of Buddhism in America* (1998, co-edited with Kenneth Tanaka), and *A Survey of Vinaya Literature* (1994). He is a founding co-editor of the *Journal of Buddhist Ethics* and in 1997-98 was Rockefeller Fellow at the University of Toronto.

Damien Keown is Reader in Buddhism at Goldsmiths College, University of London. He has published widely on Buddhist ethics and is the author of *The Nature of Buddhist Ethics* (1992) and *Buddhism and Bioethics* (1996), and the editor of *Buddhism and Abortion* (1999). He is a founding co-editor of the *Journal of Buddhist Ethics*.

Paul Waldau is a faculty member at Tufts University School of Veterinary Medicine, where he teaches ethics and works with graduate students in the Center for Animals and Public Policy. He is the author of the forthcoming book *The Specter of Speciesism: Early Christian and Buddhist Views of Animals* (Scholars Press, 1999-2000), and co-editor of the forthcoming *A Communion of Subjects: Religion and Animals*, the edited papers of the

May 1999 conference 'Religion and Animals' at Harvard University for which he was the principal organizer. His course 'Religion, Science, and Other Animals' is one of the 1999 award winners in the international competition sponsored by the Center for Theology and Natural Sciences and the John Templeton Foundation.

Ian Harris is Reader in Religious Studies at the University College of St. Martin, Lancaster. His books include *The Continuity of Madhyamaka and Yogācāra in Early Indian Mahāyāna Buddhism* (1991) and an edited volume entitled *Buddhism and Politics in Twentieth Century Asia* (1999). He has written extensively on aspects of Buddhist environmental ethics and is currently working on a History of Buddhism in Cambodia since 1863.

Robert Florida is an Emeritus Fellow at the Centre for the Study of Religion and Society at the University of Victoria in Victoria, British Colombia. He recently was Dean of Arts and Professor of Religion at Brandon University in Brandon, Manitoba. Dr. Florida is currently preparing a book on Buddhism and Human Rights for Greenwood press. Previous publications include numerous articles and book chapters on Buddhist ethics.

Pinit Ratanakul is Director of the Center of Human Resources Development, Mahidol University, Bangkok. He is the author of *Bioethics, An Introduction to the Ethics of Medicine and Life Sciences*, and has published widely on medical ethics from a Thai Buddhist perspective.

David Bubna-Litic is Lecturer in Strategic Management and Responsible Business at the School of Management in the University of Technology, Sydney. He is completing a PhD in Social Inquiry at the University of Western Sydney on Buddhist Economics. He is a long time meditation practitioner and lives in Sydney with his partner Subhana Barzaghi Roshi. David has published several book chapters on Buddhist perspectives on Business and is known in the Strategy area for his postmodern writings and research. Feedback and comments are welcome via David.Bubna-Litic@uts.edu.au

Introduction

Damien Keown

As Buddhism continues to spread in the West its views on contemporary issues are increasingly sought. Both its own followers and outsiders are curious about how this ancient Asian tradition will respond to the moral dilemmas confronting the modern world. This book is an attempt to lay the foundations for such a response. It examines a range of contemporary moral issues from a Buddhist perspective and brings together the views of leading scholars on a range of controversial subjects. Six chapters address specific issues in applied ethics, namely human rights, animal rights, ecology, abortion, euthanasia, and contemporary business practice. Two chapters explore the sources, nature, and proper classification of Buddhist ethics, and trace its ethical teachings back to their ancient roots in order to discover the appropriate foundations for Buddhist ethics in the modern world.

The contributors to this volume have undertaken a major and unique work of revisioning and reinterpretation. The topics discussed in these pages are rarely mentioned in ancient sources, and have received scant attention down the centuries within the tradition itself. The task that faces students of Buddhist ethics today, therefore, is to generate a response to new problems that is consistent with the spirit of Buddhist values and in harmony with its extensive scriptural tradition. This is no easy task since there are very few signposts or landmarks in this new terrain. After all, the earliest Buddhist canonical literature is well over two thousand years old, and many of the problems we face today are the result of modern social, economic and technological developments which could scarcely have been imagined in ancient times. In building a bridge from the old to the new there are many possible pitfalls and dangers, and it is far too early to speak of definitive solutions.

The problem of chronology, furthermore, is not the only one that confronts us. It must also be remembered that Buddhism is a culturally

1

diverse phenomenon spanning the major countries of Asia. It cannot be assumed that Buddhists in India, Southeast Asia, Tibet, China, Korea, Japan and elsewhere with their different histories and cultures will think alike or speak with one voice. There are thus many reasons to proceed with caution.

Proceed, however, we must, since if Buddhism does not rise to the challenge of the modern world it will atrophy and die. Heretofore, Buddhism has reacted productively to its encounter with new cultures, and there is every reason for optimism as it engages the attention of the West at the turn of the second millennium. To withdraw from these challenges, moreover, is not an option. There is, certainly, within Buddhism a strand that seeks to turn its back on 'worldly things' and withdraw to the seclusion of the forest or the cloister. This option is favoured by many who have renounced the household life and taken monastic vows. The view is sometimes expressed in this quarter that issues of the kind addressed in this book are 'not the kind of thing a monk should be concerned with.' The Buddhist order of monks has historically been the backbone of the tradition, and many in the Order (*saṅgha*) have felt (and still do) that the life of the monk should be untouched by mundane considerations, such as those which affect civil society and family life. After all, did they not enter the monastery precisely to escape from those distractions and devote themselves single-mindedly to the search for liberation?

The view just described has not been without influence down the centuries in traditional Buddhist societies, but it cannot survive in the modern West. For Western Buddhists, the Order is not the touchstone of their religious life as it is in more traditional cultures. One of the prominent features of contemporary Western Buddhism is an increasing emphasis on lay organization and participation. Group members discuss their understanding of Buddhist teachings in a free and informed manner, and are more ready to challenge, criticise and reform notions that seem outdated or mistaken. Different conceptions of the role of women, for example, have led to change and innovation in the structure and practice of Buddhist groups. As the momentum of modernisation gathers pace, moreover, it is increasingly difficult, even in traditional societies, to maintain an ostrich-like attitude and hope that the problems of modernity will simply 'go away' and allow monks to resume an untroubled medieval pace of life. Global developments in science and medical technology have meant that the modern world intrudes whether we like it or not. Hospitals from Benares to Birmingham now employ physicians trained in Western methods and practices, and along with the new technology go new moral dilemmas. The only way to deny these developments is to cut oneself off from the world as far as possible. But is that a proper Buddhist response? Certainly, it is not one the Buddha adopted or recommended, other than for short periods of practice. On the contrary, his lifetime's work was directed towards the wellbeing of the world and was carried out in a social milieu. He was on hand to teach, direct, and guide his followers when they faced dilemmas or problems in their lives. Those who shrink from confrontation with 'worldly' issues, therefore, can hardly be said to be following the example of the founder.

Perhaps, in some cases, the explanation for the lack of discussion within the tradition is simply that issues of the kind discussed in this book are difficult and tendentious, and rather than confront them in a careful and critical manner it is easier to avoid them altogether. There is a risk that the authority of monks will be undermined if they are seen to be unable to respond to requests for moral guidance because they are simply uninformed about the issues. Safer, then, not to become involved in these questions at all and to leave them to politicians, economists, and medical personnel. But in doing that, there is inevitably a price to be paid – the price of irrelevancy. For as the status and authority of the secular world grows, and as the voice of religion falls quieter each day, there will soon come a time when the monastery is so divorced from the daily life of ordinary folk that it has no more relevance than a museum exhibit or historical theme park.

If we take the Buddha himself as our exemplar, we see that as a teacher he was neither evasive nor equivocal, and seemed to have held the view that solutions to moral dilemmas existed and could be found. The Buddha was thus certainly no moral sceptic, and was critical of those of his contemporaries who denied (as many do today) that there can be an objective foundation for moral judgements. He taught the existence of an eternal moral law (known as 'Dharma'), and believed that through reason, analysis, reflection, and meditation one could come to know the requirements of this law in any given set of circumstances. His philosophical position can thus be described as 'moral realism.'

Moreover, in engaging with contemporary issues rather than with-drawing from them there is much to be gained in terms of a deeper understanding of Buddhism itself. To interrogate the scriptures for guidance on new problems is to constantly rediscover and renew them, and in so doing to deepen one's insight into their meaning. It is remarkable how a text which at first glance has nothing to say about an issue can speak eloquently to the matter when read from a new perspective. The answers are certainly available, if not at the surface level then not too far below it. In this respect, developing a Buddhist perspective on modern issues is a bit like assembling a jigsaw. A reference in one source, a commentator's aside in another, a story or parable somewhere else – these things can quickly go together to compose a picture which had never been seen before, simply because the material had never been read or arranged in that particular way. This kind of work requires imagination and creativity, not the passive 'transmission' of scripture but an active engagement with it. This is the kind of creative endeavour that has been undertaken by the authors whose views are presented in this volume. Much reflection has gone into the following chapters, almost always without the benefit of precedent to guide it. How well the readings offered resonate with Buddhist values is a question the reader will have to decide. They are all, at least, serious academic attempts to engage with complex issues of interest to Buddhists and non-Buddhists alike.

In terms of the structure of the book, the first two chapters introduce the reader to important issues regarding the theoretical nature of Buddhist ethics and the sources of Buddhist moral precepts. An obvious question to ask at the outset is: How are we to classify Buddhist ethics in terms of the categories evolved in the study of the ethics in the West? As James Whitehill observes in the first chapter, contemporary Buddhism increasingly seeks to make itself understood in modern terms and to respond to contemporary conditions. In his view, Buddhism's legitimation in the West can be partially met by demonstrating that Buddhist morality is a virtue-oriented, character-based, community-focused ethics, and has much in common with the Western 'ethics of virtue' tradition.

Whitehill takes the view that the earlier generation of the study of Buddhist ethics focused on escape from Victorian moralism, and was incomplete. He now sees a new generation of Western Buddhists emerging, for whom the 'construction' of a Buddhist way of life involves community, commitment and moral 'practices.' By keeping its roots in a character formed as 'awakened virtue' and a community guided by an integrative soteriology of wisdom and morality, he believes that Western Buddhism can avoid the twin temptations of rootless liberation in an empty 'emptiness,' on the one hand, and universalistic power politics, on the other.

In describing Buddhist ethics as an 'ethics of virtue,' Whitehill is pointing to consistent and essential features of the Buddhist way of life. But, perhaps more importantly, he is describing Buddhist ethics by means of an interpretative framework very much alive in Western and Christian ethics, namely that interpretation of ethics most recently associated with thinkers like Alasdair MacIntyre and Stanley Hauerwas. Whitehill suggests that the virtue ethics tradition is the most congenial Western counterpart to Buddhism. Virtue ethics, he believes, provides a means of understanding Buddhist ethics, and reciprocally Buddhist ethics offers the West a way of expanding its scope, which in the past may have been been too elitist, rationalistic, and anthropocentric. On this basis Whitehill predicts some likely future directions and limits for Buddhism in a postmodern world.

In the following chapter Charles Prebish explores the foundations of traditional Buddhist ethics as found in the twin strands of the Vinaya, or Monastic Code, and in *śīla*, commonly translated as 'morality,' or 'moral virtue.' Prebish draws the following distinction between them: 'Unlike the Vinaya, which is externally enforced, *śīla* refers to the internally enforced ethical framework by which the monk or nun structures his or her life.' So on which of these foundations should contemporary Buddhist ethics be based? Many scholars incline towards the Vinaya as the primary source for ethical norms, but Prebish finds *śīla* to be 'an incredibly rich concept for understanding individual ethical conduct.' Clearly, the two cannot be entirely unrelated, but the precise nature of their relationship has been a puzzle for scholars. Are the 227 or so monastic precepts found in the Vinaya simply an extension of the basic 'five *śīlas*' or Five Precepts that lay Buddhists observe? The problem here is that many monastic precepts seem to have no clear moral content, for example those relating to the kind of robes that must be worn and matters of general etiquette. Scholars therefore now incline to the view that the central concern of the Vinaya is not morality *per se*, but the harmonious internal regulation of the order of monks, and its proper and decorous conduct in the eyes of the laity.

Advancing beyond this, Prebish poses a further question. Granted that *śīla* is the proper foundation for Buddhist ethics, how does *śīla* itself relate to the other important soteriological components of the Buddhist path to nirvana? The Eightfold Path, which is the royal road to nirvana, is traditionally divided into three component parts: Morality (*śīla*), Meditation (*samādhi*), and Wisdom (*prajñā*). Some scholars have seen morality as simply a preliminary step on the way to nirvana, one that is subsequently transcended or left behind. This view is nowadays less influential, and Prebish emphasizes that all three components of the path are interrelated and, when developed, collectively constitute nirvana.

Having established the priority of *śīla* for any analysis of Buddhist ethics, Prebish goes on to examine the understanding of the term in early *Sūtra* and *Abhidharma* literature, and then in Mahāyāna texts. The latter pose a number of interesting challenges, for certain sources seem to authorise the transgression of the traditional moral precepts in special circumstances. In doing this they invoke the doctrine of 'skilful means' (*upāya-kauśalya*) by way of justification. This holds that when motivated by compassion and informed by wisdom, a bodhisattva (or saint) may – in exceptional circumstances – violate even the most basic precepts, such as the one against taking life. These sources seem to be moving in the direction of a 'situation ethics,' albeit with certain strict provisos.

Having researched the early material, Prebish next turns his attention to its relevance for the modern world. As noted above, many of the concerns we face today are not discussed in the ancient texts. How do we bridge the gap between the moral foundations of the tradition and contemporary ethical dilemmas? Drawing on ideas from postmodernism and elsewhere, Prebish discusses various strategies that can be adopted to make the texts speak to our present needs. Referring to recent work by Harold Coward, he proposes the notion of dialogue with an 'open canon' after the style of the Mahāyāna, which continued to produce new literature to speak to new situations. What is required is a way of approaching the literature that is 'is truly transtemporal and transcultural.' Moreover, since the vast majority of Western Buddhists are laity rather than monks, any new methodology must tailor its message to the concerns of lay life, and take into account developments such as democratization, feminism, and alternative lifestyles.

Prebish concludes by identifying two key traditional ethical frameworks that should have a place in fashioning a bridge between the old and new. The first is the four *brahmavihāras* or 'Divine Abodes,' consisting of love (*maitrī*), compassion (*karuṇā*), sympathetic joy (*muditā*), and equanimity (*upekṣā*). The second is that of the six *pāramitās* or 'perfections,' of giving (*dāna*), morality *(śīla)*, patience (*kṣānti*), vigour (*vīrya*), meditation (*samādhi*), and wisdom (*prajñā*). The first of these is drawn from the Theravāda tradition and the second from the Mahāyāna. His hope is that together 'they might be reinterpreted conjointly through an entirely new commentarial literature' in order to reconfigure Buddhist ethics for the modern world.

Turning to the first of the six applied ethical issues to be considered in the book, it is difficult to think of a more urgent or topical question for Buddhism in the late twentieth century than human rights. Human rights issues in which Buddhism has a direct involvement, notably in the case of Tibet, feature regularly on the agenda in superpower diplomacy. The political, ethical and philosophical questions surrounding human rights are debated vigorously in political and intellectual circles throughout the world. Yet despite its contemporary significance, the subject has merited hardly a footnote in mainstream academic research and publication in the field of Buddhist Studies. Why is this? One reason would seem to be the lack of a precedent within Buddhism itself for discussing issues of this kind; scholars, by and large, continue to follow the tradition's own agenda, an agenda which appears to some increasingly medieval in the shadow of the twenty-first century. If Buddhism wishes to address the issues that are of concern to today's global community, it must begin to ask itself new questions alongside the old ones.

With respect to human rights, an important preliminary question would seem to be whether traditional Buddhism has any understanding of what is meant by 'human rights' at all. Indeed, it may be thought that since the concept of 'rights' is the product of an alien cultural tradition it would be utterly inappropriate to speak of rights of any kind – 'human' or otherwise – in a Buddhist context. Even if it was felt that these objections were overstated, and that the issue of human rights does have a legitimate place on the Buddhist agenda, there would still remain the separate and no less difficult question of how human rights were to be grounded in Buddhist doctrine, particularly in the light of the fact that the tradition itself provides little precedent or guidance in this area. This chapter offers a preliminary exploration of the questions raised above. It concludes that it is legitimate to speak of both 'rights' and 'human rights' in Buddhism, and proposes a ground for human rights in Buddhist doctrine.

But are human beings the only creatures that have rights? One feature of Buddhism that has attracted much attention in the West is its different evaluation of the importance and status of animals. Although often expressed in a humorous context, the fact that according to Buddhism a person 'can come back as an ant' or as a member of another animal species, is one of the better known – if least well understood – Buddhist beliefs among Westerners. This notion, known to Buddhists as the doctrine of 'rebirth,' has profound implications for the way Buddhists view and respond ethically to the animal kingdom. In his chapter on 'Buddhism and Animal Rights' Paul Waldau sets out to discuss three questions: (1) What does 'animal rights' involve? (2) What are the Buddhist tradition's views of other animals? and (3) How might we relate Buddhist insights to the admittedly modern notions and terminology used when the many versions of 'animal rights' are discussed?

After clarifying what the notion of 'animal rights' means, Waldau explores the attitude of the Buddhist tradition towards non-human animals. References to animals are abundant in Buddhist literature, but the texts display complex and at times inconsistent views about the animal kingdom. Waldau identifies two 'faces' of Buddhism in this respect. In terms of the first, Buddhism does not restrict moral protection to the human species alone. Thus the First Precept, unlike the Sixth Commandment (as almost universally interpreted in the Christian tradition), prohibits intentionally killing or causing harm to animals as well as to humans. From this perspective, there would appear to be a moral parity between human and other species. The second 'face' of Buddhism, however, is less benign, and in many respects this general view of animals in Buddhism may be characterised as negative. This is because to exist as an animal is – in terms of the hierachical Buddhism doctrine of rebirth – to be reborn in a state of woe. It is a kind of purgatory produced by bad karma, and is a punishment for evil conduct in former lives. Existence as an animal has few positive aspects: life is perilous and likely to be cut short at any time by human or other predators. Furthermore, there is little chance of improving one's lot in terms of spiritual development, since animals lack the intellectual capabilities to enable them to advance in the Dharma. The best that can be hoped for is that in the course of time whatever evil karma caused one to be reborn as an animal will exhaust itself and one will return again to the human world. Buddhism appears to take little interest in the different capacities and abilities of the diverse animal species, preferring instead to lump them together and contrast them as a group with human beings, invariably in a negative way. Furthermore, Buddhism does not appear to object to the instrumental use of animals, as in the case of elephants that are kept in captivity and used for manual labour after being subjected to often painful techniques of training.

Although the Buddhist view of non-human animals is thus a mixed one, Waldau concludes on a positive note, observing that 'the insights and approaches which Buddhism offers for respecting other animals as real world entities entitled to the privilege of life without human interference do justify some of the optimistic statements made about the tradition and other animals.' He also believes that Buddhism 'has great potential for a contribution to environmental ethics and to the benefits which increased environmental awareness entails for other animals' lives.'

Environmental ethics is the subject of the following chapter by Ian Harris. Harris makes an important point at the outset, a point also made elsewhere in this collection. This takes the form of a caution against succumbing to the dangers of anachronism when confronting ancient texts and traditions with the concerns of modernity. Contemporary concerns such as animal rights and ecology simply did not feature as distinct topics in the philosophical agenda of the ancients. For this reason, there is little sustained discussion of these matters in the texts. Moreover, given that the texts often seem to present a 'blank screen,' there exists the danger of projecting onto them contemporary ideologies which are based on alien cultural foundations and contain inappropriate elements. The tendency to apply convenient contemporary tags – for example labelling Buddhism 'eco-friendly' – may only serve to obscure what is in reality a different set of attitudes or underlying concerns. As Harris notes:

> ... ecological concerns are quintessentially modern concerns with origins that can be traced to the collapse of traditional Western cosmological certainties under the impact of science. Indeed, there may be some justification in the view that the eco-catastophist outlook is the contemporary inheritor of Judaeo-Christian eschatology with its great emphasis on the events leading up to the 'end of history.' If this geneaology is accepted, the lack of any explicit discussion of environmental ethics in the foundational documents of Buddhism is understandable. We simply should not expect to find coherent discussion of a topic that, strictly speaking, is not crucial to the Buddhist understanding of reality.

Having sounded this warning, Harris goes on to note the feature of Buddhism which seem to be in harmony with the concerns of contemporary ecology. The First Precept is of importance here, as is the thrifty and frugal lifestyle of the monks, which contrasts with the 'untrammeled consumerism' of modern life. The existence of a monastic rule which obliges monks to avoid causing injury to plants and animals also seems to point in the direction of a rudimentary ecological concern. In the light of other factors, however – such as that monks are not required to be vegetarian – Harris takes the view that 'None of this seems closely tied to an explicitly ecological ethic.'

Certain aspects of Buddhist teaching seem to favour ecological concerns. The notion of an 'extended kinship' among all spheres of existence – animal, human, and divine – serves to foster solidarity with other forms of life. The Buddhist virtue of 'loving-kindness' (*mettā*) which is to be practised towards all beings, seems to strengthen further the bonds with other creatures. Harris, however, detects an ambiguity in these Buddhist beliefs and practices. Meditation, as an inward practice, is not at all like ecological activism, and loving-kindness has individuals as its object rather than species. The ideas that species must be valued in their own right is a cornerstone of modern ecology, but appears to be absent in Buddhism.

There is also evidence that early Buddhism is 'fundamentally dysteleologic.' The doctrinal teaching that all life is suffering, and that the world is impermanent and in decline, hardly seems a good foundation on which to construct an environmental ethic. In the light of this world-view the obvious question is 'Why bother?' If there is no intrinsic purpose or direction to time or history it is difficult to attach any ultimate value or meaning to the things of this world. This recalls a tendency within Buddhism, referred to earlier, which maintains that the priority is not to improve the world but to escape from it into nirvana at the earliest possible opportunity.

The prospects for a more positive set of ecological credentials seem greater in East Asian than Indian Buddhism. Here is found the notion that all things – even trees, grass and inanimate objects like the earth – have the capacity to reach nirvana. This is because all reality is permeated by the 'Buddha nature,' and contains within itself the 'seed of enlightenment' (*tathāgatagarbha*). This is nicely expressed in the Zen haiku of Kaga no Chiyo (1701–1775 CE):

All I pick up
At the ebb tide
Is alive!

It is this ecologically-friendly face of East-Asian Buddhism that has been received most favourably in the West amongst ecologists. The tendency has been to contrast the enlightened 'naturalism' of Buddhism with the more aggressive and destructive attitude towards nature supposedly evinced by the Judaeo-Christian tradition, which is seen by influential writers such as Lynn White as a major culprit in the contemporary eco-crisis. Here again, however, Harris sounds a note of caution against adopting too readily what may be 'romanticised and nostalgic' visions found in art and literature which have more to do with local cultural and historical circumstances than with the deep structure of Buddhist thought. He concludes by questioning the intellectual pedigree of what has come to be termed 'ecoBuddhism':

In fact, much that masquerades under the label of ecoBuddhism, a neologism employed to denote the contemporary Buddhist response to the challenge of ecological degradation premised on the prioritisation of 'mental states,' on analysis, turns out to be an uneasy partnership between Spinozism, New Age religiosity and highly selective Buddhism.

Our attention is turned in the following three chapters from the world of animals and nature back to human-centred issues. The next two chapters are concerned with issues in medical ethics: the first deals with an issue at the beginning of life, and the second with a moral dilemma at the end of life.

In chapter six, Robert Florida provides an overview of Buddhist approaches to abortion, one of the most controversial and divisive of contemporary moral issues. Rather surprisingly, and in complete contrast to the voluminous literature and abundant pronouncements and position statements available on this topic in the West, there has been little debate on the matter in the Buddhist cultures of Asia. Florida suggests some of the reasons for this curious hiatus and makes a point which strikes many observers, namely the apparent reluctance of those in positions of religious authority within Buddhism to take a position on controversial moral questions. The profile of the Buddhist establishment on questions of this kind could scarcely be lower (this applies not only to Thailand), and in many respects their pronouncements and public statements seem geared to a bygone age rather than the needs of today.

Florida then turns his attention to traditional Buddhist teachings on ethics, embryology, and abortion. Drawing mainly on Theravāda sources supplemented by Tibetan teachings, he explains how traditional Buddhist notions of rebirth generate a distinctive yet quite clear position on this question. Since conception marks not the beginning of personal existence but a continuation of it, the moral status of a new conceptus is held to be equal to that of its recently-deceased predecessor. In other words, there is no moral distinction to be drawn between the entity in the womb, a young child and a mature adult. The basic Buddhist position, therefore, is that abortion is included along with other acts of homicide as a breach of the First Precept against taking life.

At the same time, Buddhist ethics places a great deal of emphasis on the motivation with which an act is performed, so the intention of those involved has a large part to play in assessing moral culpability in individual cases. Furthermore, in the light of the doctrine of dependent origination (*paṭicca-samuppāda*), which holds that all phenomena are causally interrelated, it would be pertinent to look at the total context and the impact on all those affected rather than to evaluate the significance of the act in isolation.

The Buddhist perspective on abortion is further nuanced by the influence of the different Asian cultures with which Buddhism interacted over the course of the past two millennia. In order to provide as balanced and representative a picture as possible, Florida surveys the contemporary situation in three different countries: Thailand, Japan, and Korea. Thailand receives the most attention, and it quickly becomes clear that in practice the official or canonical stance on abortion is more respected in the breach than the observance. Florida provides useful information on the legal regulation of abortion in Thailand as well as statistics on the number of abortions performed per annum. Somewhat surprising for a country in which Buddhism – a religion renowned for its respect for life – is the state religion, and in which 90 per cent of Thais are Buddhists, abortions are running at some 50 per cent higher than the number in the USA for the equivalent number of citizens. 'Thailand', he writes, 'essentially has therapeutic abortion on demand.' 85 per cent or more of abortions are obtained by married women, the majority employed in agricultural work, who appear to use it as a means of birth control. Florida refers to an estimated 300,000 abortions per year, the majority of which are illegal. While only an estimate, the figure represents an increase of two thirds on the annual total for the United Kingdom (Thailand has a population of 60 million, one or two million higher than the United Kingdom).

Under Thai law abortion is permitted for therapeutic reasons where 'it is necessary for the sake of the woman's health,' or if the pregnancy is the result of rape. Under the current law, the Penal Code of 1956, strict penalties are prescribed for abortions performed illegally outside of these exceptions: three years in prison and/or a heavy fine for the woman, and five years imprisonment and/or a heavy fine for the abortionist. The heavy penalties reflect the traditional Buddhist disapproval of abortion, but the high abortion statistics show there is another side to the matter. This is confirmed in opinion polls which, Florida notes, 'reflect the marked dissonance between Thai religious theory, which judges abortion to be an unskilful violation of Buddhist principles, and Thai practical reality, which is that abortion is very common.' The Thai attitude to abortion is paradoxical, since while most Thais regard abortion as immoral, a majority also believe the legal grounds for obtaining it should be relaxed.

The situation in Japan, where Buddhism is not the state religion, also shows interesting variations from the canonical norm. Florida takes as the focus of his discussion the recent phenomenon of *mizuko kuyō*, a memorial service performed following an abortion or miscarriage. He explains the Buddhist context of the ritual, which emerged in the 1960s, and summarises the different scholarly opinions and interpretations of this social phenomenon, including feminist and other readings. Interestingly, the practice has also been adopted by at least one Zen Buddhist group in the United States.

From Japan, Florida turns to neighbouring South Korea, sometimes described as an 'abortion paradise.' Although abortion is officially illegal, it is, as in Thailand, widely practised. More than half of married women in Korea have had at least one abortion, with one third reporting two or more. In particular, so many female fetuses have been aborted that it is estimated there will be a shortage of wives for males of a certain age group. After a long silence, Buddhists have recently begun to express views on the subject of abortion. Particularly notable are the pro-life publications of a Buddhist monk, the Venerable Sok Myogak, and the post-abortion ceremonies held by the nun Venerable Sŏngdŏk.

Turning from the beginning of life to its end, Pinit Ratanakul's chapter 'To Save or Let Go: Thai Buddhist Perspectives on Euthanasia' returns us to Thailand to consider another important contemporary moral problem in a specific cultural setting. New medical technology has raised issues which traditional Thai ethics – based largely on early Buddhism – do not seem well equipped to deal with. The author notes that 'The new life-support technologies have blurred the line between prolongation of life and prolongation of the dying process, and have raised questions about the adequacy of the traditional definition of death as the cessation of all vital signs.' Although Buddhism has long been concerned philosophically with death as a feature of the human condition, it has not heretofore had a problem about distinguishing the living from the dead. Apart from the empirical issues presented by the new technology, like the problem of defining death, a host of thorny ethical ones cluster around the final stages of life. For example:

> Is the refusal of life-preserving treatment by artificial means a morally acceptable option or does it constitute a kind of suicide prohibited by Buddhist teachings? Is it morally wrong for doctors, nurses and families to withdraw life-preserving treatments or to stop such treatment, once these have begun? Are such actions the same as 'killing' patients or are there important ethical distinctions to be made between 'letting-go-of-life' by withholding or stopping treatment, and actual 'killing' or causing death?

The case of the late Thai monk Venerable Buddhadāsa Bhikkhu brought these issues to the attention of the Thai public in recent times. Buddhadāsa made a 'living will' stating that he did not wish his life to be prolonged by extraordinary means and preferred a natural death. However, when he suffered a serious stroke in 1993 at the age of 86 after earlier minor ones, a debate arose among his disciples as to whether he should be hospitalised. In the end he was, and the doctors insisted on continuing with treatment that contravened his wishes as expressed in the advance directive he had made. Although both sides – devotees and doctors – sought to do what was best, the incident came to be seen as providing a stark example of the contrast between the values of modern medicine and those of traditional Buddhism.

The case of Buddhadāsa also engendered a lively debate among Thai Buddhists on the question of euthanasia, and Ratanakul locates his discussion of this issue within the context of the Buddhist doctrine of karma (Pali: *kamma*). This teaches that the moral and physical are intertwined, and that physical conditions may have moral or psychological causes. As such, treating only the physical symptoms of a disease may not result in a cure. What is important is that the whole person should be well, both spiritually and physically. But what if a cure is impossible, as in the final stages of terminal illness? Is 'mercy killing' ever justified in these contexts? Ratanakul suggests an interesting psychological dynamic may be at work in the case of physicians who perform euthanasia. Despite the good motivation of wishing to prevent suffering, in Buddhist terms the physician may well be acting out of aversion (*dosa*) to the patient's suffering. As such, it is fundamentally his own repugnance and 'hidden hatred' of the patient's pain and suffering which leads him to perform euthanasia. This line of reflection leads Ratanakul to the conclusion: 'Therefore from the view of Buddhist psychology "mercy-killing" is not really a benevolent act. It is done from ill will and thus has bad kammic effects both for the doctor and the patient.'

So much for what has become known as 'active euthanasia.' But what about 'passive euthanasia'? Ratanakul sees this as a more complex issue, and one about which the majority of lay Thai Buddhists are uncertain. 'Some Thai Buddhists,' he notes, 'recognize that there is a real moral distinction between "letting-go-of-life" or allowing a patient to die and directly and intentionally taking life. For them, allowing a patient to die does not violate the precept and is considered an altruistic action for those involved.' Buddhist ethics places great emphasis on intention, and in the case of euthanasia much depends on the motivation of those in whose hands the decision rests. For example, is it done from a desire to relieve suffering, to speed the inheritance of an estate, or to harvest organs for transplantation? The moral assessment of each of these situations may vary, and so a case-by-case approach to the problem seems wisest. Given the increasing number of cases of patients who recover from so-called 'irreversible' comas, and the obvious scope for abuse, lay Thai Buddhists take the view that it would be unwise to adopt general policies on passive euthanasia. Instead, Buddhism emphasises the principle of interrelatedness (*paṭicca-samuppāda*) when assessing situations of this kind. As noted above, this is a universal principle that states that everything exists in mutual dependency. As such, it discourages unilateral decisions and calls for dialogue and discussion with full recognition of the effects our actions have on others. The most appropriate environment for the care of terminal patients, and the one most congenial to Buddhist values, Ratanakul concludes, is the hospice, for the following reasons:

The success in pain-relief and the atmosphere and policies of the hospice movement indicate that no one needs die neglected, alone, shunted aside by doctors and nurses, busy with the living yet unconscious and hooked to machines, kept from their families. The hospice movement shows that death with dignity and humane treatment is still possible in our time.

Clearly, had hospice care been available in the case of the Venerable Buddhadāsa, the tragic course of events surrounding his death could have been avoided, and the suffering of all concerned reduced.

Developments in medical science present a unique set of problems, but so do other facets of the modern world. Business, commerce, and economic concerns have come to dominate modern life. What is the proper role of Buddhism in this new era where, as one writer puts it, 'corporations rule the world'? This is the question David Bubna-Litic sets out to answer in the final chapter. He begins by reminding us just how rapid the changes have been in modern times:

In the two hundred or so years since the Industrial Revolution began, the world has seen a period of unprecedented change. Our capacity to transform raw materials into products has grown exponentially. For example, total global economic output has expanded by more in *each* of the past four decades than from prehistory to the middle of this century.

The impact of these changes on individuals has been significant, and it is surely true that 'the dominance of work in our lives leaves gaps in our humanity.' The giddy pace of modern life seems to leave less and less time for spiritual pursuits. In society as a whole, the gap between rich and poor seems every wider, and in the world economy poor nations resort to sweat-shop industries, corruption, violence and political repression to meet the needs of more affluent countries.

In seeking a Buddhist response to these concerns, Bubna-Litic draws a parallel between the Buddha's rejection of a life of comfort and luxury and the increasing dissatisfaction of many people today with a contemporary ethos which values only status and material success. The central theme in the legend of the Buddha's life, however, is not out-and-out rejection but the search for a productive 'middle way.' It was when he adopted the 'middle way' after six years of austerity that the Buddha quickly gained enlightenment. So what is the proper role of 'the bodhisattva in business?' It would seem to call for a relationship with the everyday world rather than a flat rejection of it. But what form of organizational structure is most appropriate for this? The monastery, the corporation, or does some new communal framework need to be developed as a suitable vehicle for Buddhism in the modern world? To answer this question, Bubna-Litic turns back to the fundamental doctrines and moral teachings of the Buddha. The principle of interdependency must surely be acknowledged in any organisational structure. So too must the vows of refuge and the Precepts. Modern business techniques that are compatible with Buddhist teachings, like Julian Gresser's methodology for negotiation, can be incorporated. Using the Samurai technique of approaching new situations at work with 'a stance of open awareness' can allow us to respond intuitively, without expectations or prejudice. Work situations also provide the opportunity to cultivate the spiritual virtue of integrity through 'a spiral pathway of learning.' Given the short-term focus of modern organisations they can be chaotic, and full of conflict. The practice of Buddhism can help us withstand the pain and disappointment which arises from the over-identification with projects and plans we become involved with by stripping away the projections and emotional over-investment we make in them.

Integrity is also important in dealing with the success and financial and other rewards which business acumen can bring. Buddhism teaches how wealth should be distributed and emphasises an attitude of inner detachment so that our inner integrity is undisturbed and unthreatened either by failure or success. Bubna-Litic suggests that 'it is possible to develop an alternative framework for navigating work life that resonates well with Buddhist precepts and may shed new light on "right livelihood".' This framework contains two important and interrelated elements. The first is the development of detachment, and alongside this a lifestyle that is simple, healthy, and frugal. The second element is to live and work with integrity. Work cannot be separated from other areas of life, and the workplace can become just as much a forum for personal growth and spiritual development as the monastery. In terms of organisations, also, integrity is capable, like DNA, of forming many different structures depending on the local environment. The encounter with the West provides a new challenge regarding the integration of Buddhist practice and commerce.

The assumptions of the world of commerce, basically those of egoism and sensual materialism, are quite different from those which underlie the Dharma, namely selflessness and detachment. Can they co-exist, or will one overcome the other? Bubna-Litic is optimistic and concludes:

> As more Buddhist join the commercial world and negotiate their work lives with integrity, changes will naturally emerge at the collective level. These cannot be prescribed. What will emerge from this new growth of Buddhism in the West hopefully will express itself with the grace and beauty of nature in the market place.

What general conclusions can be drawn from this book about contemporary Buddhist ethics? The overall tone of the chapters can be described as one of guarded optimism. The authors on the whole seem to feel cautiously optimistic about the prospects for Buddhism in the modern world, and believe that Buddhism can make a useful contribution to contemporary moral issues. At the same time, they also point out the many pitfalls and problems that face those who seek today to tap the spring of Buddhist moral wisdom for guidance.

In large part these dangers fall into two groups. The first concerns the hermeneutical problems of making ancient scriptures speak to new contexts. This is a challenging but not insuperable task, and it is one that is at present being undertaken in other religious traditions. There is no reason why Buddhism cannot meet this challenge in the same way, perhaps in dialogue with other faiths.

The second danger is more subtle, and concerns what might be termed 'cultural misappropriation.' This occurs when contemporary Western views are 'read back' into an Asian tradition. Many Westerners, for example, find Buddhism attractive because it seems congenial to their own liberal ideology. Thus, in contrast to much of what is perceived as negative in Western religion, Buddhism appears to be open-minded, rational, eco-friendly, kind to animals, pacifist, and neither authoritarian nor doctrinaire. The 'voluntary' or 'optional' nature of the Buddhist precepts, for example, is frequently contrasted with the 'Commandments' of Christianity. The essays in this book, however, show that such a conception – which for convenience we might term 'liberal Buddhism' – is really only a construct which depends largely for its existence on Western culture, and, in particular, Christianity. Buddhist sources, as noted above, reveal a much more untidy and at times contradictory picture made up of different strands. To select only those which are in harmony with fashionable trends in Western society is to treat Buddhism superficially, and fail to engage seriously with its views. It is, however, an understandable and common mistake to project the assumptions of one's own culture onto another, and to make invisible those parts of it which do not seem to fit well with our own preconceptions. Buddhism as a reality is far from monolithic, and even at the level of individual schools one encounters nuanced and divergent points of view. This complexity must be reckoned with in any dialogue with Western ethics.

The purpose of this book is to open such a dialogue across a broad front. The views expressed here are far from the last word or the only voices that deserve attention. The collection as a whole, however, constitutes one of the first major contributions to a range of contemporary moral issues from a Buddhist perspective, and may serve as a representative example of the present state of reflection on the issues surveyed.

CHAPTER ONE

Buddhism and the Virtues[1]

James Whitehill

My purpose in this chapter is to speculate about the optimal, future development of Buddhism in the West. To speculate about the future is, of course, to reach beyond the narrow protections of expertise into the vulnerability of guesswork. My guesswork about Western Buddhism's future takes the form of two hypotheses for scholarly consideration by interested philosophers and ethicists, Buddhist or not. The two hypotheses can also be viewed by Western Buddhists as recommendations on the future course of their Buddhist practices and communities.

The first hypothesis and recommendation is that Buddhism must begin to demonstrate a far clearer *moral form* and a more sophisticated, *appropriate ethical strategy* than can be found among its contemporary Western interpreters and representatives, if it is to flourish in the West. This hunch is to me almost certainly correct, so I will treat it only briefly at the beginning.

My second conjecture is that Buddhism's success in the West is most likely if Buddhist ethics is specifically grafted to and enriched by the 'ethics of virtue' approaches of Western tradition, approaches recently revived in Christian thinkers like MacIntyre and Hauerwas.[2] This second guess is more specific, tentative, and provocative, and, therefore, more interesting, so it will be my dominant theme.[3]

Viewing Buddhist morality and ethics in the light of virtue theory is, I believe, true to the central core of Buddhism. The virtues approach also generates a wide range of analytical comparisons with Western philosophical and theological tradition, and helps us foresee and plan for the limits of Buddhism's Western pilgrimage.

Returning for a moment to my first and most general hypothesis, I will begin by saying that I am persuaded that Buddhism is on the threshold of a more significant future in the West. It will increasingly play practical, heuristic, balancing, and liberating roles in the lives of Western people and their societies. But, in order for this to happen, philosophers, Buddhist and non-Buddhist, must help more to clarify the *moral and ethical* terms of Buddhism's soteriological project, in ways coordinate with Western intellectual tradition. For more than two decades, Buddhist philosophical talent in the West has been focused almost exclusively on ontology and hermeneutics. One result is that Buddhist philosophy in the West has ballooned off into the clouds of *śūnyatā*-focused dialectics. I propose that our philosophical soaring needs the *ballast* of Buddhist moral practices and the *landmarks* of a refreshed Buddhist ethics to bring Buddhist philosophy more into a practical relationship with the on-the-ground, everyday realities of people's lives. I am moved to this recommendation by my deductive understanding of Buddhist teaching, but also by the fact that American Buddhists, since the early 1980s, have increasingly puzzled over moral and/ or political choices and issues, without much help from Buddhist philosophers and scholars who are also well-grounded in Western moral and political thought.

When Christians translated their Gospel into Chinese contexts, the Greek 'Logos' became the Chinese 'Tao,' a daring and radical translation, transmuting the Gospel as it transmitted it. A similar translation *problematique* faces us now as Buddhism transmits the 'Dharma' to the West. But, in the matter of that part of the Dharma which can be called 'Buddhist ethics,' no proposal in Western philosophical terms on the shape of Buddhist ethics currently commands wide attention, much less agreement.[4] As a result, the legitimization of the Buddhist Dharma *as a whole* is at risk in the West, for no religious or soteriological philosophy without a developed ethic can be fully and widely legitimized in Western culture.

A variety of philosophical proposals relevant to the Western shaping of Buddhist ethics can be seen across the spectrum of Buddhist thinkers. Happily, no one argues that Buddhist ethics or morality are sui generis, a unique and inviolate form of Buddhist tradition to be transplanted whole and entire into Western cultural soil. Also, few are suggesting that Buddhist morality and ethics are so much embedded in Asian cultures that they cannot be transplanted.

Both in theory and in practice, most Western Buddhists appear to look for and accept a grafting or hybridizing process, assimilating Buddhist moral stock to a plausible, compatible Western moral root. Some are tempted to confuse this process, by reversing it, as if the task is to graft Western moral concerns to a Buddhist root of compassion or, worse, transcendental wisdom. This confusion is like 'growing a lotus without planting it in the mud,' or 'putting the spiritual cart before the moral horse.' More simply, this confusion assumes that ethics follows spirit or theory, a rather un-Buddhist notion, given the Buddha's existential impatience with metaphysical gymnastics.

In the 1960s, Buddhist ethical reflection, and morality in the broad sense of 'a way of life,' were grafted by Western apologists to the stem of existentialism and to some branches of the human potential movement.[5] These early efforts fell short of a satisfactory ethical development of Western Buddhism, in my opinion, because they failed to include much critical, communal, or practical guidance for would-be Buddhist existentialists (or existentialist Buddhists?) and other Aquarians. Recently, more politically relevant splicings have been attempted by several Buddhists within the peace, environmental, and feminist movements.[6]

Only a few Western *philosophers* have attempted grafting work recently in Buddhist ethics, usually by asserting and working out conceptual analogies between Buddhist ethics in general and particular Western philosophers and theologians. Examples of this comparative work include David Kalupahana's proposal that Buddhist ethics melds interestingly with William James' pragmatism, and Christopher Ives' explorations of opportunities to develop a Zen Buddhist social ethic in contrast with Reinhold Niebuhr's Christian social ethics. Also noteworthy, if less comparative in its analysis, is Robert Thurman's proposal to find a relevant recipe for contemporary social activism in a specific text of Nāgārjuna.[7]

While I do not find these proposals sufficiently developed to be compelling to Western ethicists, they are thought-experiments that address some issues of interest to Western philosophical and theological ethics, while taking interpretive risks for the sake of Buddhist relevance. I regret that none of the proposals can withstand the kind of friendly critique that comes quickly and easily from ethicists grounded in Christian and Western ethical studies; Winston King, for example, has long been helpful in raising a variety of critical and disturbing questions about the strengths and weaknesses of Buddhist philosophy in a Western ethical milieu dominated by demands for human rights and individual autonomy.[8]

Assuming the under-developed condition of the domain of Buddhist ethics in Western context, I now address at length my second, more tentative conjecture on the future prospect of Western Buddhism. I propose that the most appropriate analogy, the most fruitful grafting prospect for a Western Buddhist ethics, will be with the Western tradition of the 'ethics of virtue.' By 'ethics of virtue' I mean simply an ethics that is *character-based* (rather than principle-driven or act-focused), *praxis-oriented, teleological,* and *community-specific.* More fully, I mean the complex tradition of ethics that stretches in the West from Socrates and Aristotle to Alasdair MacIntyre, Philippa Foot, and other contemporary virtues theorists.[9]

This proposal does not originate with me. The conceptual and heuristic linkage of Buddhist ethics with Aristotle's is a key to Damien Keown's approach in his well-argued, revisionist view of Buddhist ethics, *The Nature of Buddhist Ethics.*[10] Earlier, Robert Bellah favored grafting Buddhism to the virtues approach as a possible path to meet his concern to renew an American ethic of community. Specifically, Bellah has called for a 'cultural symbiosis' of Zen and modern Aristotelianism as a way of re-asserting 'a teleological understanding of the order of human life' and bringing about 'the creation of actual communities' that can resist:

> a *modern* Western culture that is destroying the natural habitat, undermining any kind of social solidarity, and creating a conception of the individual person which is utterly self-destructive.[11]

The utopian spirit of his call for Buddhist-like communities of personal and civic virtue suggests that these communities would almost certainly be 'marginalized,' growing only at the edges of the dominant socio-cultural structures of Western individualism or bureaucratic nation-states. Its utopian character does not seem to dissuade Bellah from making his recommendation. Nor am I. Indeed, such 'contrast' communities already exist, however tenuous their rooting in the Western 'soul and soil.'[12]

Before taking up this proposal, that Buddhist 'morality' and 'ethics' can be appropriately transplanted in the West by assimilating them to our own virtues tradition, I need to define Buddhist *morality* more precisely, in the terms of 'awakened virtue.' 'Awakened, compassionate virtue-cultivation' is a more accurate phrasing of what I mean, but, for simplicity's sake, I will avoid using it. 'Awakened virtue' usefully describes the process and goal of Buddhist morality. It affirms the intertwined correspondence of the moral and the spiritual, in fresh language, by referring to Buddhist moral vision and praxis in the language of virtue theory, and by retaining the Buddhist insistence on spiritual awakening as a necessary, although not sufficient, condition of moral maturity. Second, I will simply define Buddhist ethics as 'philosophical reflection upon Buddhist morality, including descriptive, normative and meta-ethical reflections.'[13]

My purpose in this essay about 'awakened virtue' is not to engage in historical and textual analysis. I will not exegete the comparative analogies of *śīla* or the *pāramitās*[14] to *phronesis, arete,* or *virtus.*[15] My aim is more philosophical, practical, and even policy-oriented: to probe constructively the implications of 'awakened virtue,' the goal of Buddhist morality and the object of Buddhist ethics, in connection with the future prospects of Western Buddhism. The effort to construct a Western Buddhist ethics by means of a virtues approach is not without exemplars. For example, Robert Aitken relies on it often in his homiletical text, *The Mind of Clover: Essays in Zen Buddhist Ethics.* Aitken fashions refreshing sermons on Buddhist ethics, with a Zen twist, framing most of his chapters as expositions of 'The Ten Grave Precepts' of Buddhist morality. He also writes briefly about the Six Perfections, the six *pāramitās* of generosity, morality, patience, vigour, meditation, and self-realization, and discusses 'virtue' as a way of understanding the Zen life.

Aitken opens his chapter, 'The Way and Its Virtue,' with a saying of his teacher, Yamada Koun Roshi: 'The purpose of Zen practice is the perfection of character.' Aitken proceeds to discuss briefly but provocatively the six *pāramitās*, relating them to contemporary experience and applications.[16] But his teacher's saying is overlooked and the focus on virtue collapses as, in the perennial fashion of most Zen interpreters, he concludes that:

> At the same time, 'virtue,' 'the Six *Pāramitās*,' 'perfection of character' – these are simply labels for an organic process. Breathing in and out, you let go of poisons and establish the serene ground of the precepts.[17]

Aitken here falls into a common pitfall in the path of ancient and contemporary Zen interpreters, what I call 'the transcendence trap.' The trap misleads them and us into portraying the perfected moral life as a non-rational expressiveness, something natural, spontaneous, non-linguistic, and uncalculating. This is a 'Taoist-like' view of virtue as 'natural, intuitive, skill/power' (Chin. *te*; Jap. *toku*), a view Aitken shares with some influential, but late Mahāyāna *sūtras*. This ethical conception results in the kind of ontological dismissal of morality and ethics preached by Aitken at the end of his chapter: 'Thus, in the world, too, there is nothing to be called virtue.'[18] The common corollary, 'there is also nothing to be called character,' is unstated by Aitken, although it is part of the same syllogistic net of claims deduced ostensibly from 'no-ego' and *śūnyatā* axioms. This net is true and helpful only within the 'deconstructive' mood and context of *śūnyatā* dialectics and metaphysics. When the net of 'no-self' is thrown to catch truth in an ethical context, villains laugh and demons thrive.

A good beginning by Aitken, in taking a virtues approach to interpreting Buddhist ethics, is later swamped by the *śūnyatā*-weighted dialectical anamorphisms of Mahāyāna and Zen thought. Aitken is enmeshed in what I have called 'the satori perspective' in Zen philosophy, the position most clearly seen in D.T. Suzuki's vigorous anti-rationalism and antinomianism. The 'satori perspective' characteristically over-emphasizes the 'awakening' dimensions of Buddhist soteriology, to the detriment of the moral, 'virtuous' dimensions.[19] Consequently, a view of the Buddhist virtues from this standpoint tends insistently to relativize and diminish the 'virtue' in the summum bonum of 'awakened virtue,' until there is only the 'awakened One,' beyond good and evil.

A clear and egregious example of this spiritualizing over-emphasis on 'awakening,' comes to us in the writings of Gerta Ital, in her book, *On the Way to Satori*, where she offers us this advice:

> This is something that cannot be repeated often enough: no one who has not completely erased themselves as an ego can do anything to help liberate anyone else, and the attainment of the goal is not easy. The journey is very long. ... Until one is liberated oneself one is simply not capable of helping anyone else.[20]

This is not a complete Buddhism, I believe, and certainly not one that can expect a significant future in the West, except as an individualistic, private, and mainly 'therapeutic' mysticism. Buddhism is far more and other than that.

A fuller and more finely articulated virtues approach to Buddhist ethics guides Ken Jones' *The Social Face of Buddhism*. I consider this the best available *ethical* manual on Buddhist social ethics by a Westerner.[21] I recommend it, convinced that it is a touchstone philosophical text in Buddhist ethics. It is unlike Aitken's, because Jones' seriously pays attention to key philosophical, moral, and psychological issues. Regrettably, Jones, like Aitken, walks into 'the transcendence trap,' by devaluing the roles of will and deliberation in the life of awakened virtue.

Jones affirms in good virtues theory fashion that Buddhist morality is a matter of character and cultivation, and that it focuses on cultivating character rather than evaluating particular acts.[22] But quickly he slides toward 'the transcendence trap,' beginning with a too casual substitution of the word 'personality' for 'character':[23]

> The emphasis in Buddhist morality is therefore on the cultivation of a personality which cannot but be moral, rather than focusing upon the morality of particular choices and acts. But, to repeat, it is not the will that can create such a personality, no more than I can pick myself up from the ground by my collar. It is to the training that the will must be applied, from which virtue will naturally flow.[24]

Jones's disclaimer on the power of will may only be a rejection of Nietzschean or Sartrean voluntarism. If so, he would be correct from a Buddhist point of view, which dialectically affirms both the deterministic weight of karma or character dispositions and our freedom from them in the concomitant 'emptiness' of *śūnyatā*. And he is certainly correct to assert that the will in Buddhist practice, rather than serving a 'creative' role in free self-creation, serves mainly to restrain and hold oneself in the various forms of moral and intellectual practice.

However, the fuzziness of the phrase, 'from which virtue will naturally flow,' places Jones on the lip of the 'transcendence trap.' He later falls in by constructing virtue as a kind of *natural* 'grace,' emergent from the *forms* of moral discipline and repetition, *yet* different from them, somehow transcendent, natural and free. As Robert Scharf suggests, this transcendent view of virtuous activity is a mystification of what in Buddhist practice is simply a repetitive and normal process of learning to *perform* in certain ways with skill; Hee-jin Kim, discussing what he calls the 'heart of Dogen's thought,' refers to the process of Buddhist practice as essentially something prosaic, 'the ritualization of morality.'[25]

More than Jones can or will admit, schooling in the forms of virtue is a social, emotional, and cognitive process. Becoming good is hardly a natural process in the sense suggested, of being the non-voluntary, non-deliberative unfolding of a natural goodness. Aristotle would agree: 'While it is Nature that gives us our faculties, it is not Nature that makes us good or bad.'[26] The goal of ethics is to become a person who does good or virtuous things freely from the ground of a well-tempered character, supported by a matured, resolute, and reasonable knowledge of what one is doing. The path of Buddhism does not dissolve character (which is different from ego and personality). It awakens and illuminates moral character and establishes a 'noble' selfhood in the wide, deep, expressive freedom of creative forms of life and its perfections.

Jones' view of virtue echoes the Christian moral doctrine of 'infused virtue,' but without dependence on St. Thomas Aquinas' transcendent, theistic assumptions and absent his clear sense of the endurance of the 'natural' virtues in the perfected saints. I venture the guess that, like Alan Watts and others who fall into 'the transcendence trap,' Jones devalues the will in preferring 'natural expressiveness' (in the sense of what we are born with, *natus*), in his beliefs about learning to be good, because of things that have little to do with Buddhism, the *Diamond Sūtra*, and Mahāyāna dialectics. I suspect that many a Westerner's 'Taoist-like' misreading of Buddhist ethics, as a form of individualistic naturalism, is mostly and often a reaction to the West's residual Victorian morality – morality characterized by and hated for its conceived overemphasis on individual, rational self-discipline, strength of will, rigidity of personality, and psychophysical repressions – and from which middle-aged and older Western Buddhists seem to be still trying to make their escape. In their desire to escape, they share in a broader, late twentieth-century Western shift to a moral outlook that prizes a rather passive, non-judgmental tolerance of others, combined with a preference for the spontaneous or ecstatic expression of impulses – at least, and especially, in contrast with the much maligned Victorians.

To disdain the necessary roles of will and reason in the Buddhist moral process is to overlook the importance of both in early Buddhism. Early Buddhism did not abandon reason, although it did not rely on reason alone. Neither did early Buddhists overlook the necessity of a steady will, even in the stages of Buddhist meditation training. That will and reason were requisite accompaniments of the good person is also evident in later additions to the six *pāramitās* list, namely, the *pāramitās* of resolution, determination, strength, and skillful means. Obviously, strength of will is necessary even in *samādhi* exercises, in making the Bodhisattva vow, or in responding to exhortations of the Zen masters to throw one's whole self and attention into *zazen* or *kōan*. Buddhist cultivation requires a constant dose of what William James called 'animal spirits' and doing the difficult thing against our inclinations.

Now, having by-passed the 'transcendence trap' on the way to a Buddhist virtues perspective, I wish briefly to describe what I mean by Buddhist 'awakened virtue' in the context of general virtues theory, distinguishing it somewhat from traditional Western views. Following this description, I will conclude by exploring some implications for the West of viewing Buddhist ethics and the Buddhist 'way of life' in a virtues perspective.

Buddhist morality as awakened virtue

The Buddha's Dharma or teaching was authoritatively divided in early times into three groups, but they were interdependent facets of one process leading to deliverance (*vimutti*). The Buddhist investigated and cultivated *śīla* (morality), *samādhi* (deep meditation), and *prajñā* (transcendental wisdom).[27] Each of the three facets of self-cultivation evolved appropriate practices: of moral intent...... of meditation method and mapping; of t............ness. We may speak of these practices as .... transformative *pāramitās*. The last, the .... oncerned with practices that alter consci.................... Nirvanic' level, while the contemplative *p*........................ evelopment of powers of concentration, s.................... editation. The moral *pāramitās* involve pr............................ re aroused and acted upon in the light .... good and of situations. With repetition and correction these practices severally and together nurtured the dispositions, both karmic and salvific, that together constitute Buddhist character.

The question why *these pāramitās* as the specific Buddhist virtues, rather than others, invites a fuller treatment than I will give here.[28] The *pāramitās*, as methods of attending, energizing, pacifying and relating the self to others, work together to wean the self from egocentricity. Beyond ego-weaning, the goal of the *pāramitās* is positive: to foster a character that increasingly encounters each moment, each space, each being, as a 'mother' enjoys and protects her only child – to use a traditional simile attributed to the Buddha.

Since moral intentions are always elastic, they need shaping by forms and disciplines, taught by teachers and learned in communities. The virtuous practices that in Buddhism characterize a good person were often defined as at least the six *pāramitās* of generosity or gift-giving (*dāna*), morality or the Five Precepts (*śīla*), patience and forgiveness (*kṣānti*), courage and vigour (*vīrya*), concentration (*dhyāna*), and wisdom (*prajñā*). Some held that the six *pāramitās* constituted a progressive order of training in virtue, from generosity to wisdom. These may be said to be the necessary moral, mental, and spiritual touchstones of the Buddhist virtues tradition, notwithstanding later additions to, and analytical divisions of, the six. Enrichment of virtue-like practices beyond the *pāramitās* is seen in the development of the well-known Four Immeasurables (the *Brahmavihāras* or 'divine abodes') of Buddhist friendliness, compassion, joy, and peace, which further mapped out, stimulated, and idealized Buddhist moral praxis.

These practices, moral and otherwise, were more often than not 'methodologized,' that is, formalized, ritualized and institutionalized in ways to promote habitual performances in a general program of self-cultivation and character development, conceived to stretch over many aeons of time (thus requiring the *pāramitā* of patience!). Methods would differ somewhat between monk and layperson, and from culture to culture. Some practices were Buddhist adaptations of pre-existing practices and rituals in the surrounding non-Buddhist culture, as Nath shows in her study of the Buddhist transformations of Hindu *dāna*, gift-giving rites.[29]

Buddhist moral self-cultivation tends to encompass not only the formation of good intentions in the heart and mind (reminding us of Kant). Practices also include physical postures and breath-speech techniques. This holistic 'psycho-pneumo-physical' approach to moral self-cultivation results, for example, in attention to helping others not only by forming a good will, but also by expressing kind words and offering the material things that they also need. A more holistic self-training also opens a way to fuse moral practice with aesthetic practice, as an early concern in Buddhism with how gracefully to give gifts demonstrates.

Practice of the moral *pāramitās* is said to create and accumulate 'merit,' or favorable karma dispositions within the psyche, which lead to a better life and higher rebirth. The 'ethics of karma,' focused upon by Melford Spiro and Winston King as the key to understanding Theravādin Buddhist societies is, when looked at closely, but an 'ethics of karma-cultivating virtues and practices.'[30] Spiro and King, reflecting an interpretation within the Theravādin tradition, highlight the ostensibly traditional split between the karmic and the Nibbānic motives in Buddhist life, one for goodness and reward, the other for salvation and transformative liberation. The two motives are personalized in layperson and monk, respectively.[31]

The tension between moral and religious motives appears also in Mahāyāna Buddhism. At one point the tension was reconciled in the bodhisattva image of a virtuous layman-sage, Vimalakīrti. The *Vimalakīrti Sūtra* affirms that a breach between moral effort and spiritual awakening constitutes bondage and delusion.[32] The center of Buddhist tradition affirms that moral effort, mainly through practicing the *pāramitās*, must be conjoined with meditative and transformative practices to be ultimately effective for oneself and for others. It also affirms that the practices of awakening have little foundation and less result, for oneself or others, without the frame, skills, and habit of moral practice. Moral virtue without *śūnyatā*, or transforming liberation, may be shallow and weak; but *śūnyatā* without moral virtue is blind and dangerous. She who has accomplished awakened virtue, the merging of skilled, well-disposed, rational moral agency with self-transforming spirit, is, in contrast, deep, strong, ever-maturing, and rational – by her character and deeds she reduces suffering and promotes friendliness, compassion, joy, and peace.

In contrast with Western virtues tradition, the Buddhist *pāramitās* viewpoint tends, in matters of self and community, to be *biocentric and ecological*. First, Buddhism does not begin with the premise of the substantial, separable, and distinctive self of Aristotelian and Christian thought. In Buddhism, the idea of the atomistic, self-empowering monad-godling of Western individualism is well known, but understood as a delusion born of ignorant desires and fears, resulting in a wish-fantasy for domination. Compared to Western concepts, the self-concept of Buddhism is processional, relational, and 'fuzzy.'[33]

While the moral saint as individualized hero, above and apart from others, is not unknown in Buddhism, the open, relational nature of selfhood stresses the solidarity of those who act virtuously with those for whom they act, or better, with whom they practice the perfecting goods of generosity, patience, and so forth. For Buddhist thought the self is fundamentally incomplete, evolving, and interpenetratively co-dependent with others. Since we are imbedded in mutual dependent community, training in the *pāramitās*, moral and otherwise, is necessarily a training with others and for others. Because of this solidarity and because *pāramitās* practice nurtures body, speech, and the mind-heart, the Buddhist believes her moral efforts flow necessarily into the community on many levels, materially, verbally, and mentally, in a subtle, looping reciprocity.

Second, Buddhist tradition differs from the Western in defining *membership* in the moral community, the 'considered others' to whom *pāramitās*-defined practices are to be extended. In the dominant traditions of Western culture, at least since Aristotle, the community of character and virtue has clearly been the *human* community. The politics in which an individual's ethics and virtue find their completion is a human politics – almost always an anthropocentric, urban politics. The Buddhist community of virtue is biocentric, far more inclusive of animals and other sentient beings as objects of moral consideration (in the practice of the six *pāramitās*, for example, giving aid to animals) than Western virtues tradition.[34] Because of this biocentric orientation, Buddhist moral practices must include specific training and self-cultivation in our relations with nature, as well as human society, extending *dāna*, *śīla*, *kṣānti*, and so on to non-human sentient beings and to the biosphere itself as a community of communities.[35]

Given the exurban settings of Buddhist monasteries and universities, and other factors, Buddhist ethics did not elaborate itself often into urban, class-oriented political theory, a theory of revolutionary change, or a theory legitimizing divine rule – although Buddhist thinkers did propose all three. The community scale imaged by the *saṅgha* was smaller and more nurturing of personal development, perhaps that of a village set within nature. Perhaps this goes to explain partially why even urban Buddhists have tended to re-create or simulate in the grounds of their city temples a contrasting, natural refuge, for people, animals, fish, birds, and even insects. A Japanese tea ceremony garden and hut in the middle of Tokyo express this microtopic, exurban focus most eloquently and ironically.

Like the Aristotelian virtues tradition, Buddhist ethics tends to be ahistorical, in that it regards human life as having an important and profound constancy in its nature and goal, persistent amidst the general flow and struggles of actual personal and historical forces. That constancy for the Buddhist lies not in a substantial or eternal self, but in our common, almost irrefragable experience of suffering and in our inherent capacity to work toward an awakened, moral virtuosity, in wisdom and fellow-feeling.

With respect to the question of historicity, I think that, in comparison with the Christian virtues tradition, Buddhist ethics did not develop so extensive a quasi-historical hagiography, a 'sense of narrative,' concerning the lives of the virtuous and their exemplars, the saints. The *Jātaka* tales, while we classify them as 'animal' fables, may be similar in appearance to a 'Lives of the Saints.' But we should probably resist calling them 'narrative' because they display a narrow range of the Buddhist reality picture, and we should hesitate to call them unqualifiedly Buddhist, because the stories are from a pre-Buddhist tradition. This comparative absence of emphasis on individual 'drama,' which may be more of degree than type, applies even to the most obvious Buddhist saint, the Buddha, whose 'story' does not serve for Buddhists the whole range of functions that we find centered in the Gospels, in Roman Catholic hagiography or in Muslim *hadith* tradition.[36]

On another theme of contemporary virtues theory, I begin by acknowledging without apology that Buddhism makes moral claims that are universalistic. Buddhists have imagined utopian times and settings for the virtuous, the perfected, the awakened – and projected a utopic future when 'all beings are awakened.' But, like all ethical traditions centered on virtues, Christian, Muslim, Confucian, or Aristotelian, the Buddhist *pāramitā* tradition looks to the establishment of particular and appropriately designed communities to optimize favorable conditions for self-cultivation and happiness in the good life. Virtue ethics traditions, often focused in small groups engaged in voluntary training, tend to spend little time on the ethical strategies necessary in non-voluntary, pluralistic, very large, or coercive societies. Consequently and not surprisingly, they tend to lack a viable social ethic in modern terms, that is a policy-generating set of principles that can be institutionalized on a mass scale, while protecting individual rights-claims with coercive means.

So, while espousing the general tenets and principles of a universal ethics, Buddhist ethics tends, in practice, to define and effectuate *pāramitā*-cultivation in community-specific terms. At the mind-and-heart level, the broad intention 'to help others' may be similar across many communities, but at the levels of linguistic and physical practice, the *pāramitās* have a local aspect, and in that sense display a modest 'historical' quality. For example, while the virtue of giving, *dāna-pāramitā*, may show local nuances of expression in almsgiving rites, these local forms are practiced with recognition of their universal applicability in their intention, but not in their formal, material, local features. A tolerant awareness of distinctions between inner and outer aspects of Buddhist practices may result in much less zealous enforcement of verbal, symbolic, and physical conformity in moral (and contemplative) practices in Buddhist contexts. The resulting diversity, flexibility, and tolerance sustain the Buddhist tradition, at the risk of appearing very soft and highly 'contextual' in social ethics and politics.

Nevertheless, one does find conformity in the moral forms and practices within Buddhist voluntary communities, of which the *saṅgha* is the classical exemplar. Conformity is in keeping not only with the needs of any community for the standardization and predictability of behaviours that enhance trust and efficiency. Shared forms are especially necessary and appropriate to a community guided by virtue ethics. The Buddhist's cultivation of the *pāramitās* requires a community designed to respond to awakened virtue practices with specific structures of support and correction.

Each Buddhist community has a distinctive shape and style, governed primarily by a common goal, the awakened virtue of each member-in-community. This perfectionist aim is universalized and idealized by extending it to encompass the awakening of 'all sentient beings.' But, on-the-ground, the community's purpose is realized in the details – of distinctive forms of etiquette, and in the characters of exemplary individuals; in shared schedules, and a common submission to rules; in rituals of giving and receiving, and procedures for correcting and expelling delinquent member. These are communities where one learns and practices what it quite precisely means, mentally and physically, morally and psychologically, to act as an 'awakened virtue being.' That is, one learns to act, to perform, to talk, walk, sit, sort things out, and take out the garbage like a Buddha.

It should be obvious by now that learning to act like a Buddha means something other than becoming spontaneous, inventive, and free of Victorian inhibitions. The practice of awakened virtue in Buddhist communities requires diligent learning of the forms in and through which one can perform like an awakened virtue being. In the moral sphere, these practices require repeated experiences in learning how to give, to listen patiently, to call up courage in overcoming fear and desire, to observe non-violence in the way one walks, to steady the mind and heart, to make friends with the seasons, and so on. In the meditative sphere, similar forms of practice are observed, submitted to, tasted, repeated, tested, and perfected, in cultivation of the contemplative virtues.

28

Finally, the Buddhist community, like any virtue-oriented community, is defined in the characters of its persons, as well as in their stories and the forms of their practices. Its continuation and success depend necessarily upon the degree to which community members become successful practitioners of the community's full repertoire of virtues. Thus, Buddhism will flower in the West only when Western Buddhists take up a fully balanced Buddhist way of life, by cultivating both the moral and the contemplative *pāramitās* in proper balance. 'Awakened virtue' is the balanced platform upon which to practice the ultimate, transformative, Nirvanic virtues constituting the flowering of the spiritual life of Buddhists.

Implications for Buddhist ethics in the West

If we accept the propositions that Buddhist ethics is ineluctably and essentially an 'ethics of virtue' and, second, that the Buddhist life is necessarily *at every stage* integrative of moral and spiritual practices, several implications emerge for Buddhism as it grows in the West. Some of these implications are corrective of recent Western Buddhist troubles, while others may indicate real limits to Buddhism's success in and impact on the West.

Soon, with the passing away of the pioneering, older generations of Western Buddhists, I hope we will see Buddhism in the West turning from its role as a raft carrying Westerners away from the eroding shores of Victorian – or Judaeo-Christian – or technological – or imperialist – or patriarchal culture. While the function of Buddhism, as a means of liberation from suffering and oppression is a central one, it is not the only one. The other function of Buddhism is to carry the suffering to the 'Other Shore,' to awakened virtue, to becoming a Buddha in Buddha-fields where Buddhas flourish. This means working to construct and preserve relationships and communities, as much as cultivating oneself. And this means the renewal of a *pāramitās*-approach in Buddhist thought and life.

One corrective consequence of renewing the *pāramitās* in Buddhist lives and communities will be the denial of authority to imbalanced Buddhist teachers by the communities that support them. Too many Buddhist teachers in the West in the 1980s have demonstrated that they cannot balance well the moral and the spiritual.[37]

However, a virtues-oriented ethic has limitations in meeting problems caused by the vices of individuals in the practicing community. This is because a virtue ethic focuses on the person-as-agent developing over time, in a learning process often of trial and error. This long-term focus devalues the moral significance of particular acts, even transvaluing them into 'teachable moments,' while often overlooking the consequences of flawed or vicious acts for others and the community. A particular moral failure is excused as 'out-of-character.' The result is a greater tolerance of isolated acts of harming others, for example, unless the acts constitute an intolerable 'pattern' of vice that forces community or individual reaction – perhaps too late.

Every virtue ethics guides us to the good life by means of models of 'the good person.' The model may be a living person or a narrative character (i.e., the Buddha, Vimalakīrti, Vessantara, Queen Śrīmālā, one's roshi, etc.). A focus on character tends to obscure or override the role of general principles and rules as guides to decision-making and mutual regulation.

But rules, however flawed, sometimes have a place. For example, a rule-orientation is preferable in some circumstances and relationships to counter teacher-disciple abuses and distortions. Traditionally, Buddhism depends heavily on its teachers and on the belief that profound qualities of an awakened teacher can be passed directly, through 'mind-to-mind' transmission, to her students. Of course, teachers are capable of transmitting the forms of the *pāramitās*, moral and contemplative, through imitation, familiarization, direct instruction, and, I will grant, a kind of psychic 'osmosis.' But, far more difficult to transmit to one's students and friends are the all-important *balance* and *integration* of the *pāramitās* in a given person, because they are partly contingent on the individuality of the novice's personality. It is wrong to believe that this balance can be given to the student, rather than earned by self-effort in the corrective view of a vital community.

Buddhist tradition poses to each Buddhist a momentous question: 'Who is Buddha?' How do we know that someone is advanced in the practices of 'awakened virtue'? That she's a 'good person'? The answer is critical, for it is these people one turns to for instruction, advice, example, confidence, and even faith. A *pāramitās*-oriented approach carries us some distance to the answer, because of its dual focus on character and communally validated moral practices. Consequently, the living meaning of awakened virtue is less dependent on the character of single persons upon whom a community focuses, and more dependent on several persons and the community (the *saṅgha*-community) in its evolving solidarity. Viewing the practicing community as Buddha, as itself a virtue-oriented awakening being, reduces personality cults and deepens community resources.

The *pāramitās* emphasis I am advocating will tend to develop protective standards of a more public nature, to test those who seek to join or lead communities. But a Buddhist virtues approach requires shoring up with useful ethical strategies developed in the West both to assess particular acts and to generate moral rules. The Western Buddhist milieu may also require a *heuristic* recovery of the Vinaya tradition of Buddhist monastic regulation. The Vinaya may have strayed into the trap of legalistic casuistry, but it did define and set procedures for adjudicating particular acts of monks that could not be tolerated, that had to result in suspension or expulsion. Western Buddhist communities are only now beginning to face up to this kind of decision-making, for which a virtues-orientation is sometimes inadequate.

Having said all this, I acknowledge that act-evaluations and rule-adjudications must be secondary instruments in Buddhist ethics, necessary as they may be in particular moments of particular communities. Essentially, Buddhist ethics is centered in and on 'character in community.' This focus needs to be kept, for upon it depends the future development of a Buddhist ethics more aimed at relationships than principles, more interested in mutual support than a defense of rights, more empathic than rational, more compassionate than just.

Ethical strategies focusing on rational rules and judgments of particular outward acts are the essential feature of groups so large that they constitute a *society* of strangers, threatened by the Hobbesian shadows of competition and governed by laws of contract, restraint, coercion, property, and command.[38] Laws are secondary to virtue in a Buddhist setting (and in this I agree with Western Buddhists who resist 'code' or rule-oriented moralizing as a dominant approach to self- or community-discipline). Nevertheless, while secondary, they are not dispensable.

The primary focus on persons, character, and virtuous practices in Buddhist ethics cannot be sustained without *community*, places where we know each other well enough to call each other into the intimacies of an ethics of intention and practice, as in a family. This means that Buddhist communities must ever be small, small enough that people intimately know each other and the other sentient beings sharing their life and death. I propose that they can be too small, in that a group of four or six can hardly challenge and support the full range of self-cultivation practices necessary to awakened virtue.

The problem of size for many Buddhists in the West lies at the 'too small' end of the spectrum. But that is better than to be at the 'too large' end. I cannot identify a practicing community that has become too large (say, more than 200 active members), unless one looks at the large metropolitan communities in San Francisco and Los Angeles, which are arguably too large, too complex, and too absorbed in the entropic tasks of organization maintenance of buildings, mortgages, and so on.

We know from reading Aristotle and MacIntyre that an ethics focused in virtue does not picture the way to the good life in abstract or individual or universal terms. The paths of virtue are marked by lived practices special to each community. Virtue-oriented groups and communities, if we are to believe MacIntyre and Hauerwas, depend more on their traditional 'narrative' reality-frames, their memories and stories of good persons practicing the good life, than on their laws or universal principles.[39] But, we also know that Western Buddhists today live in a post-Nietzschean world, where the 'stories' are many and 'memory' is tattered. It is not at all clear to many Western people that their chosen or inherited stories invoke human reality in a coherent and compelling way.

31

In the postmodern West, the Buddha's story or the life of awakened virtue can be told and tested only in small, marginalized zones appropriately distanced from the dominant power and value structures. The criteria of testing are two: 1) the plausibility of the story of a person who, through specific practices in a certain kind of community, 'awakened, by and through virtuous practices, in wisdom and compassion;' and 2) the evident goodness in the people and communities now engaged in practices of the Dharma. These people are the Buddha. Their story is the Buddha's story.

Acceptance of the virtues approach in ethics presents specific challenges and advantages to Buddhist thinkers and other scholars. For example, we need to develop a more historical scholarship of the *pāramitās* dimension in Buddhism. But, hopefully, we can also help people in today's Buddhist communities to think through the tensions among the *pāramitās*, the problems of priorities, the meanings of practicing in lay life, and a host of other on-the-ground issues. We need to help Western Buddhists distinguish among therapeutic, aesthetic, moral, economic, political, and spiritual practices and choices. What is the optimum balance of attention and consideration between self and others? What is Buddhist friendship? Does it include mosquitoes? How and why do Buddhists fail morally after years of practice? How does a virtues orientation link up with social justice issues and the development of a Buddhist social ethics? Far more moral and ethical questions buzz in Western Buddhists' lives, awaiting creative, practical inquiry by philosophers, new-generation Buddhologists, and others.

I have been recommending the virtues approach. It needs a fuller development, in order to carry Buddhist morality into an inevitable, serious and mutually constructive dialogue with Western philosophers and theologians. My recommendations may appear too straitlaced, or even atavistically Victorian, but what seems clear to me so far is this: the most constructive future of Buddhism in the West rests on its manifestation in the characters of people, not in eloquent prose, fundraising efforts, temple-building, or incomplete life modeling. Hopefully, a new generation will increasingly take the path of balancing *samādhi*-exercise with *pāramitās*-practices. Put simply, the future depends on a few good women and men who reveal a balanced, integrative life of 'awakened virtue' practices, in families, jobs, and communities. It is through good lives that the Buddha's Dharma can fully flower in the West, transforming our sufferings and awakening in us, each and all, that which is best, inch by inch, moment by moment, breath by breath.

Notes

1 First published in the *Journal of Buddhist Ethics* vol.1 1994:1–22. Reprinted here with permission and minor editorial changes.

2 Alasdair MacIntyre, *After Virtue* 2nd ed. (Notre Dame, Ind.: University of Notre Dame Press, 1984; Stanley Hauerwas, *A Community of Character* (Notre Dame, Ind.: University of Notre Dame Press, 1981).

3 For my judgment that Buddhism will fail to bear fruit in the United States unless it develops moral practices and ethical reflection more in concert with American realities, see James Whitehill, *Enter the Quiet* (San Francisco: Harper & Row, Publishers, 1980), pp. 60–74, and Whitehill, 'Is There a Zen Ethic?' *The Eastern Buddhist (New Series)* 20 (Spring 1987), pp. 9–33.

4 A promising and brief sketch of the philosophical roots of Buddhist ethics in the doctrine of 'dependent co-arising' (*paṭicca-samuppāda*), with a good discussion of 'moral agency,' is Joanna Macy's 'Dependent Co-arising: The Distinctiveness of Buddhist Ethics,' *The Journal of Religious Ethics*, Vol. 7 No. 1 (Spring 1979), pp. 38–52. But Macy did not explicitly acknowledge the commensurability of Buddhist ethics with virtue ethics, in terms of key similarities with respect to the nature of the self, dispositions (kamma, *saṅkhāras*, etc.), and freedom.

5 I think here first of the San Francisco Renaissance figures of Jack Kerouac and Gary Snyder, but also of Erich Fromm, William Barrett, Alan Watts, Thomas Merton, and other writers who probed parallels between Zen and their own home-grown existential concerns.

6 Relevant sources include: (on feminism) Rita Gross, 'Buddhism and Feminism: Toward their Mutual Transformation,' *The Eastern Buddhist* 19 (Autumn 1986), pp. 62–74; Sandy Boucher, *Turning the Wheel: American Women Creating the New Buddhism* (San Francisco: Harper & Row, Publishers, 1988); (on environmentalism) Allan H. Badiner, ed., *Dharma Gaia* (Berkeley: Parallax Press, 1990); J. Baird Callicott and Roger T. Ames, eds., *Nature in Asian Traditions of Thought* (Albany: SUNY Press, 1989); James Whitehill, 'Ecological Consciousness and Values: Japanese Perspectives,' *Ecological Consciousness*, eds J. Donald Hughes and George Schultz (New York: University Press of America, 1980), pp. 165–182; (on the peace movement) Fred Eppsteiner, ed., *The Path of Compassion: Writings on Socially Engaged Buddhism* (Berkeley: Parallax Press, 1988).

7 See David J. Kalupahana, 'The Buddhist Conceptions of "Subject" and "Object" and their Moral Implications,' *Philosophy East and West* 33 (July 1988), pp. 290–304; Christopher A. Ives, 'A Zen Buddhist Social Ethic,' (Unpublished Ph.D. dissertation, Claremont Graduate School, 1988) and *Zen Awakening and Society* (Honolulu: University of Hawaii Press, 1992); Robert A. Thurman, 'Guidelines for Buddhist Social Activism Based on Nāgārjuna's *Jewel Garland of Royal Counsels*,' *The Eastern Buddhist (New Series)* 16 (Spring 1983), pp. 19–51. For a Kantian approach, see Philip Olson, *The Discipline of Freedom: A Kantian View of the Role of Moral Precepts in Zen Practice* (Albany: State University of New York, Press, 1993).

8 See Winston L. King, 'Buddhist Self-World Theory and Buddhist Ethics,' *The Eastern Buddhist* (New Series) 22 (Autumn 1989), pp. 14– 26; 'A Buddhist Ethic for the West?' (unpublished manuscript, 1990).

9 A large bibliography of contemporary writings in virtues theory is in Robert B. Kruschwitz and Robert C. Roberts, ed., *The Virtues: Contemporary Essays on Moral Character* (Belmont, Calif.: Wadsworth Publishing Company, 1987), pp. 237–63. For a discussion of the translatability and commensurability of one ethical tradition (e.g. Buddhist) with another (e.g. Western virtues tradition), see Stephen E. Fowl, 'Could Horace Talk with the Hebrews? Translatability and Moral Disagreement in MacIntrye and Stout,' *The Journal of Religious Ethics* Vol. 19 No.1 (Spring, 1991), pp. 1– 20.

10 Damien Keown, *The Nature of Buddhist Ethics* (New York: St. Martin's Press, 1992). See especially Chap. 1, 'The Study of Buddhist Ethics,' and Chap. 8, 'Buddhism and Aristotle.'

11 Robert N. Bellah, 'The Meaning of Dogen Today,' *Dogen Studies*, ed. William R. LaFleur (Honolulu: University of Hawaii Press, 1985), pp. 157–8.

12 'Soul and soil' because a complete virtue ethics not only refers to the capacities of 'human beings in general,' but also the particular limitations for expressing those capacities in terms of the 'soil,' literally and metaphorically, in which those capacities for 'humanity at its best' are grown. Virtue is formed by 'place,' and a change of place or soil requires appropriate transformation of the virtues. Ivan Illich and others have called for a 'philosophy of soil,' because 'our generation has lost its grounding in both soil and virtue. By virtue, we mean that shape, order and direction of action informed by tradition, bounded by place, and qualified by choices made within the habitual reach of the actor; we mean practice mutually recognized as being good within a shared local culture which enhances the memory of a place.' See, 'Declaration of Soil,' *Whole Earth Review*, No. 71 (Summer, 1991), p. 75.

13 By 'awakened,' I mean the process and state of an empowering liberation of the self, by means of ego-transforming praxis. By 'virtue,' I mean the ideal cultivated set of rational discernments, personal skills, and dispositions of character regarded as ideal and relevant to relations with self and others in a known and shared community, in this case the Buddhist community. In Buddhism as I understand it, moral virtue and spiritual awakening are coordinate and mutually necessary; neither alone is sufficient for attaining Buddhahood.

14 *Śīla*, 'custom or manner,' but usually referring to the Five Precepts, avoidance dicta, such as, 'Avoid harming living beings,' etc. *Pāramitā*, 'high,' 'complete,' or 'perfect,' but usually in the context of a list of 'perfections,' akin to the virtues, characterizing the praxis and character of those pursuing the Buddhist goals of selflessness, insight, compassion, and liberation or 'salvation.'

15 Several works can provide historical and textual framework for Buddhist ethics, including H. Saddhatissa, *Buddhist Ethics* (New York: George Braziller, 1970), and Gunapala Dharmasiri, *Fundamentals of Buddhist Ethics* (Antioch, Calif.: Golden Leaves Publishing Company, 1989). Lopez's recent discussion of virtues and sainthood from the Mahāyāna bodhisattva perspective, with comparisons to Roman Catholic tradition, is detailed enough to be helpful; Donald S. Lopez, Jr., 'Sanctification on the Bodhisattva Path,' *Sainthood*, eds. Richard Kieckhefer and George S. Bond (Berkeley: University of California Press, 1988).

16 For a classic discussion of the *pāramitās*, Śāntideva, *The Path of Light*, trans. L.D. Barnett (AMS Press, 1990). A more recent translation of Śāntideva's *Bodhicārya-avatāra* is Marion Matics' *Entering the Path of Enlightenment* (London: Macmillan Company, 1970).

17 Robert Aitken, *The Mind of Clover: Essays in Zen Buddhist Ethics* (San Francisco: North Point Press, 1984), p. 158.

18 Aitken, *The Mind of Clover*, p. 159.

19 See Whitehill, 'Is There a Zen Ethic?'

20 Gerta Ital, *On the Way to Satori: A Women's Experience of Enlightenment*, trans. Timothy Green (Dorset, England: Element Books, Ltd., 1990), p. 276.

21 Ken Jones, *The Social Face of Buddhism: An Approach to Political and Social Activism* (London: Wisdom Publications, 1989).

22 Dharmasiri, interestingly, argues that Buddhist ethics is best understood as a peculiar, non-hedonic form of act utilitarianism; *Fundamentals of Buddhist Ethics*, pp. 26–27.

23 Much confusion in thinking about Buddhism in the West results because the Asian cultures from which it comes focus morality in the 'roles' people play in hierarchical, organic relationships, while modern Westerners who have taken up Buddhism are often urged by their traditions to view morality from the perspective of the autonomous, isolated self, understood as an expressive 'personality.' This cross-cultural difference needs to be more carefully used and understood by Buddhist interpreters. On the contemporary American shift of interest from 'character' to 'personality,' see Anthony Quinton, 'Character and

Culture,' in *Vice and Virtue in Everyday Life*, ed. Christina & Fred Sommers (New York: Harcourt Brace Jovanovic, Publishers, 1989), pp. 613–22.

24 Jones, *The Social Face of Buddhism*, p. 157.

25 Robert H. Scharf, 'Being Buddha: A Performative Approach to Ch'an Enlightenment' (unpublished manuscript, 1989). Hee-jin Kim, *Dogen Kigen: Mystic Realist* (Tucson: The University of Arizona Press, 1987), pp. 172–3. Martin Southwold argues, in the instance of Sinhalese Buddhism, that ethical behavior is the focus and vehicle of the 'ritual impulse' for Buddhist laypeople in Sri Lanka. Absent a transcendent focus of religious worship and ritual reference, Buddhists have made of ethics and the Dharma the object of ritual activity. Of course, the form of ethics most congenial to ritualization is, of course, virtue ethics. See Southwold, *Buddhism in life: the anthropological study of religion and the Sinhalese practice of Buddhism* (Dover, N.H.: Manchester University Peress, 1983), pp. 162–80.

26 *Nicomachean Ethics*, Book II, Chap. 4. See M.F. Burnyeat, 'Aristotle on Learning to Be Good,' *Essays on Aristotle's Ethics*, ed. Amelie Oksenberg Rorty (Berkeley: University of California Press, 1980), pp. 69–92.

27 I am taking a rather casual approach to the spelling of these terms, choosing between the Pali and the Sanskrit renderings on the basis of which seems easiest to pronounce and remember in English. I am casual with an excuse however, for I think it must soon be necessary to coin English phonetic neologues for these terms, and I am merely choosing those I like (e.g., I think *paññā* is weak-sounding in English when referring to a powerfully transforming insight, or *prajñā*-insight).

28 I hope someone with perseverance can attempt an analysis of the *pāramitās*, in comparative light, akin to Lee Yearley's arduous study of the theories of virtue in Mencius and Aquinas. Yearley takes the study of virtue deep into comparative terrain, marking assiduously more distinctions between Aquinas and Mencius than I care to know, because I cannot see readily what difference they make. Lee Yearley, *Mencius and Aquinas: Theories of Virtue and Conceptions of Courage* (Albany: State University of New York Press, 1990).

29 Vijay Nath, *Dāna: Gift System in Ancient India* (New Delhi: Munshiram Manoharlal Publishers, 1987).

30 See Melford Spiro, *Buddhism and Society* (New York: Harper & Row, Publishers, 1970); Winston L. King, *In the Hope of Nibbana* (LaSalle, Ill.: Open Court, 1964). Spiro and King, while admiring many of the personal qualities of Buddhist laypeople, tend to diminish their moral achievements as self-regarding, because lay Buddhists link good deeds and good character with favorable rebirths. Scholars from Christian cultures that have given the highest moral value to self-sacrificing altruism, agape, are not likely to regard the Buddha's injunction, to avoid the extremes of self-indulgence and self-mortification, as the most heroic spiritual advice.

31 Some scholars believe King and Spiro make too sharp a distinction between layperson and monk, between kamma-motives and Nibbāna-motives, in Theravāda Buddhism. See, Harvey B. Aronson, 'The Relationship of the Karmic to the Nirvanic in Theravada Buddhism,' *The Journal of Religious Ethics*, Vol. 7 No. 1 (Spring 1979), pp. 28–36; Donald K. Swearer, 'Bhikkhu Buddhadasa on Ethics and Society,' *The Journal of Religious Ethics*, Vol. 7 No. 1 (Spring 1979), pp. 54–64. Southwold makes his argument against this 'elitist' and 'modernist' interpretation of a dualistic Buddhism the center of his work, Buddhism in Life. See also, Damien Keown, *The Nature of Buddhist Ethics*, pp. 83–105.

32 Robert A. Thurman, trans., *The Holy Teaching of Vimalakīrti* (London: The Pennsylvania State University Press, 1976).

33 This self-concept gives trouble to ethical systems, like Kant's, and social-political traditions, like Western liberalism (of progressive or conservative varieties), that function in terms of rights-claims, human rights, etc. Buddhist ethics, insofar as it is grounded in the

processional, ecological self-in-community, and articulated teleologically in terms of the specific *pāramitās* and their cultivation, must be in tension with Western tradition on this issue, so long as Western ethics and legal structures are primarily designed to serve individual and corporate property interests. This is not to claim that Buddhist ethics overlooks or radically discounts individual human rights. The origins of Buddhism clearly reflect a vision of human life that is prejudiced toward individual release from social, as well as psychic, oppression of the human spirit. Buddhist ethics supports democracy and human rights protection as a preferable arrangement of social, legal, and religious tolerance. However, Buddhist ethics views such tolerance and protection as only two of the conditions for a good human life.

34 See Joanna Macy, 'The Ecological Self: Postmodern Ground for Right Action,' *Sacred Interconnections*, ed. David Ray Griffin (Albany: State University Press of New York, 1990), pp. 35–48.

35 David E. Shaner develops the Japanese Buddhist connection between cultivation of character and a 'biophilic' experience of nature in an excellent article, 'The Japanese Experience of Nature,' *Nature in Asian Traditions of Thought*, ed. J. Baird Callicott and Roger T. Ames (Albany: State University of New York Press, 1989), pp. 163–82.

36 See Shaner's review of recent biographies of the Buddha, in which he discusses the nature and limits of Buddhist hagiography; David E. Shaner, 'Biographies of the Buddha' *Philosophy East and West* 37 (July 1987), pp. 306–22.

37 Helen Tworkov's *Zen in America: Profiles of Five Teachers* (San Francisco: North Point Press, 1989) discusses moral concerns in connection with the behavior of some American Zen teachers, but avoids using the words 'moral' and 'ethical' and makes little use of Buddhist moral tradition to clarify the concerns discussed. Sandy Boucher reports moral concerns of many American women growing out of their experiences in American Buddhist centers; Boucher, *Turning the Wheel: American Women Creating the New Buddhism*.

38 Frank Kirkpatrick and I have ventured a comparative philosophical discussion of Buddhist and Christian models of community in our 'Mutual/Personal Community: Buddhist and Christian Models' (unpublished manuscript, 1990). See Kirkpatrick's *Together Bound: God, History, and the Religious Community* (New York: Oxford University Press, 1994).

39 See, for example, Alasdair MacIntyre's much referred to chapter, 'The Virtues, The Unity of a Human Life and the Concept of a Tradition,' in *After Virtue*. His emphasis on the 'narrative' quality of life is not common to all virtue theorists. The Buddhist notion of 'narrative' is, I presume, sufficiently different from the Christian notion to offer a useful test of MacIntyre's claims. For example, is the story of Jesus' life, death and resurrection more 'plausible' (MacIntyre's criterion) than the story of Siddhārtha Gautama?

CHAPTER TWO

From Monastic Ethics to Modern Society[1]

Charles Prebish

The topic of Buddhist ethics has become sufficiently timely and consequential that it now provides the occasion for sponsoring international conferences. In 1990, the first Chung-Hwa Institute of Buddhist Studies International Conference on Buddhism was organized by its director, Venerable Sheng-Yen, and convened at Taipei's National Central Library with 'Buddhist Ethics and Modern Society' as its essential focus. The papers presented at the conference were collected into a volume entitled *Buddhist Ethics and Modern Society*, edited by Charles Wei-hsun Fu and Sandra A.Wawrytko. It is perhaps the most useful of all recent books on the subject due to the breadth and scope of its twenty-nine papers spanning the past, present, and future. The success of the initial conference enabled the Chung-Hwa Institute to hold a second conference in summer 1992.

Venerable Sheng-Yen, in the Prologue to *Buddhist Ethics and Modern Society*, says 'The precepts (*Vinaya*) form the basis of Buddhist ethics.' He goes on to say that 'Buddhist lay members need obey only 5, or at the most 8, Buddhist novices must obey 10, while adult monks and nuns have to obey anywhere from 250 to more than 300.'[2] Although Sheng-Yen is wrong in not distinguishing the basis of ethical conduct for the laity as separate from the monastic code of the *Vinaya*, a traditional association in East Asian Buddhism where the terms *śīla* and *Vinaya* are compounded, his mistake is rather commonly made even the Indian tradition where the terms are indeed separate and never compounded. Akira Hirakawa has offered considerable insight on the need to separate the traditional compound *śīla/vinaya* into its component parts for a proper understanding of each term,[3] but it is rather ordinary and regular, I think, for scholars to associate *Vinaya* rather than *śīla* with ethics.

It is critical for our study to understand why the distinction between these terms is so important, and precisely how the distinction impacts on our original topic. The technical term *Vinaya*, derived from the Sanskrit prefix *vi+√nī*, is often rendered as (some variant of) training, education, discipline, or control. John Holt, utilizing another etymologically valid approach suggests, '*Vinaya*, the reified noun form of the verb *vi+√nī* therefore leads us to the general meaning of "that which separates," or "that which removes."'[4] Holt goes on:

> Our translation of the term *vinaya* begs the question: what is being removed? To answer that question in the simplest terms, that which is being removed are wrong states of mind, the conditions of grasping, desire and ignorance which stem from the delusion that we have a 'self' that can be satiated. The discipline of the *Vinaya Piṭaka* represents a systematic assault on the idea of 'ego-consciousness.'[5]

Charles Wei-hsun Fu, utilizing Hirakawa's etymological analysis which captures the essence of both meanings cited above, comes to the same conclusion: '*Vinaya* referred to the established norms of the Sangha that all members were expected to observe to maintain the monastic order and insure its continuation.'[6] In other words, the *Vinaya* was as much concerned with the *pariśuddhi* or complete purity of the community, individually and organizationally, as it was with the specifics of ethical conduct.[7] Under no circumstances should we presume that ethical concerns were superseded in the *Vinaya*, but rather were included in a series of tiered concerns that focused on institutional, but not exclusively ethical conduct.

Śīla, more difficult etymologically than *Vinaya*, is probably derived from the verb *√śīl* and generally translated as virtue, moral conduct, morality, or some similar variant (although Buddhaghosa in the *Visuddhimagga* traces it to a different verb root, associated with 'cooling' and Vasubandhu in the *Abhidharmakośa* suggests it derives from the verb *√śī*, which he too associates with cooling).[8] As such, it is a highly ethical term, almost exclusively applied to the individual, and referenced to his or her self-discipline. Additionally, one finds such references continually in the literature.[9] Unlike the *Vinaya*, which is externally enforced, *śīla* refers to the internally enforced ethical framework by which the monk or nun structures his or her life.[10] Taken in this light, we can see that *śīla* is an incredibly rich concept for understanding individual ethical conduct. Thus, as Fu points out, with respect to *śīla* and *Vinaya*:

> Hirakawa's analysis of the two words seems to have enormous significance for Buddhist ethics. Our present inquiry into the essential meaning of Buddhist ethics and morality, to address the task of its constructive modernization, demands that we give serious considera-tion to the means for maintaining a balance between autonomy (*śila*) [sic], expressing the inner spirit of Dharma, and the heteronomous norms or precepts (*vinaya*) of the Buddhist order.[11]

Although the *Sūtravibhaṅga* and its paracanonical precursor, the *Prātimokṣa* (that portion of the *Vinaya Piṭaka* devoted to precepts for the individual monks and nuns), contain many rules reflective of significant ethical awareness and concern, is it appropriate to identify the *Sūtravibhaṅga* as an exclusively ethical document? If we could establish that the canonical *Vinaya* texts, of which the *Sūtravibhaṅga* is a critical part, have their basis in the precepts of *śīla*, then such an argument might be well taken. In this regard, one of the pioneers of comparative *Prātimokṣa* study, W. Pachow, argues for precisely that position in asserting that the Buddhist disciplinary code was little more than an embellishment of the traditional, widely known, and quite early, *Pañcaśīla* or five ethical precepts. Pachow says:

> It would not be unreasonable to say that the code of discipline of the *Saṅgha* is but an enlarged edition of the *Pañcaśīla* which have been adopted by the Buddhists and the Jains from the Brāhmaṇical ascetics. And under various circumstances, they have developed subsidiary rules in order to meet various requirements on various occasions. This appears to us to be the line of development through which the growth of these rules could be explained.[12]

He then attempts to identify a clear developmental relationship between the individual precepts of the *Pañcaśīla* and the lesser, secondary rules of the *Prātimokṣa*. Pachow's interesting approach is cited by most scholars researching the problem. Holt, for example, says, 'If this hypothesis were absolutely sound, we could somehow relate all of the disciplinary rules in some way to the four *pārājikas* or to the *pañaśīla*. Unfortunately, we are not able to do this.'[13] Using the Pāli text as the benchmark, 139 of the 227 *Pātimokkha* rules can be explained. Nonetheless, 88 rules cannot be reconciled! Undaunted, Pachow simply creates new categories to accommodate them.[14] The problem is further exacerbated by the fact that the *Pañcaśīla* largely mirror the rules for Brāhmaṇical ascetics and Jain monks. Holt summarizes well:

> Thus, if we are to argue that the fundamental basis of Buddhist discipline consists of the primary concerns of *śīla*, we would have to admit that the basis of Buddhist discipline is not exclusively Buddhist, nor Śramaṇic, not even monastic for that matter: not a very satisfying finding.[15]

In the beginning of his important chapter on 'Aspects of *Sīla*' in *The Nature of Buddhist Ethics*, Damien Keown clearly identifies the impact of the above argument: 'Overall, there seems to be no reason to assume that the *Vinaya* is either derived from a simpler set of moral principles or founded upon a single underlying principle or rationale.'[16] The remarks of Holt and Keown mirror what Prebish said rather directly in 1980: the '*Prātimokṣa* is not just monastic "glue" holding the *saṅgha* together, but the common ground on which the internally enforced life of *śīla* is manifested externally in the community.'[17] More recently, and aggressively, Lambert Schmithausen has made the same point. He notes, 'The *Vinaya* is not concerned, primarily, with morality proper but rather with the internal harmony and external reputation of the Order.'[18] He goes on to say, 'One of the main purposes of the *Pātimokkha* (though some of its prohibitions do also refer to morality proper) is no doubt, besides internal harmony, the correct and decorous behaviour of the Order and its members in society.'[19] If Upāli's recitation of the first council of Rājagrha has as much to do with communal administration and conduct as it does with individual moral behavior, and if the canonical *Vinaya Piṭaka*, even in the *Sūtravibhaṅga*, devotes more than one-third of its regulations to matters that could at best be referred to as etiquette, where, if anywhere in the Buddhist canon, can we find a fuller exegesis of *śīla*, acknowledged to be a more comprehensive, apt, and better descriptive term for Buddhist ethical concerns than *Vinaya*? Further, although the commentarial tradition associated with the *Vinaya* presents an immense literature in Pāli, replete with *ṭikās*, sub-*ṭikās*, and the like, it remains somewhat limited in scope with regard to more modern issues.[20] Thus, it becomes necessary to question whether it is possible for the textual material on *śīla* to be functional in a transtemporal and transcultural fashion.

If we acknowledge that the most general and consistent treatment of ethics in Buddhism is revealed by its expositions on *śīla*, then it also becomes critical for an accurate understanding of Buddhist ethics to ask the question clearly put by Winston King in 1964: 'What is the relation of ethics to the total structure of Buddhist doctrine and practice, particularly with regard to the definition of moral values, their metaphysical status if any, and the nature of ultimate sanctions?'[21] The traditional way of expressing King's question considers the relationship between the three aspects of the eightfold path, *śīla*, *samādhi*, and *prajñā*, and their connection to *nirvāṇa*. Damien Keown reviews several longstanding notions on how these soteriological elements relate.[22] Keown first cites the most common view that *śīla* leads to *samādhi* which leads to *prajñā*, and that *prajñā* is identified with *nirvāṇa*. In this context, the ethical concerns expressed by *śīla* are at best subsidiary to the others, and are generally thought to be transcended with the attainment of *nirvāṇa*. Secondly, it may be argued that ethical enterprise may facilitate enlightenment, and following the attainment of *nirvāṇa*, once again become operative. Thirdly, ethics and knowledge (i.e., *prajñā*) may both be present in the attainment of the final goal. About his review Keown concludes:

> The three possibilities outlined above represent very different visions of the role of ethics in the Buddhist soteriological programme. In the first two cases, which I have bracketed together, ethics is extrinsic to

nibbāna, dispensable, and subsidiary to *paññā*. In the third it is intrinsic to *nibbāna*, essential, and equal in value to *paññā*.[23]

Although the prevailing viewpoint in Buddhist scholarship has tended toward a utilitarian conclusion on the issue of *śīla*, especially with regard to Theravāda studies, and despite the contrariness of Mahāyāna-based testimony, an ever-increasing volume of new scholarship has rejected the so-called 'transcendency thesis,' in favor of a more valued role for those practices collected under the categorical term *śīla*.[24] In so doing, it becomes possible to consider those principles categorized as *śīla* collectively, as a synthetic reflection of both *nikāya* Buddhism and Mahāyāna, and perhaps to at least reconsider, and at most dispel, such notions as *śīla* representing a purely mundane goal, largely considered as the highest pursuit for the laity, and practiced by monks and nuns only as a preparation for *samādhi*. If we summarize the relationship between *śīla*, *samādhi*, and *prajñā*, it becomes possible to delineate a clear and precise connection:

> The fact that the Eightfold Path begins with *śīla* does not mean that morality is only a preliminary stage. The Eightfold Path begins with *śīla* but ends with *śīla* and *paññā*. *Sīla* is the starting point since human nature is so constituted that moral discipline (*śīla*) facilitates intellectual discipline (*paññā*). Until correct attitudes, habits, and dispositions have been inculcated it is easy to fall prey to speculative views and opinions of all kinds. This does not mean that there is a direct line leading through *śīla* to *paññā*, or that morality is merely a means of limbering up for the intellectual athlete. No: morality is taken up first but constantly cultivated alongside insight until the two fuse in the transformation of the entire personality in the existential realisation of selflessness.[25]

Finally, the author of the above quotation integrates the role of *samādhi* in the progression as well. He says, 'In the scheme of the Eightfold Path, *samādhi* stands between *śīla* and *paññā* and supplements them both. It is a powerful technique for the acceleration of ethical and intellectual developments towards their perfection in *nibbāna*.'[26]

Having established the efficacy of *śīla* rather than *Vinaya* as the primary and most essential category of inquiry for matters pertinent to the ethical tradition in Buddhism, and having established *śīla* as critical throughout the Buddhist path to enlightenment and after its attainment, we can now proceed to an examination of the *sūtra*, and to a lesser extent, *Abhidharma* literature fundamental to the *śīla* tradition.

The clearest and most detailed exposition of *śīla* in the Pāli Canon can be found in the first thirteen suttas of the *Dīgha Nikāya*, a section collectively referred to as the *Sīlakkhandhavagga*. The first, and perhaps most important of these thirteen texts cited above, is the *Brahmajāla-sutta* or the 'Discourse on Brahma's Net.' The preliminary, critical portion of this text is divided into three sections termed, respectively, the short (*cūla*), medium (*majjhima*), and long (*mahā*) divisions. These three sections occur in each of the thirteen *suttas* of the *Sīlakkhandhavagga*. Thomas W. Rhys Davids, in the notes to his translation of these sections of the *Dīgha Nikāya*, refers to them as the '*Sīla Vagga*,' and says that 'the tract itself must almost certainly have existed as a separate work before the time when the discourses, in each of which it recurs, were first put together.'[27] The short tract (as Rhys Davids calls the division) contains twenty-six items of moral conduct, the medium tract ten, and the long tract seven, and while each tract is important for understanding the developing notion of Buddhist morality, it is the short tract that is most most critical. Compared to the various codes of precepts that have become the standard of proper Buddhist conduct, namely, the (in Pāli) *pañcasīla* (five precepts), *aṭṭhaṅgasīla* (eight precepts), *dasasīla* (ten precepts), *dasakusalakammapatha* (ten good paths of action), and *Pātimokkha* (formal monastic disciplinary code), one can correlate four of the five *pañcasīla* to the short tract, seven of the eight *aṭṭhaṅgasīla*, nine of the ten *dasasīla*, seven of the ten *dasakusalakammapatha*, and, as we have seen above, 139 of the 227 offenses of the *Pātimokkha*. This close correspondence is important because '...the conduct of the ideal *samaṇa* as defined in the Short Tract becomes the foundation of Buddhist ethics.'[28] Although the *Brahmajāla-sutta* is possibly the clearest exposition of all the discourses in the *Sīla Vagga*, a number of other texts are also especially important for understanding *sīla* in a contextual framework consistent with Buddhist soteriology. The *Sāmaññaphala-sutta* or 'Discourse on the Fruits of the Religious Life,' for example, links the practice of *sīla* to meditative attainment, destruction of the imperfections known as *āsavas* (usually translated as 'outflows' or 'cankers'), and the achievement of arhanthood. The famous eightfold path, with its division into *sīla*, *samādhi*, and *paññā*, is mentioned in the *Mahāli-sutta* ('Discourse to Mahāli') and the *Kassapasīhanāda-sutta* ('Discourse on the Lion's Roar to Kassapa'). Nor should we conclude that ethicality is not emphasized in the other parts of the canon, as the *Maṅgala-sutta* of the *Khuddaka Nikāya*, *Metta-sutta* of the *Suttanipāta*, and *Sigālovāda-sutta* of the *Dīgha Nikāya* are among the most important Theravāda texts on this subject.

It would also be incorrect to presume *sīla* as topically important only in the *sūtras*. It is also of much interest to *Abhidharma* and later commentarial authors as well. Nowhere is this more plainly visible than the Theravādin *Abhidhamma*, the first text of which (i.e., the *Dhammasaṅgaṇī*) classifies mental elements around a markedly ethical base. According to G.S.P. Misra, the *Puggalapaññatti* as well 'deals with the task of the classification of human types in which ethical consideration, among others, is the most dominant principle.'[29] Anuruddha's *Abhidhammattha-saṅgaha* offers a list of fourteen immoral and nineteen moral mental constituents (*cetasikas*).[30]

Additionally, ethical concerns abound in the appropriate sections of Buddhaghosa's *Visuddhimagga* and virtually throughout the *Milindapañha*. In the *Sarvāstivādin* tradition too, twenty-eight of the forty-six *caittas* have clear ethical import: ten positive mental constituents known as *kuśala-mahābhūmika-dharmas* and eighteen negative mental constituents (composed of six *kleśas* or defilements, two *akuśala-mahābhūmika-dharmas* or universally bad elements, and ten *upakleśas* or secondary defilements).[31] The ethical considerations in Vasubandhu's *Abhidharmakośa* are simply too numerous to cite. What it boils down to is this: 'The *Abhidharma* posits two classes of mental forces which produce either defilement or purification of the mind.'[32]

How does the above present a consistent, harmonious picture for the early Buddhist? In the *Kassapasīhanāda-sutta*, Buddha says, of his own ethical attainment:

> Now there are some recluses and Brahmans, Kassapa, who lay emphasis on conduct. They speak, in various ways, in praise of morality. But so far as regards the really noble, the highest conduct, I am aware of no one who is equal to myself, much less superior. And it is I who have gone the furthest therein; that is, in the highest conduct (of the Path).[33]

Of course the Pāli word utilized to indicate 'highest conduct' is *adhisīla*. The implication of Buddha's statement is clear enough: Buddha's attainment was unquestionably motivated by compassion and fueled by moral development of the highest order, but also that the attainment of Buddhahood (or, for that matter, arhantship) does not preclude ethical propriety. No doubt the cultivation of meditational attainment, as we indicated earlier, bridges the proverbial gap between *sīla* and *paññā*, and not only does this suggest that meditational experience has serious impact on the moral life, but also that '*Sīla* is a central feature of the conduct of the enlightened...'[34] Keown notes that 'the Arahat certainly has not gone beyond *kusala*, and *kusala* is the term which par excellence denotes ethical goodness.'[35] Ethical goodness, as manifested by Buddha or any serious practitioner, is a reflection of his sympathy (*anukampā*) for all sentient beings and manifested by cultivation of the four *Brahmavihāras* or 'Divine Abodes,' as Aronson has amply demonstrated.[36]

If the above paragraph demonstrates that Buddhist ethical development takes its inspiration from Buddha's personal example, it is not unreasonable to conclude about the Buddha, as Lal Mani Joshi does, that:

> His love of solitude and silence was matched only by his universal compassion towards the suffering creatures. Hīnayāna seems to have laid emphasis on the former while Mahāyāna on the latter aspect of the Buddha's personality and ideal.[37]

Such an approach lead Joshi and others to identify the ethical approach of the Buddhist *nikāyas* as narrower and more limited in scope than Mahāyāna. About Mahāyāna, Joshi remarks, 'Its aim is higher, its outlook broader, and its aspiration more sublime than that of Hīnayāna.'[38] One should not read Joshi's evaluation too aggressively, or as a rejection of the earlier understanding of *śīla*, but rather as what Keown aptly calls a 'paradigm shift.'[39] This paradigm shift is of course reflected by the Mahāyāna emphasis on the bodhisattva ideal.

Nalinaksha Dutt, in his still important *Aspects of Mahāyāna Buddhism and Its Relation to Hīnayāna*, notes that the Chinese pilgrim I-ching 'who was chiefly interested in the *Vinaya*, remarks that the Mahāyānists had no *Vinaya* of their own and that theirs was the same as that of the Hīnayānists.'[40] Dutt, however, goes on to list a large number of Mahāyāna sūtras that deal with ethical issues, including the *Bodhisattvacaryānirdeśa*, *Bodhisattva-prātimokṣa-sūtra*, *Bhikṣu Vinaya*, *Ākāśagarbha-sūtra*, *Upāliparipṛcchā-sūtra*, *Ugradattaparipṛcchā-sūtra*, *Ratnamegha-sūtra*, and *Ratnarāśi-sūtra*.[41] Of these, the *Bodhisattva-prātimokṣa-sūtra* and the *Upāliparipṛcchā-sūtra* are clearly the best known. The former was edited by Dutt and published in *Indian Historical Quarterly*,[42] but to my knowledge, has never been translated into English. It is a *sūtra* only in name, comprised primarily of fragments taken from the *Upāliparipṛccha-sūtra* and the *Bodhisattvabhūmi*.[43] Nonetheless, it is not a code of monastic rules for bodhisattvas, as its name implies, but rather a general ethical guide for both lay and monastic bodhisattvas. The *Upāliparipṛcchā-sūtra* has benefitted from the fine scholarly translation of Pierre Python.[44]

There is little doubt that at least three major texts form the basis of Mahāyāna ethics: the (1) (Mahāyāna) *Brahmajāla-sūtra*, an apocryphal Chinese work[45] (2) *Śikṣāsamuccaya* of Śāntideva, and (3) *Bodhicaryāvatāra* of Śāntideva. The *Śikṣāsamuccaya* was of sufficient importance to prompt Joshi to state, 'The fundamental principle of Mahāyāna morality is expressed in the first verse of the *Śikṣāsamuccaya*: "When to myself as to my fellow-beings, fear and pain are hateful, what justification is there that I protect my own self and not others?"'[46] Structurally, the text is organized into three parts, beginning with twenty-seven *kārikās* outlining the ethical ideal of the bodhisattva. A second part offers an extensive commentary on these verses, with the third part offering a huge compendium of supporting quotations from additional Buddhist texts. Taken collectively, its three parts form a comprehensive statement on bodhisattva ethics.

The *Bodhicaryāvatāra* is possibly the best known Mahāyāna text associated with the conduct of the bodhisattva. It is arranged in ten chapters, five of which address the *pāramitās*, but with mindfulness (*smṛti*) and awareness (*samprajanya*) substituted for the traditional *dāna* and *śīla*. This does not mean to say that the *śīla-pāramitā* is omitted, for Chapter V, Verse 11 mentions it by name.[47] Specifically ethical concerns are also considered in Chapter II, known as '*Pāpa-deśanā*' or 'Confession of Evil.' Overall, an incredible breadth and scope of ethical issues are considered.

Curiously, it is not from these famous Mahāyāna ethical texts alone that we find the key which unlocks the major emphasis of bodhisattva conduct. Two further texts are critically important here: the *Mahāyānasaṃgraha* and the *Bodhisattvabhūmi*, and it is on the basis of their evidence that many authors, Buddhist and otherwise, have advanced the theory of the superiority of Mahāyāna ethics over that of *nikāya* Buddhism. In fact, the tenth or 'ethical' chapter of the *Bodhisattvabhūmi* was the focus of a complete translation and study by Mark Tatz.[48]

Keown, in *The Nature of Buddhist Ethics* (pp. 135–157), provides an extremely careful exposition of the argument. The *Mahāyānasaṃgraha* suggests that Mahāyāna morality is superior to Hīnayāna in four ways: (1) in its classifications (*prabheda-viśeṣa*), (2) in its common and separate rules (*sādhāraṇa-asādhāraṇa-śikṣā-viśeṣa*), (3) in breadth (*vaipulya-viśeṣa*), and (4) in depth (*gāmbhīrya-viśeṣa*).[49] The first category is the most important of the four since it supports the other three, and is itself composed of three sections: (a) morality as temperance (*saṃvara-śīla*), (b) morality as the pursuit of good (*kuśala-dharma-saṃgrāhaka-śīla*), and (c) morality as altruism (*sattva-artha-kriyā-śīla*).[50] The threefold categorization of morality as temperance, the pursuit of good, and altruism is further developed by the *Bodhisattvabhūmi*, concluding that it is the element of altruism that enables Mahāyāna morality to surpass its *nikāya* Buddhist counterpart. The extreme importance of the issue of altruism in asserting the superiority of Mahāyāna ethics has not gone unnoticed by modern Theravādins. Walpola Rahula, for example, says

> The *bhikkhu* is not a selfish, cowardly individual thinking only of his happiness and salvation, unmindful of whatever happens to the rest of humanity. A true *bhikkhu* is an altruistic, heroic person who considers others' happiness more than his own. He, like the Bodhisattva Sumedha, will renounce his own *nirvāṇa* for the sake of others. Buddhism is built upon service to others.[51]

Other Theravādin authors echo Rahula's sentiment.[52] Regarding the specific conduct of bodhisattvas, the *Bodhisattvabhūmi* postulates a code having fifty-two rules, of which only the first four are categorized (as *pārājayika-sthānīya-dharmā*) and a number of which allow the violation of (some of) the ten good paths of action. The second category explores the differentiation between serious and minor offenses, emphasizing that while both bodhisattvas and *Śrāvakas* are enjoined to observe all the major rules of conduct, bodhisattvas may breach minor matters of deportment while *Śrāvakas* may not. Of course the circumstances under which a bodhisattva may engage in this kind of behavior are also stated. The third category is essentially a summary. Finally, the fourth category is the most innovative, focusing on the notion of skill-in-means (*upāya-kauśalya*) in relation to Mahāyāna ethics.

In the fourth chapter of the *Bodhicaryāvatāra*, one reads 'The son of the Conqueror, having grasped the Thought of Enlightenment firmly, must make every effort, constantly and alertly, not to transgress the discipline (*śikṣā*).'[53] In the next chapter: 'Thus enlightened, one ought to be constantly active for the sake of others. Even that which generally is forbidden is allowed to the one who understands the work of compassion.'[54] How can these two conflicting views appear in the same text, and in such close proximity? The answer lies in a proper understanding of *upāya-kauśalya* and its role in Mahāyāna ethics: it is a theme that permeates Śāntideva's writings. Throughout the eighth chapter of the *Śikṣāsamuccaya* on 'Purification from Sin' (*Pāpaśodhanā*), citations abound, especially from the *Upāliparipṛcchā-sūtra* and the *Upāyakauśa-lya-sūtra*, in which ethical trangressions are allowed and sanctioned in the name of skill-in-means.[55] Keown concludes from all these examples 'that the freedom allowed to a bodhisattva is enormous and a wide spectrum of activities are permitted to him, even to the extent of taking life.'[56] He goes on, however, to say:

> When actions of these kinds are performed there are usually two provisos which must be satisfied: (a) that the prohibited action will conduce to the greater good of those beings directly affected by it; and (b) that the action is performed on the basis of perfect knowledge (*prajñā*) or perfect compassion (*karuṇā*).[57]

The relationship between *śīla* and *prajñā* in Mahāyāna is thus parallel to that noted above with respect to *nikāya* Buddhism in which it was remarked that 'the two fuse in the transformation of the entire personality in the existential realisation of selflessness' (see note 25). What seems not to be parallel is that the *nikāya* Buddhist adept is at no time allowed to breach the practice of proper morality while the Mahāyāna bodhisattva may, under certain circumstances invariably linked to altruistic activities and based on *karuṇā*, *upāya-kauśalya*, and *prajñā*, transcend conventional morality. G.S.P. Misra, for example, notices that, 'In the *Bodhisattvabhūmi* we find an enumeration of the circumstances under which a Bodhisattva may justifiably commit transgressions of the moral precepts; the governing factor, however, is always compassion and a desire to save others from sinful acts.'[58] The above passages notwithstanding, parallel references can be also found[59] emphasizing a strict observance of the precepts for bodhisattvas. As a result, we find ourselves confused over the apparent incongruency in the textual accounts of Mahāyāna ethical conduct, and wondering just how breaches of conventional ethical behavior are sanctioned.

The solution emerges from the postulation of two uniquely different types of *upāya-kauśalya*. About the first, which he categorizes as normative ethics and calls *Upāya*$_1$, Keown says:

> *Upāya*$_1$ does not enjoin laxity in moral practice but rather the greater recognition of the needs and interests of others. One's moral practice is now for the benefit of oneself and others by means of example. Through its emphasis on *karuṇā* the Mahāyāna gave full recognition to the value of ethical perfection, making it explicit that ethics and insight were of equal importance for a bodhisattva.[60]

The second type of *upāya* has nothing to do with normative ethics or ordinary individuals. It is the province of those who have already perfected ethics and insight. Thus:

> ... it is the *upāya* of bodhisattvas of the seventh stage (*upāya-kauśalya-bhūmi*) and beyond, whose powers and perfections are supernatural. *Upāya*$_2$ is depicted as an activity of the Buddhas and Great Bodhisattvas (Bodhisattva-Mahāsattvas) and it is only they who have the knowledge and power to use it. It is by virtue of *upāya*$_2$ that bodhisattvas transgress the precepts from motives of compassion and are said to do no wrong.[61]

There can be little doubt that *upāya*$_2$ is not the model by which ordinary beings perfect themselves but rather the pragmatic moral outcome of the attainment of the seventh stage of the bodhisattva path. *Upāya*$_2$ is the social expression of a genuine understanding of the notion of emptiness (*śūnyatā*) in which no precepts can even be theorized. It is emphasized throughout the Mahāyāna literature on emptiness, but nowhere as eloquently as in the discourse between Vimalakīrti and Upāli in the third chapter of the *Vimalakīrtinirdeśa-sūtra*:

> Reverend Upāli, all things are without production, destruction, and duration, like magical illusions, clouds, and lightning; all things are evanescent, not remaining even for an instant; all things are like dreams, hallucinations, and unreal visions; all things are like the reflection of the moon in water and like a mirror-image; they are born of mental construction. Those who know this are called the true upholders of the discipline, and those disciplined in that way are indeed well disciplined.[62]

As such, it represents the far extreme of the ethical continuum, a Buddhist situation ethics established not simply on love, as in Fletcher's system, but on the highest and most profound manifestation of compassion.

Having concluded in the above pages that *śīla* is operative throughout the individual's progress on the *nikāya* Buddhist path, even after the attainment of *prajñā*, and that the same claim can be made for Mahāyāna, enhanced by the altruistic utilization of $upāya_1$ up to the attainment of the seventh bodhisattva stage, after which $upāya_2$ becomes operative, albeit in rather antinomian fashion, it now becomes important to address the issue of whether textually based Buddhist ethics can be truly current; whether an ethical tradition solidly grounded on the textual heritage can serve as the foundational basis for a socially engaged Buddhism, effective in addressing the complex concerns cited in the growing literature on the subject.

The relative vitality of Buddhist ethics in today's world is a concern that cannot be minimized. Indeed, Kōshō Mizutani, in the Prologue to *Buddhist Ethics and Modern Society* asserts, 'I submit that a study of Buddhism that emphasizes its ethical aspects will be the most important task facing Buddhists in the twenty-first century.'[63] Studies abound stressing the difficulties of living effectively in a postmodern society that is becoming increasingly pluralistic and secular. This dilemma is further exacerbated for Buddhists in that 'Buddhists today face the question not only of how to relate to other religions, but also how to relate to other forms of Buddhism from different traditions.'[64]

In 1987, Rick Fields delivered a paper on 'The Future of American Buddhism' to a conference entitled 'Buddhism and Christianity: Toward the Human Future,' held at the Graduate Theological Union in Berkeley, California. Although case specific to the American Buddhist situation, Fields concluded his presentation with a sketch of eight features that he felt would be critical in the on-going development of American Buddhism. All eight points were directly or indirectly related to issues of Buddhist ethics, prompting Fields to comment: 'The Bodhisattva notions of direct involvement in the world will tend to overshadow tendencies towards renunciation and withdrawal. Buddhist ethics, as reflected in the precepts, the paramitas, and the Bodhisattva vow, will be applied to the specific problems of day-to-day living in contemporary urban North America.'[65] It is difficult to consider Fields' words, and those of similar, like-minded individuals such as the contributors to works in the genre of *The Path of Compassion* edited by Fred Eppsteiner without feeling much sympathy for the predicament facing Buddhists in Asia and America as they try to confront ethical dilemmas directly. Consequently, when we read articles by Sulak Sivaraksa, Thich Nhat Hanh, Jack Kornfield, Joanna Macy and others we must commend them for the depth of their sincerity and commitment, the expanse of the timely issues they confront, and wonder why there is rarely a footnote, hardly a textual reference in their writings which might provide additional and persuasive authority to their arguments.

In an exciting new article, drawing heavily on the work of recent biblical scholarship, Harold Coward points out that:

> The relationship between a religious community and its scripture is complex, reciprocal and usually central to the normative self-definition

48

of a religion. The awareness of this relationship is the result of postmodern approaches that no longer see scriptures as museum pieces for historical critical analysis, but recognize them to be the products of human perception and interaction – both in their own time and in today's study by scholars.[66]

The problem of precisely how ethical guidelines can be appropriately reinterpreted in the context of changing times and cultures was confronted early on in Buddhist religious history. By including only the presumed words of Buddha, referred to as *Buddhavacana*, within a closed canon, *nikāya* Buddhism in general and Theravāda in particular made a clear statement about the relationship of community and scripture in the early tradition. Mahāyāna chose the opposite approach. As Coward points out: 'Rather than closing off the canon as the Theravāda school had done, Mahāyāna maintained an open approach and added to the "remembered words" of Ānanda new *sūtras* such as the *Prajñāpāramitā Sūtras* and the *Lotus Sūtra*.'[67] This openness allowed Buddhists the occasion to utilize Buddha's own approach in transmitting the substance of his teaching if not his exact words. Robinson and Johnson point this out clearly in *The Buddhist Religion*: 'Both strictness in preserving the essential kernel and liberty to expand, vary, and embellish the expression characterize Buddhist attitudes through the ages toward not only texts but also art, ritual, discipline, and doctrine. The perennial difficulty lies in distinguishing the kernel from its embodiment.'[68]

The openness in creating new scripture emphasized by Mahāyāna, and the utilization of an on-going commentarial tradition, as fostered by earlier Buddhism, conjointly provide the potential for a profoundly current Buddhist ethics that is also textually grounded. Such an approach is solidly in keeping with the program outlined by Charles Wei-hsun Fu (in a slightly different context). Fu says, 'The Buddhist view of ethics and morality must be presented in the context of open discussion in a free and democratic forum.'[69] To be successful, it requires that:

> A philosophical reinterpetation of the Middle Way of *paramārtha-satya/samvṛti-satya* must be undertaken so that the original gap between these two can be firmly bridged, thereby accomplishing the task of constructive modernization of Buddhist ethics and morality. On the theoretical level, a new ethical theory based on the Middle Way of *paramārtha-satya/samvṛti-satya* can meet the challenge of modern times[70]

When I wrote *American Buddhism*, I suggested that much of the future of Buddhism in the 1970s, or for that matter, in longer term perspective, would be dependent on the changing face of American religious life in general. This is especially important in examining Buddhism's situation with regard to everyday life. By the late 1970s, America was in the throes of severe social anomie, largely fueled by the vast ethical uncertainty that gripped the cultural and religious landscape. At that time, I maintained that Buddhism's traditional view of *Vinaya* and *śīla*, monastic and individual guidelines for everyday, institutional and ethical conduct, was grossly ineffective and needed serious commentary and reform. I believe that significant reform is taking place in American Buddhist communities. Needless to say, in this short context, I cannot pursue the many, varied ways Theravāda, Mahāyāna, and Vajrayāna Buddhist groups in America are specifically engaging the ancient tradition in a new dialogue that elevates precepts beyond a facile understanding merely as *śikṣā*, as rigid regulations. Such an exposition would require an elucidation of new approaches to the literature so as to provide a result that is truly transtemporal and transcultural. In his earlier mentioned 1987 paper Fields also commented Buddhism's future in America was intimately tied up with its ability to develop a *Vinaya* for lay people, its concern for promoting a just and compassionate society, and its regard for identifying an ethical pattern for women.[71] Fields is by no means the first to say this[72], but he is absolutely correct in his assertion.

In the nearly two decades that I have been writing about Buddhism in America, I have consistently argued that since the vast majority of Buddhists in this country were members of the laity, for Buddhism to be truly American, it would need to address the dilemma of tailoring the major emphasis of Buddhist practice to lay rather than monastic life. Initially, the suggestion was rather widely and aggressively attacked by what seemed to me like most of the Buddhists groups in America. The substance of the critique presumed that I ignored the monastic *saṅgha*, the very basis and foundation of Buddhist community life. Of course I did nothing of the kind. I simply acknowledged what Buddhists in Asia have recognized for more than two millennia. Most practitioners, for an enormous variety of entirely valid reasons, cannot make the full and complete commitment to the rigorous practice associated with monastic life. That doesn't mean we should ignore the monastic tradition, or exclude it from American Buddhist life, but rather that we provide the context for all Buddhists in America to practice in a fashion appropriate to their choice of approach. In so doing, we would simply be following, and perhaps adapting, an Asian Buddhist model predicated on the notion that there have always been more members of the laity than members of the monastic tradition, but that both endeavours needed to be affirmed and endorsed for the successful development of Buddhist religious life. Such an approach has not always been clear in the popular literature.

In Spring 1992, the *Tricycle* editorial observed that 'Just now, ours is not predominantly a Buddhism of removed monasticism. It is out of robes, in the streets, in institutions, workplaces, and homes.'[73] The editorial closed with this remark: 'While Buddhist history is steeped in monasticism, our own democratic traditions compel us to share the burden of social problems.'[74] For some Buddhists in this country, monastic and otherwise, the above comments may be perceived as highly inflammatory, possibly even reflective of a rejection of the entire monastic vocation. To be sure, American Buddhism might redefine somewhat the nature of the symbiosis between the two main component groups of the Buddhist *saṅgha*, but neither enterprise would ever be disparaged by the other. In Don Morreale's 1988 volume *Buddhist America*, Jack Kornfield called the same process integration, and along with democratization and feminism, considered it one of three major themes in North American Buddhism.[75] So, within a decade, many writers, mostly identified with non-ethnic American Buddhism, had begun to echo my own sentiment. No one, however, has made the argument so eloquently, and with such awareness of the complexity of the task, as Rita Gross, in her extremely important book *Buddhism After Patriarchy*.[76] Gross recognizes that what she refers to as 'monasticism after patriarchy,' while understanding that new and vital archetypes must replace Buddhism's current 'very weak models for meaningful lay life,' must forge new monastic paradigms that are androgynous and free of prejudice or discrimination.[77] The movement to a truly post-patriarchal monastic tradition is at least as threatening to traditional Buddhism in Asia as to the conflict between the 'Two Buddhisms' in America, and of course Gross argues persuasively for an androgynous lay Buddhism as well. Additionally, Gross identifies, addresses, and validates the emphasis of those Buddhists who are trying to work out an intermediary lifestyle that incorporates both monastic and lay features into serious, rigorous Buddhist practice.

Associated with the struggle to redefine community life in American Buddhism, accommodating both ethnic and largely non-ethnic groups, is a new emphasis on active expressions of compassion as perhaps the major component of a revitalized Buddhist ethics that has been called 'socially engaged Buddhism.' In an interesting recent book titled *Inner Peace, World Peace*,[78] the editor Kenneth Kraft provides an interesting survey chapter in which he chronicles many of the activities collected under the above rubric, such as the founding of the Buddhist Peace Fellowship in 1978, Thich Nhat Hanh's many significant endeavours in North America, the Dalai Lama's efforts, and, most importantly, the growing body of literature that has accompanied the effort. Kraft shows how socially engaged Buddhism in America has utilized well-known methods of social action in this culture: voter mobilization, letter writing campaigns, volunteer charity work, tax resistance, product boycotts, and so forth. What is most puzzling here is that one of the major foci of socially engaged Buddhists in the West consists of providing aid and support to ethnic Buddhist groups, both here and in Asia, while, with few exceptions, ethnic Buddhists in America seem not to be especially active in the movement.

A creative commentary on Buddhism's attempt to renew its commitment to generating and practicing a revitalized, value-oriented ethical life is the development of Thich Nhat Hanh's 'Order of Interbeing,' the successor to Vietnam's Tiep Hien Order. It tries to provide a creative (even experimental) individual and collective methodology for the application of Buddhist principles to today's world. The major thrust of the group is to practice the traditional five vows of the laity, in conjunction with fourteen additional precepts that amplify and augment the values underlying the original five. Moreover, Nhat Hanh has struck a careful balance between meditational training and political activism, emphasizing each activity as mutually influencing. In so doing, both ethnic and non-ethnic American Buddhist groups are provided with an agenda for activism that benefits all Buddhists. Despite its clever use of what Fields calls 'cross-cultural borrowing' and genuine potential for an honorable rather than politically correct multi-culturalism in American Buddhism, this approach has not been uniformly accepted.

One of the most fruitful approaches to understanding the attitudinal differences between ethnic and non-ethnic American Buddhists can be extracted from Kenneth Kraft's work in *Inner Peace, World Peace*. He suggests that Buddhists in Asian and Third World countries are often engaged in serious struggle for political and cultural survival. He notes that 'Those involved in such conflicts typically have little interest in the theoretical implications of nonviolence or the latest innovations in spiritual/activist practice.'[79] Most Western Buddhists have never shared that tragic experience; it is a form of suffering they've never experienced. Yet their teachers have. Chögyam Trungpa's *Born in Tibet* remains a chilling testament to the fallout of a world filled with suffering. Thich Thien-an's work with Vietnamese refugees both before and after the fall of Saigon documents how suffering sometimes fosters what one writer called 'the exigencies of a major transplantation of human beings to a totally new environment.'[80]

Recently, in the Introduction to my edited 1992 volume *Buddhist Ethics: A Cross-Cultural Approach*, I suggested that Buddhists could look to the synthesis of two traditional ethical frameworks in fulfilling the suggestions noted by Fields: (1) the four *brahmavihāras* or 'Divine Abodes,' consisting of love (*maitrī*), compassion (*karuṇā*), sympathetic joy (*muditā*), and equanimity (*upekṣā*), and (2) the six *pāramitās* or 'perfections,' of giving (*dāna*), morality (*śīla*), patience (*kṣānti*), vigor (*vīrya*), meditation (*samādhi*), and wisdom (*prajñā*). Although the *brahmavihāras* are more generally applied to Theravāda thought, and the *pāramitās* to Mahāyāna thought, they might be reinterpreted conjointly through an entirely new commentarial literature in reconfiguring a modern American Buddhist ethics. In so doing, American Buddhism will arrive at a wisdom that is grounded in equanimity, understanding properly that, '... although fully liberated beings have abandoned all the negative emotions of attachment, hatred, and delusion, they have not destroyed all emotion and feeling. They have the ability to develop a whole range of rich and satisfying emotions and are encouraged in scripture to do so.'[81] Consequently, a powerful new ethical tool is developed that stands outside of time and culture.

Not to beg the original question, the above more than argues for the composition of new commentarial literature focusing on those significant texts mentioned earlier and including especially, the: thirteen *suttas* constituting the *Sīlakkhandhavagga* of the *Dīgha Nikāya, Maṅgala-sutta, Metta-sutta, Sigālovāda-sutta, Dhammasaṅgaṇī, Puggalapaññatti, Abhidhammmattha-saṅgaha, Visuddhimagga*, and *Milindapañha* of the Theravādin tradition. Mahāyāna texts worthy of new consideration would also include those with the richest heritage of ethical underpinnings, for example, the: *Brahmajāla-sūtra, Śīkṣā-samuccaya, Bodhicaryāvatāra, Mahāyānasaṃgraha, Bodhisattvabhūmi, Bodhisattva-prātimokṣa-sūtra*, and *Upāliparipṛcchā-sūtra*. Certainly this does not mean to say that there are no other texts of ethical import for Buddhism, but simply that the ones cited above represent the most fertile, reasonable place from which to begin a new and revitalized textual tradition. The process would be a high expression of what Coward calls 'the reciprocal relationship between text and tradition in Buddhism,'[82] a profound demonstration that Buddhist ethics can indeed be meaningfully current and textually supported.

Notes

1 Portions of this paper appeared earlier in 'Text and Tradition in the Study of Buddhist Ethics,' *Pacific World*, NS 9 (1993), pp. 49–68.

2 Charles Wei-hsun Fu and Sandra A. Wawryto (eds), *Buddhist Ethics and Modern Society* (Westport, Conn.: Greenwood Press, 1991), p. 4.

3 Akira Hirakawa, *Studies in Primal Buddhism: The Original Model of the Organization of the Buddhist Order* (Tokyo: Shunshusha Press, 1964), pp. 107–108. In the body of this paper, I regularly present technical terminology in Sanskrit, except when discussing the Theravāda tradition, in which case Pāli terms are utilized.

4 John Holt, *Discipline: The Canonical Buddhism of the Vinayapiṭaka* (Delhi: Motilal Banarsidass, 1981), p. 3.

5 Ibid. p. 4.

6 Charles Wei-hsun Fu, 'From *Paramārtha-satya* to *Samvṛti-satya*: An Attempt at Constructive Modernization of (Mahāyāna) Buddhist Ethics,' in *Buddhist Ethics and Modern Society*, edited by Charles Wei-hsun Fu and Sandra A. Wawrytko (Westport, Conn.: Greenwood Press, 1991), p. 315.

7 See, for example, Charles S. Prebish, 'The Prātimokṣa Puzzle: Fact Versus Fantasy,' *Journal of the American Oriental Society*, 94, 2 (April-June, 1974), pp. 168–176. Holt, *Discipline: The Canonical Buddhism of the Vinayapiṭaka*, p. 125 makes the same point.

8 See Henry Clarke Warren and Dharmananda Kosambi (eds), *Visuddhimagga of Buddhaghosācariya* (Cambridge, Mass.: Harvard University Press, 1950), p. 7 (Chapter I.19), and Louis de La Vallée Poussin (tr.), *L'Abhidharmakośa de Vasubandhu* (Paris: Paul Geuthner, 1924), Vol. 3, p. 47 (Chapter IV.16a-b).

9 For example, see Charles S. Prebish, *Buddhist Monastic Discipline: The Sanskrit Prātimokṣa Sūtras of the Mahāsaṃghikas and Mūlasarvārvastivādins* (University Park: The Pennsylvania State University Press, 1975), p. 42. The text reads:
śīlena yukto śramaṇo tireti śīlena yukto brāhmaṇo tireti /
śīlena yukto naradevapūjyo śīlena yuktasya hi prātimokṣaṃ //

10 See Charles S. Prebish, *American Buddhism* (North Scituate, Mass.: Duxbury Press, 1979), p. 45.

11 Fu, 'From *Paramārtha-satya* to *Samvṛti-satya*: An Attempt at Constructive Modernization of (Mahāyāna) Buddhist Ethics,' p. 315.

12 W. Pachow, *A Comparative Study of the Prātimokṣa* (Santiniketan: Sino-Indian Cultural Society, 1955), p. 37.

13 Holt, *Discipline: The Canonical Buddhism of the Vinayapiṭaka*, p. 64. Keown, in *The Nature of Buddhist Ethics*, p. 33, notices the same dilemma.

14 Pachow, *A Comparative Study of the Prātimokṣa*, Appendix I, pp. 1–2.

15 Holt, *Discipline: The Canonical Buddhism of the Vinayapiṭaka*, p. 65.

16 Damien Keown, *The Nature of Buddhist Ethics* (New York: St. Martin's Press, 1992), p. 34.

17 Charles S. Prebish, 'Vinaya and Prātimokṣa: The Foundation of Buddhist Ethics,' in *Studies in the History of Buddhism*, edited by A.K. Narain (Delhi: B.R. Publishing Corporation, 1980), p. 248.

18 Lambert Schmithausen, *Buddhism and Nature* (Tokyo: The International Institute for Buddhist Studies 1991), *Studia Philologica Buddhica Occasional Paper Series*, 7, p. 43.

19 Lambert Schmithausen, *The Problem of the Sentience of Plants in Earliest Buddhism* (Tokyo: The International Institute for Buddhist Studies, 1991), *Studia Philologica Buddhica Monograph Series*, 6, p. 16.

20 Charles Prebish (ed.), *Buddhist Ethics: A Cross-Cultural Approach* (Dubuque, Iowa: Kendall/Hunt, 1992), p. vii.

21 Winston King, *In the Hope of Nibbana* (LaSalle, Ill.: Open Court, 1964), p. v.

22 Keown, *The Nature of Buddhist Ethics*, pp. 8–23.

23 Ibid., pp. 10–11.

24 Here I have in mind especially the work of Harvey Aronson, *Love and Sympathy in Theravāda Buddhism* (Delhi: Motilal Banarsidass, 1980) and Nathan Katz, *Buddhist Images of Human Perfection* (Delhi: Motilal Banarsidass, 1982).

25 Keown, *The Nature of Buddhist Ethics*, pp. 111–112.

26 Ibid., p. 76.

27 Thomas W. Rhys Davids (tr.) *Dialogues of the Buddha*, Part I (London: Luzac & Co., Ltd., 1899), pp. 3–4, note 1.

28 Keown, *The Nature of Buddhist Ethics*, p. 29.

29 G.S.P. Misra, *Development of Buddhist Ethics* (Delhi: Munshiram Manoharlal, 1984), p. 67.

30 See Shwe Zan Aung (tr.), *Compendium of Philosophy* (London: Luzac & Co., Ltd., 1910), pp. 95–97.

31 See, for example, Th. Stcherbatsky, *The Central Conception of Buddhism and the Meaning of the Word 'Dharma,'* 2nd ed. (Calcutta: Susil Gupta, 1956), pp. 84–86.

32 Keown, *The Nature of Buddhist Ethics*, p. 81.

33 Thomas W. Rhys Davids (tr.), *Dialogues of the Buddha*, Part I, p. 237.

34 Keown, *The Nature of Buddhist Ethics*, p. 112.

35 Ibid., p. 124.

36 Aronson, *Love and Sympathy in Theravāda Buddhism*. See especially pp. 3–10 on 'Buddha's Sympathy,' pp. 11–23 on 'Disciples' Sympathy,' pp. 60–77 on 'The Sublime Attitudes,' and pp. 78–96 on 'Equanimity.'

37 Lal Mani Joshi, *Studies in the Buddhistic Culture of India*, 2nd revised ed. (Delhi: Motilal Banarsidass, 1977), p. 91.
38 Ibid., p. 93.
39 Keown, *The Nature of Buddhist Ethics*, p. 130.
40 Nalinaksha Dutt, *Aspects of Mahāyāna Buddhism and Its Relation to Hīnayāna* (London: Luzac & Co., 1930), p. 290.
41 Ibid., pp. 290–291.
42 *Indian Historical Quarterly*, 7 (1931), pp. 259–286.
43 Nalinaksha Dutt, 'Bodhisattva Prātimokṣa Sūtra,' *Indian Historical Quarterly*, 7 (1931), p. 261.
44 See Pierre Python (tr.), *Vinaya-Viniścaya-Upāli-Paripṛcchā* (Paris: Adrien-Maisonneuve, 1973), which offers Tibetan (with Sanskrit fragments) and Chinese text along with a French translation of the Chinese (taken from *Taishō* 310, 325, 326, and 1582). Python notes on page 1 that the Sanskrit fragments are taken from Dutt's edition of the *Bodhisattva-prātimokṣa-sūtra*. Python's text is an entirely different text than Valentina Stache-Rosen (tr.) *Upāliparipṛcchā sūtra: Ein Text zur buddhistischen Ordensdisziplin* (Göttingen: Vandenhoeck & Ruprecht, 1984), which offers a translation from Chinese (*Taishō* 1466) with parallels to the Pāli.
45 See, for example, James R. Ware, 'Notes on the Fan Wang Ching,' *Harvard Journal of Asiatic Studies*, 1, 1 (April, 1936), pp. 156–161. Paul Groner makes a similar case, in Robert E. Buswell, Jr. (ed.), *Chinese Buddhist Apocrypha* (Honolulu: University of Hawaii Press, 1990), pp. 251ff.
46 Joshi, *Studies in the Buddhistic Culture of India,* p. 93. The Sanskrit reads:
    yadā mama pareṣāṃ ca bhaya duḥkham ca na priyam /
    tadātmanaḥ ko viśeṣo yattaṃrakṣāmi netaram //
47 See Marion Matics (tr.), *Entering the Path of Enlightenment* (London: Macmillan, 1970), p. 163.
48 See Mark Tatz, *The Complete Bodhisattva: Asanga's Chapter on Ethics with the Commentary by Tsong-kha-pa, The Basic Path to Awakening* (Lewiston, New York: Edwin Mellen Press, 1987).
49 Keown, *The Nature of Buddhist Ethics*, p. 136.
50 Ibid., pp. 137–138.
51 Walpola Rahula, *The Heritage of the Bhikkhu* (New York: Grove Press, 1974), p. 126.
52 See, for example, Buddhadāsa, *Me and Mine*, edited by Donald K. Swearer (Albany: State University of New York Press, 1989), pp. 141–145.
53 Matics, *Entering the Path of Enlightenment*, p. 157 (verse 1). The Sanskrit, from P.L. Vaidya (ed.), *Bodhicaryāvatāra of Śāntideva with the Commentary Pañjikā of Prajñākaramati* (Darbhanga: Mithila Institute, 1960), p. 44, is
    evaṃ gṛhītvā sudṛḍham bodhicittaṃ jinātmajaḥ /
    śikṣānatikrame yatnaṃ kuryānnityamatandritaḥ //
54 Ibid., p. 169. The Sanskrit, from P.L. Vaidya, *Bodhicaryāvatāra*, p. 69, is
    evaṃ buddhvā parārtheṣu bhavetsatatamutsthitaḥ /
    niṣiddhamapyanujñātaṃ kṛpālorarthadarśinaḥ //
55 See Cecil Bendall and W.H.D. Rouse (trs.), *Śiksha-Samuccaya: A Compendium of Buddhist Doctrine* (Delhi: Motilal Banarsidass, 1971), pp. 157–174. For the Sanskrit, see P.L. Vaidya (ed.), *Śikṣā-samuccaya of Śāntideva* (Darbhanga: Mithila Institute, 1961), pp. 90–99.
56 Keown, *The Nature of Buddhist Ethics*, p. 154.
57 Ibid.
58 G.S.P. Misra, *Development of Buddhist Ethics* (Delhi: Munshiram Manoharlal, 1984), p. 137. He refers to Nalinaksha Dutt (ed.), *Bodhisattvabhūmi* (Patna: K.P. Jayaswal Research Institute, 1966), 'Śīlapaṭalam,' pp. 112–116.

59 See, for example, *Bodhicaryāvatāra*, Chapter IV, verses 8–10; Matics, *Entering the Path of Enlightenment*, p. 158.

60 Keown, *The Nature of Buddhist Ethics*, p. 159.

61 Ibid., p. 157.

62 Robert A.F. Thurman (tr.), *The Holy Teaching of Vimalakīrti: A Mahāyāna Scripture* (University Park: The Pennsylvania State University Press, 1976), p. 31.

63 Fu and Wawrytko, *Buddhist Ethics and Modern Society*, p. 7.

64 David W. Chappell, 'Buddhist Responses to Religious Pluralism: What are the Ethical Issues?' in *Buddhist Ethics and Modern Society*, edited by Charles Wei-hsun Fu and Sandra A. Wawrytko (Westport, Conn.: Greenwood Press, 1991), p. 355.

65 Rick Fields, 'The Future of American Buddhism,' *The Vajradhatu Sun*, 9, 1 (October–November, 1987), p. 26.

66 Harold Coward, 'The Role of Scripture in the Self-Definition of Hinduism and Buddhism in India,' *Studies in Religion*, 21, 2 (1992), p. 129.

67 Ibid., p. 142.

68 Richard H. Robinson and Willard L. Johnson, *The Buddhist Religion: A Historical Introduction*, 3rd edition (Belmont, Calif.: Wadsworth Publishing Company, 1982), p. 39.

69 Fu, 'From *Paramārtha-satya* to *Samvṛti-satya*: An Attempt at Constructive Modernization of (Mahāyāna) Buddhist Ethics,' p. 327.

70 Ibid.

71 For the published version of this paper, see Rick Fields, 'The Future of American Buddhism,' *The Vajradhatu Sun*, 9, 1 (October-November, 1987), pp. 1, 22, 24–26.

72 See, for example, Robert Aitken, *The Mind of Clover: Essays in Zen Buddhist Ethics* (San Francisco: North Point Press, 1984), or Prebish, 'Karma and Rebirth in the Land of the Earth Eaters.'

73 See: Helen Tworkov, 'The Formless Field of Buddhism,' *Tricycle*, 1, 3 (Spring, 1992), p. 4.

74 Ibid.

75 Kornfield, in Don Morreale (ed.), *Buddhist America: Centers, Retreats, Practices* (Santa Fe, New Mexico: John Muir Publications, 1988), p. xv.

76 See: Rita Rita M. Gross, *Buddhism After Patriarchy* (Albany, N.Y.: State University of New York Press, 1993).

77 Ibid., pp. 240–49.

78 See: Kenneth Kraft (ed.), *Inner Peace, World Peace: Essays on Buddhism and Nonviolence* (Albany: State University of New York Press, 1992), and especially pp. 1–30.

79 Ibid., p. 24.

80 This statement was made by Lenore Friedman.

81 Harvey Aronson, *Love and Sympathy in Theravāda Buddhism* (Delhi: Motilal Banarsidass, 1980), p. 95.

82 Coward, 'The Role of Scripture in the Self-Definition of Hinduism and Buddhism in India,' p. 143.

CHAPTER THREE

Buddhism and Human Rights[1]

Damien Keown

In the autumn of 1993 the Parliament of the World's Religions met in Chicago to determine whether a consensus on basic moral teachings could be found among the religions of the world. The meeting was attended by representatives of the major world religions as well as ethnic and other minority groups. Representatives of many Buddhist schools, including Theravāda, Mahāyāna, Vajrayāna, and Zen were present and the main closing address was given by the Dalai Lama in Grant Park on September 4th.

One of the major fruits of this interfaith convention was a document known as the Declaration towards a Global Ethic.[2] The Global Ethic sets out the fundamental moral principles to which it is thought all religions subscribe. Many of these principles concern human rights, and the Global Ethic sees the universal recognition of human rights and dignity by the religions of the world as the cornerstone of a 'new global order.'

A related aim of the Global Ethic was to provide 'the basis for an extensive process of discussion and acceptance which we hope will be sparked off in all religions.'[3] The present chapter is a contribution to this process from a Buddhist perspective. Its aims are limited to an exploration of some of the basic issues that must be addressed if a Buddhist philosophy of human rights is to develop. I say 'develop' because Buddhism seems to lack such a philosophy at present. Buddhism is a latecomer to the cause of human rights, and for most of its history has been preoccupied with other concerns. It might be suggested, in defense of Buddhism, that concern for human rights is a postreligious phenomenon which has more to do with secular ideologies and power-politics than religion, and it is therefore unreasonable to accuse Buddhism of neglect in this area.[4] I will suggest below that such an understanding of human rights is mistaken, but leaving the specific issue of human rights to one side there is no doubt that Buddhism lags far behind religions such as Christianity and Islam in

57

developing the framework for a social gospel within which questions of this kind can be addressed. For such an intellectually dynamic tradition Buddhism is a lightweight in moral and political philosophy. A fig-leaf of a kind may be found in the suggestion that since much Buddhist literature remains untranslated there may be hidden treasures in these areas awaiting discovery. Such appeals to the unknown, however, lack credibility. For one thing, it would be curious if only texts on these subjects had been lost to history while literature on all manner of other topics abounds. Nor can it be a coincidence that these subjects are absent from the traditional monastic curricula. The absence of a discipline of philosophical ethics in Indian culture as a whole makes it much more likely that Buddhism simply invested little time in questions of these kinds.[5]

Political events in the course of this century, however, have forced the issue of human rights to the top of the agenda.[6] The Chinese invasion of Tibet, the bitter ethnic conflict in Sri Lanka, and the experience of military dictatorship in countries such as Burma have all provided contemporary Buddhism with first-hand experience of the issues at stake. Another development which has done much to focus attention on social and political themes is the emergence of 'socially engaged Buddhism,' a movement whose very name implies a critique of the more traditional (presumably 'disengaged') forms of Buddhism. Leading Asian and Western Buddhists now routinely express their concern about social injustice in the Western vocabulary of human rights. What I wish to consider here is how appropriate this language is for Buddhism, and what grounds there are for supposing that Buddhism is committed to the cause of 'human rights' or has any clear understanding of what the concept means. Given the lack of intellectual effort down the centuries in articulating, promoting and defending rights of the kind which the world (and especially the West) is now called upon to secure for oppressed groups like the Tibetans, the more cynical might suggest that this late conversion to the cause is born more of self-interest than a deep and long-standing commitment to social justice. In calling for respect for human rights today, then, is Buddhism simply riding on the coat-tails of the West or is there, after all, a commitment to human rights in Buddhist teachings?

My theme in this paper may be summed up as the conceptual and doctrinal basis for human rights in Buddhism. I am concerned with the intellectual bridgework which must be put in place if expressions of concern about human rights are to be linked to Buddhist doctrine. There are many aspects to this problem, but three related issues will be considered here: the concept of rights, the concept of human rights, and the question of how human rights are to be grounded in Buddhist doctrine. I ask first if the concept of 'rights' is intelligible in Buddhism. To answer this question it will be necessary to gain some understanding of the origin of the notion in the West. Next I ask whether the Buddhist concept of human rights (if such a thing exists) is the same as the Western understanding. Finally I consider in what specific area of Buddhist teachings a doctrine of human rights might be grounded.[7] Since the discussion is essentially theoretical, detailed reference will not be made to particular Buddhist cultures or schools, to specific human rights 'abuses,' or to the human rights 'record' of particular regimes.[8]

Before turning to these issues a preliminary point must be made about Buddhism itself. In speaking of 'Buddhism' I should make clear that I am writing with reference to an abstraction which might be termed 'classical' Buddhism. This abstraction is neither the same as nor different from Buddhism in any historical or cultural context. It is not meant to represent the views of any sect and is broad enough to include both Theravāda and Mahāyāna schools. The justification for this fiction lies in the belief that whatever concept of human rights we regard Buddhism as holding must be one that is universal in form. The essence of any doctrine of human rights is its unrestricted scope, and it would be as strange to have distinct 'Theravāda,' 'Tibetan' and 'Zen' doctrines of human rights as it would be to have 'Catholic,' 'Protestant' and 'Eastern Orthodox' ones. To insist on the priority of cultural and historical circumstances would be tantamount to denying the validity of human rights as a concept.

Rights

The concept of a 'right' has a long intellectual history in the West, and the contemporary notion of a right as an exercisable power vested in or held by an individual has its antecedents in a more impersonal understanding of what is objectively true or right. Etymologically, the English word 'right' is derived from the Latin *rectus* meaning straight. *Rectus*, in turn, can be traced to the Greek *orektos* which means stretched out or upright. As Richard Dagger notes, 'The pattern ... is for the notion of straightness to be extended from the physical realm to the moral – from rectus to rectitude, as it were.'[9] In other words, the property of a physical object, namely that of being right, straight or upright, is applied metaphorically in a moral context. Dagger suggests:

> By analogy with the physical sense, the primary moral sense of 'right' was a standard or measure for conduct. Something was right – morally straight or true – if it met the standard of rectitude, or rightness ...

Once the idea of 'rightness' had been transferred to the moral domain, the next development was to view it as denoting a personal entitlement of some kind. Dagger continues:

> From here the next step was to recognize that actions taken 'with right' or 'by right' are taken *as a matter of right*. The transition is

from the belief that I may do something because it is right, in other words, to the belief that I may do something because I *have a right* to do it ... Thus the concept of rights joins the concept of *the right*.[10]

The metaphorical moral usage of terms such as 'right,' 'straight' and 'upright' (in opposition to 'crooked,' 'twisted' and 'bent') readily suggests itself to the mind. The rationale for the transition from the moral use of 'right' to the notion of a right as a personal entitlement, however, is less obvious. Indeed, this development which took place in the West during the late middle ages, and which has been described as the 'watershed'[11] in the history of 'right,' may be a phenomenon which is culturally unique. The evolution of the concept in this direction occurs sometime between Aquinas in the thirteenth century and the jurists Suarez and Grotius in the seventeenth. The modern usage appears clearly in Hobbes, writing in the middle of the seventeenth century, and the idea of a right as a personal power occupies centre stage in political theory from this time on.

As part of this evolution in the concept of a right the notion of 'natural rights' comes to prominence towards the end of the seventeenth century, notably in the writings of John Locke. The belief that there are natural rights flows from the recognition of human equality, one of the great ideals of the Age of Revolution. Natural rights are inalienable: they are not conferred by any judicial or political process nor can they be removed by these or other means. These natural rights of the seventeenth and eighteenth centuries are the forerunner of the contemporary notion of human rights.

Two questions might be asked concerning the evolution of the doctrine of natural rights in the West. First, why did it take so long for the concept of natural rights to appear? The answer seems to lie in the fact that for much of Western history 'rights' were closely tied to social status, and were essentially a function of position or role in society. A hierarchical social structure, such as was predominant in Roman and medieval society, is antithetical to the notion of natural rights. In these circumstances a person's duties and responsibilities are determined fundamentally by the office they hold (lord, citizen, slave), offices which are to a large extent hereditary. It was only when the hierarchical model was challenged and replaced by an egalitarian one that the idea of natural rights began to gain ground.

The second and more important question for our present purposes is: Does the part played by the unique cultural matrix of social political and intellectual developments in the Enlightenment mean that human rights are essentially a function of the historical process? This conclusion need not follow, for while it may be said that in the seventeenth and eighteenth centuries the notion of natural rights was 'an idea whose time had come,' the idea itself was not entirely new. The influence of Christian doctrine can be seen in several respects,[12] such as the belief (ultimately derived from Judaism) of a 'universal moral law rooted in the righteousness of God.'[13]

Since human beings are created in the image of God and loved by him as individuals each is worthy of dignity and respect. Furthermore, since each is a member of the human community under God, all other memberships (tribe, state, nation) are secondary.[14] Apart from Christianity, ideas about the just treatment of individuals on the basis of their common humanity are found in a secular context in Stoicism and the writings of Cicero and Seneca.[15] The philosophical justification for a doctrine of human rights has thus always been available, although the ground in which this seed might flourish – a particular combination of social, political and intellectual developments – has not.

So much for historical background. What of contemporary theories of rights? The concept of a right has been analyzed in a number of ways, as evidenced by the extensive interdisciplinary literature on the subject spanning diverse fields such as politics, law, philosophy and history. Within this discourse of rights there is no single definition of a right which commands universal assent. For our present purposes, however, a basic understanding of the concept will suffice. We noted above that a right is something personal to an individual: it may be thought of as something an individual 'has'.[16] What the holder of a right has is a benefit or entitlement of some kind, and at the most general level this is an entitlement to justice. This entitlement may be analyzed into two main forms for which there are corresponding rights: rights which take the form of a claim (claim-rights), and rights which take the form of a liberty (liberty-rights).[17] A claim-right is the benefit which A enjoys to impose upon B a positive or negative requirement. A liberty-right is the benefit which A enjoys of being immune from any such requirement being imposed by B.[18] This basic understanding of a right may be summed up in the following working definition: *a right is a benefit which confers upon its holder either a claim or a liberty.*

One important feature of any right is that it provides a particular perspective on justice, in that the right-holder always stands in the position of beneficiary. This subjective aspect of the entitlement, which, as we have seen, appeared early in the history of the concept, remains crucial to the modern understanding of a right. This is brought out in the following definition by Finnis:

> In short, the modern vocabulary and grammar of rights is a many-faceted instrument for reporting and asserting the requirements or other implications of a relationship of justice *from the point of view of the person(s) who benefit(s)* from that relationship. It provides a way of talking about 'what is just' from a special angle: the viewpoint of the 'other(s)' to whom something (including, *inter alia*, freedom of choice) is owed or due, and who would be wronged if denied that something.[19]

The above brief review of the Western concept of a right was required as a preliminary to an assessment of its relevance to Buddhism. We are now in a position to ask whether the concept of a right is found in Buddhism. If it is, then talk of *human rights* in Buddhism seems legitimate.[20] If it is not, there is a danger of anachronistically foisting onto the tradition a concept which is the product of an alien culture.[21]

Buddhism and Rights

We took our cue for the discussion of rights in the West from etymology, and perhaps we can glean something further from this source. Above it was noted that the English word 'right' is derived from the Latin *rectus* meaning straight. Both 'right' and *rectus* themselves, however, have a more remote ancestor in the Sanskrit *ṛju* (straight or upright). The equivalent form in Pali is *uju* (or *ujju*) meaning 'straight, direct; straightforward, honest, upright.'[22] It would therefore appear that both the objective sense ('straight') and the metaphorical moral sense ('rectitude') of the word 'right' referred to earlier occur in Buddhist as well as Western languages. Despite a common Indo-European etymology, however, there is no word in Sanskrit or Pali which conveys the idea of a 'right' or 'rights,' understood as a subjective entitlement.[23]

Does this mean that the concept of rights is alien to Buddhist thought? Not necessarily. Alan Gewirth has pointed out that cultures may possess the concept of rights without having a vocabulary which expresses it. He suggests that it is 'important to distinguish between having or using a concept and the clear or explicit recognition and elucidation of it ... Thus persons might have and use the concept of a right without explicitly having a single word for it.'[24] Gewirth claims that the concept of rights can be found in feudal thought, Roman law, Greek philosophy, the Old Testament, and in primitive societies. In connection with the last Finnis points out that anthropological studies of African tribal regimes of law have shown that the English terms a 'right' and 'duty' are usually covered by a single word derived from the form normally translated as 'ought.' He suggests that the best English translation in these cases is 'due' because 'due' looks 'both ways along a juridical relationship, both to what one is due to do, and to what is due to one.'[25]

It seems, then, that the concept of a right may exist where a word for it does not. Could this be the case in Buddhism? In Buddhism what is due in any situation is determined by reference to the universal moral law, or Dharma. Dharma determines what is right and just in all contexts and from all perspectives. With respect to social justice the Rev Vajiragnana explains:

> Each one of us has a role to play in sustaining and promoting social justice and orderliness. The Buddha explained very clearly these roles as reciprocal duties existing between parents and children; teachers and pupils; husband and wife; friends, relatives and neighbours;

employer and employee; clergy and laity ... No one has been left out. The duties explained here are reciprocal and are considered as sacred duties, for – if observed – they can create a just, peaceful and harmonious society.[26]

From this it would seem that Dharma determines not just 'what one is due to do' but also 'what is due to one.' Thus through A's performance of his Dharmic duty B receives that which is his 'due' or, we might say, that to which he is 'entitled' in (under, through) Dharma. Since Dharma determines, for example, the duties of husbands and the duties of wives,[27] it follows that the duties of one correspond to the entitlements or 'rights' of the other. If the husband has a duty to support his wife, the wife has a 'right' to support from her husband. If the wife has a duty to look after her husband's property, the husband has a 'right' to the safe-keeping of his property by his wife. If under Dharma it is the duty of a king (or political authority) to dispense justice impartially, then subjects (citizens) may be said to have a 'right' to just and impartial treatment before the law.

Should it be concluded, then, that the notion of a right is present in classical Buddhism? The answer depends on the criteria adopted for 'having' a concept. Dagger sets out the options:

> If one is willing to look primarily for the idea or the notion, however it may be expressed, then one can confidently say that the concept of rights is virtually as old as civilization itself.

On the other hand:

> If one insists that the form of expression is crucial ... so that a concept cannot be said to exist unless there is a word or phrase that distinguishes it from other concepts, then one would have to say that the concept of rights has its origin in the middle ages.[28]

I think our conclusion should be that the concept of rights is implicit in classical Buddhism in the normative understanding of what is 'due' among and between individuals. Under Dharma, husbands and wives, kings and subjects, teachers and students, all have reciprocal obligations which can be analyzed into rights and duties. We must qualify this conclusion, however, by noting that the requirements of Dharma are almost always expressed in the form of duties rather than rights. In other words, Dharma states what is due in the form 'A husband should support his wife' as opposed to 'Wives have a right to be maintained by their husbands.' Until rights as personal entitlements are recognized as a discrete but integral part of what is due under Dharma, the modern concept of rights cannot be said to be present. In this respect, however, Buddhism is far from unique, and a similar comment could be made about many other cultures and civilizations. Finnis points out with respect to Roman law:

[I]t is salutary to bear in mind that the modern emphasis on the powers of the right-holder, and the consequent systematic bifurcation between 'right' ... and 'duty,' is something that sophisticated lawyers were able to do without for the whole life of classical Roman law.[29]

He also suggests, rightly I think, that 'there is no cause to take sides as between the older and the newer usages, as ways of expressing the implications of justice in a given context.'[30] A right is a useful concept which provides a particular perspective on justice. Its correlative, duty, provides another. These may be thought of as separate windows onto the common good which is justice or, in the context of Buddhism, Dharma. It would therefore be going too far to claim that the notion of rights is 'alien' to Buddhism or that Buddhism denies that individuals have 'rights.' In sum it might be said that in classical Buddhism the notion of rights is present in embryonic form although not yet born into history.

Whether anything like the Western concept of rights has, or would, appear in the course of the historical evolution of Buddhism is a question for specialists in the various Buddhist cultures to ponder. In many respects the omens for this development were never good. Buddhism originated in a caste society, and the Asian societies where it has flourished have for the most part been hierarchically structured. MacIntyre, citing Gewirth, mentions that the concept of a right lacks any means of expression in Japanese 'even as late as the mid-nineteenth century.'[31] The preconditions for the emergence of the concept of rights would seem to be egalitarianism and democracy, neither of which have been notable features of Asian polity before the modern era. On the other hand, a justification for the rejection of hierarchical social structures is not hard to find in Buddhism – one need look only at the Buddha's critique of caste.[32] Buddhism also holds, in the doctrine of no-self, that all individuals are equal in the most profound sense.[33] Like the Christian doctrine that all men are created equal before God this would appear to be fertile ground for a doctrine of natural rights. What seems to have been lacking in both faiths, but perhaps more so in Buddhism, was the will to incarnate this theoretical vision of man in the flesh of social institutions.

Human Rights

In the preceding section attention was focused on the concept of a right. Here we consider what it means to characterize certain rights as human rights,[34] and pursue further the discussion initiated in the preceding section as to whether Western notions of human rights are compatible with Buddhism.[35]

The point has already been made that what are today called human rights were originally spoken of as 'natural' rights, in other words, rights which flow from human nature. In the seventeenth century philosophers and statesmen began to define these rights and enshrine them in early constitutions such as the 'Fundamental Orders of Connecticut' as early as 1639. Documents of this kind inspired the publication of other declarations, charters and manifestos in a tradition which has continued into modern times. As an example of a modern charter of human rights we may take The Universal Declaration of Human Rights proclaimed by the General Assembly of the United Nations in December 1948. Since its promulgation this thirty-article code has been used as a model for many subsequent human rights charters.

What is the Buddhist position with respect to declarations of this kind? It may be useful to begin by asking whether Buddhism would endorse the Universal Declaration on Human Rights. The repeated calls by the Dalai Lama for respect for human rights give some reason to think that it would. The signing of the Global Ethic by many Buddhists also suggests that Buddhism has no reservations about subscribing to charters or manifestos which seek to secure universal human rights. Moreover, there seems to be nothing in any of the thirty articles to which Buddhism would take exception. Perera's commentary on each of the thirty articles of the Universal Declaration shows them to be in harmony with early Buddhist teachings both in letter and in spirit. In his Foreword to the commentary Ananda Guruge writes:

> Professor Perera demonstrates that every single Article of the Universal Declaration of Human Rights – even the labour rights to fair wages, leisure and welfare – has been adumbrated, cogently upheld and meaningfully incorporated in an overall view of life and society by the Buddha.[36]

But how are these rights to be justified with reference to Buddhist teachings? In asking this question I am not seeking justification by reference to textual passages which seem to support the rights claimed. There are many passages in the Pali Canon, as Perera has ably demonstrated, which support the view that early Buddhist teachings were in harmony with the spirit of the Declaration. The justification required at this point has more to do with the philosophical presuppositions underlying these passages and the overall Buddhist vision of individual and social good.

The various declarations on human rights themselves rarely offer a justification for the rights they proclaim. MacIntyre observes dryly how 'In the United Nations declaration on human rights of 1949 [sic] what has since become the normal UN practice of not giving good reasons for any assertion whatsoever is followed with great rigor.'[37] A gesture towards justification is sometimes made in recital clauses by reference to the 'inherent dignity ... of all members of the human family' or some similar form of words. The Global Ethic, which provides a fuller statement than most, echoes the Universal Declaration in its call for 'the full realization of the intrinsic dignity of the human person'.[38] It states: 'We make a commitment to respect life and dignity, individuality and diversity, so that every person is treated humanely.' This is amplified as follows:

> This means that every human being without distinction of age, sex, race, skin, color, physical or mental ability, language, religion, political view, or national or social origin possesses an inalienable and *untouchable dignity*. And everyone, the individual as well as the state, is therefore obliged to honor this dignity and protect it.[39]

Elsewhere, as part of his dialogue with world religions, Küng makes a constructive suggestion on this point to which students of Buddhism might do well to pay heed:

> Should not Buddhist thinkers, as they critically assess their own and alien traditions, make a more direct effort to establish an anthropology centered around *human dignity* (which the Buddha himself deeply respected)? Buddhists are fully aware that man can be adequately understood only as conditioned in every way, as a relational being within the totality of life and the cosmos. But should they not reflect more earnestly, especially in an ethical vein, on the problems of the unique, inviolable, noninterchangeable human self, with its roots in the past and its future destiny?[40]

It is by no means apparent, however, how human dignity is to be grounded in Buddhist doctrine. The very words 'human dignity' sound as alien in a Buddhist context as talk of rights. One looks in vain to the four noble truths for any explicit reference to human dignity, and doctrines such as no-self and impermanence may even be thought to undermine it. If human dignity is the basis of human rights Buddhism would seem to be in some difficulty when it comes to providing a justification for them. The theistic religions, on the other hand, seem much better equipped to provide an account of human dignity. Christians, Muslims and Jews typically refer to the ultimate source of human dignity as divine. Article one (paragraph 1700) of the most recent Catechism of the Catholic Church, for instance, states: 'The dignity of the human person is rooted in his creation in the image and likeness of God.' Buddhism, clearly, would not wish to make such a claim. Küng notes how leading Buddhists at the Parliament of the World's Religions felt called upon to protest at calls for 'a unity of religions under God,' and at references to 'God the Almighty' and 'God the Creator' in invocations during the proceedings. He suggests, however, that these differences are reconcilable since the Buddhist concepts of 'Nirvana, Shunyata and Dharmakaya ... fulfil analogous functions to the concept of God' and can be regarded by Christians as 'parallel terms for the Absolute.'[41]

It may or may not be the case that Mahāyāna schools recognize a transcendent reality which resembles the Christian concept of God as the Absolute, and there are those better qualified than myself to address such a question. Here I will make only three brief points regarding the problems which arise in regarding these things as the source of human dignity. The first is that since these concepts are understood differently by the main Mahāyāna schools they are unlikely to provide the common ground that is required as a foundation for human rights. The second is that it is difficult to see how any of these things can be the source of human dignity in the way that God can, since no school of Buddhism believes that human beings are created by them. The third point is that even if some metaphysical ground of the above kind can be identified in Mahāyāna Buddhism it still leaves the problem of how human dignity is to be grounded where Theravāda Buddhism is concerned. For the Theravāda, Nirvana is not a transcendent Absolute, nor do the concepts of 'Shunyata and Dharmakaya' have anything like the meaning or significance they attain later. No grounding for human rights can be truly satisfactory, I would suggest, unless it unambiguously forms part of the core teachings of classical Buddhism as a whole.

One suggestion as to how human rights can be grounded in Buddhist doctrine has been made by Kenneth Inada. In a discussion of 'The Buddhist Perspective on Human Rights,' Inada suggests 'there is an intimate and vital relationship of the Buddhist norm or Dhamma with that of human rights.'[42] He explains the relationship as follows:

> Human rights is indeed an important issue, but the Buddhist position is that it is ancillary to the larger or more basic issue of human nature. It can be asserted that the Buddhist sees the concept of human rights as a legal extension of human nature. It is a crystallization, indeed a formalization, of the mutual respect and concern of all persons, stemming from human nature. Thus, human nature is the ultimate source, the basis from which all other attributes or characteristics are to be delineated. They all have their respective *raison d'etre* in it. They are reflections and even byproducts of it. The reason for assigning human nature the basic position is very simple. It is to give human relations a firm grounding in the truly existential nature of things: that is, the concrete and dynamic relational nature of persons in contact with each other, that which [sic] avoids being caught up in rhetorical or legalistic tangles.[43]

Few would disagree with the proposition that human rights are grounded in human nature. Towards the end of the extract, however, Inada seems to move away from his initial suggestion that human nature is the 'ultimate source' of human rights towards the view that the ultimate ground is the 'dynamic relational nature of persons in contact with each other.' In other words, it is in the interrelatedness of persons rather than in the persons themselves that the justification for human rights is to be found. This is confirmed a little later:

> Consequently, the Buddhist concern is focused on the experiential process of each individual, a process technically know as relational origination (*paticca-samuppāda*). It is the great doctrine of Buddhism, perhaps the greatest doctrine expounded by the historical Buddha. It means that, in any life-process, the arising of an experiential event is a total, relational affair.[44]

How is the link between dependent-origination and human rights to be forged? The argument reaches its conclusion in the following passage:

> Like a storm which consumes everything in its wake, an experience in terms of relational origination involves everything within its purview. Hence, the involvement of elements and, in our case, human beings as entities should not be in terms of mere relationship but rather a creative relationship which originates from the individual locus of existence. In other words, each individual is responsible for the actualization of an 'extensive concern' for everything that lies in his or her path of experience. So, we may say that the sum total of the 'extensive concerns' can be referred to as a mutually constituted existential realm, and it thereby becomes a fact that there will be mutual respect of fellow beings. It is on this basis that we can speak of the rights of individuals. These rights are actually extensions of human qualities such as security, liberty, and life.[45]

In simple language, the argument seems to be as follows. Human beings, like everything else, are part of the relational process described in the doctrine of dependent-origination; since no-one exists independently we should look out for one another; looking out for one another means respecting each other's rights; examples of the rights we should respect are security, liberty and life.[46]

Although I have described this as an 'argument' it is little more than a series of assertions. Working backwards, it is difficult to know what sense to give the concluding sentence: 'These rights are actually extensions of human qualities such as security, liberty and life.' It is unclear what is meant by 'human qualities' here. In what sense is security a 'human quality' (perhaps a 'need')? Why is life described as a 'quality' of a human being? Even granted that these things are 'human qualities,' what does it mean to say that rights are extensions of 'human qualities'? In the first extract quoted above, Inada suggests that 'the Buddhist sees the concept of human rights as a legal extension of human nature.' What is left unexplained, however, is how human nature (or 'human qualities') become legal rights. Do all 'human qualities' extend into rights or only some? If so, which and why? Finally, if 'human qualities' are what give rise to rights, why invoke the doctrine of dependent-origination?

The derivation of human rights from the doctrine of dependent-origination is a conjuring trick. From the premise that we live in 'a mutually constituted existential realm' (we all live together) it has 'thereby become a fact' that there will be 'mutual respect of fellow beings.' In the twinkling of an eye, values have appeared from facts like a rabbit out of a hat. However, the fact that human beings live in relationship with one another is not a moral argument about *how they ought to behave*. By itself it offers no reason why a person should not routinely abuse the rights of others. Inada's suggestion that human rights can be grounded in the doctrine of dependent-origination turns out to be little more than a recommendation that people should be nice to one another on the ground that we are 'all in this together.'[47]

The approach adopted by Perera is rather different. Perera's main concern is to demonstrate that the articles of the Universal Declaration are adumbrated in early Buddhist teachings, rather than explore their philosophical foundations. He acknowledges that 'Buddhism credits the human personality with a dignity and moral responsibility'[48] but does not explain fully whence this arises or how it provides a foundation for human rights. In a number of places he suggests certain possibilities regarding the source of human dignity, not all of which seem to be compatible. At one point he defines 'the ethical assumption on which the Buddhist concept of human rights is founded' as the 'fundamental consideration that all life has a desire to safeguard itself and to make itself comfortable and happy.'[49]

Basing rights on desires, however, is problematic. One reason is that certain people, for example those who seek to end their lives through suicide, seem to lack the desire in question. Nor is it difficult to conceive of a justification for human rights abuses along the lines that the victims 'no longer cared what happened to them.' If they themselves had no interest in their future, whose rights would have been violated? A deeper problem is that the mere existence of desires establishes nothing from a moral point of view. Desires are many and varied and can be met in manifold ways. Moral questions arise both at the level of whether a desire *should* be met and *how* it should be met. The identification of a desire may be a starting point for moral reflection, but it is certainly not its end.[50]

On the preceding page Perera suggests an alternative foundation for human rights, one which links it to human dignity. He writes: 'Buddhism posits, as Jean Jaques Rousseau did much later, that the essence of human dignity lies in the assumption of man's responsibility for his own governance.'[51] No Buddhist sources are cited in support of this claim, and I believe it is unlikely that Buddhism would wish to link human dignity quite so closely to politics. Perhaps if this suggestion were developed a little further it would make reference to underlying human capacities such as reason and autonomy which enable individuals to constitute themselves into orderly societies, and then point to these as the underlying source of human dignity. While political institutions may be produced through the exercise of distinctively human capacities, however, it is unlikely that Buddhism would locate 'the essence of human dignity' in their creation. According to the *Aggaññasutta*, the evolution of political societies is the consequence of depravity and decline, which makes them a dubious testament to human dignity.

Where, then, should the foundations for a Buddhist doctrine of human rights be sought? The proper ground for a doctrine of human rights, I suggest, lies elsewhere than in the doctrine of dependent-origination, as suggested by Inada, or in either the desire for self-preservation or the acceptance of responsibility for self-government, as proposed by Perera. Perera, in fact, comes closest to what in my view is the true source of human rights in Buddhism in his commentary on Article 1.[52] In discussing the first sentence of the Article ('All human beings are born free and equal in dignity and rights') he comments that 'Buddhahood itself is within the reach of all human beings ... and if all could attain Buddhahood what greater equality in dignity and rights can there be?' To focus attention upon the goal, I believe, is more promising than any of the other approaches considered thus far. Perera seems to grasp its significance in a remark towards the end of his commentary on Article 1. He writes:

> It is from the point of view of its goal that Buddhism evaluates all action. Hence Buddhist thought is in accord with this and other Articles in the Universal Declaration of Human Rights to the extent to which they facilitate the advancement of human beings towards the Buddhist goal.[53]

I believe the above statement provides the key to understanding human rights from a Buddhist perspective. What is missing in Perera's commentary, however, is the explicit linkage between the goal and human dignity, and it is this which I will now try to establish. What I will suggest in general is that the source of human dignity should be sought not in the analysis of the human condition provided by the first and second noble truths but in the evaluation of human good provided by the third and fourth. Human rights cannot be derived from any factual non-evaluative analysis of human nature, whether in terms of its psycho-physical constitution (the five 'aggregates' which lack a self), its biological nature (needs, urges, drives), or the deep structure of interdependency (*paṭicca-samuppāda*). Instead the most promising approach will be one which locates human rights and dignity within a comprehensive account of human goodness, and which sees basic rights and freedoms as integrally related to human flourishing and self-realization.[54] This is because the source of human dignity in

Buddhism lies nowhere else than in the literally infinite capacity of human nature for participation in goodness.[55]

The connection between human rights and human good can be illustrated by asking what the various declarations on human rights seek to secure. Documents which speak of human rights commonly announce a list of specific rights and freedoms and proclaim them to be inviolable. The rights proclaimed by the Universal Declaration include the right to life, liberty, security of person, equality before the law, privacy, marriage and protection of family life, social security, participation in government, work, protection against unemployment, rest and leisure, a minimum standard of living, and enjoyment of the arts. The exercise of these rights is subject only to such general limitations as are necessary to secure due recognition and respect for the rights and freedoms of others and the requirements of morality, public order and general welfare (Article 29.2). Otherwise, the rights are expressed in categorical forms such as 'Everyone has . . .' and 'No-one shall . . .'. For example, Article 3: 'Everyone has the right to life, liberty and security of person.' And Article 4: 'No one shall be held in slavery or servitude; slavery and the slave trade shall be prohibited in all their forms.' The document thus understands the rights it proclaims as both 'universal' and exceptionless. Using the terminology introduced earlier it can be seen that some of these rights are claim rights while others are liberty rights. Article 2 confirms this when it speaks of an entitlement to both the '*rights* and *freedoms* set forth in this Declaration.'[56]

What do these rights and freedoms amount to? It might be said that they map the parameters of human 'good-in-community.' In other words, these rights and freedoms are what is required if human beings are to lead fulfilled lives in society. Article 29.1 recognizes this when it observes 'Everyone has duties to the community *in which alone the free and full development of his personality is possible.*'[57] In the absence of human rights the scope for human development and fulfilment through social interaction is drastically reduced. The rights specified define and facilitate aspects of human fulfilment. The right to life is clearly fundamental since it is the condition for the enjoyment of all other rights and freedoms. The right to 'liberty and security of person' (Article 3) is also basic to any understanding of human good. Without these minimum conditions the scope and opportunity for human fulfilment would be intolerably restricted. The same would apply in the case of slavery (Article 4), torture (Article 5), and the denial of rights before the law (Article 6). It can also be seen that many of the detailed rights identified are actually derived from more fundamental ones. Article 3, for example, 'No one shall be held in slavery,' is clearly implied in Article 2, 'Everyone has the right to . . . liberty.' It might thus be said that many of the thirty articles articulate the practical implications of a relatively small number of fundamental rights and freedoms which are the basis of the common good.

It may be noted that the Universal Declaration itself and modern charters like it do not offer a comprehensive vision of human good. This is not intended as a criticism, for the purpose of such charters is to secure only what might be termed the 'minimum conditions' for human flourishing in a pluralistic milieu. The task of articulating a comprehensive vision of what is ultimately valuable in human life and how it is to be attained falls to the competing theories of human good found in religions, philosophies and ideologies. Buddhism provides one view of human nature and its fulfilment, Christianity another, secular philosophies a third. To pursue any of these different paths, however, requires the substructure known as 'human rights,' a complex of fundamental rights and liberties which are the preconditions for the realization of the particular opportunities made available by the competing ideologies.

If the aim of human rights declarations is understood in the way outlined above then human rights is fundamentally a moral issue. Where there is no right to life, liberty and security of person, and where torture is routine, the opportunities for the realization of human good are greatly reduced. Freedom of religion (Article 18), for example, is vital to the Buddhist vision of individual and social good, and the consequences of the loss of these rights are all too obvious in Tibet. Human rights is thus an area in which religions have a legitimate and vital stake, and there is every reason why it would be proper for Buddhism both to endorse the Universal Declaration and call upon others to respect and implement it.[58]

If religions have a legitimate stake in human rights, we might expect to find many of the rights and liberties spelled out in human rights charters present in either an express or implied form in their moral teachings. These typically include, as in the case of the Five Precepts of Buddhism, commandments or precepts forbidding the immoral treatment of others in such ways as by killing, stealing, and lying. These evils are prohibited because it is immediately apparent that they are antithetical to human flourishing-in-community. The rationale for these prohibitions, I suggest, coincides to a large extent with that of the various human rights manifestos.[59] These manifestos, indeed, may be regarded as a translation of religious precepts into the language of rights. The process of casuistry can be seen at work in both. Just as a limited number of moral precepts can be expanded to meet the needs of different social situations (many of the extensive Vinaya rules, for example, have their source in a handful of moral precepts),[60] so the many articles in human rights charters are extrapolated from a comparatively small number of basic rights and freedoms.

It must be admitted there are grounds for scepticism towards the parallel which has just been suggested since it cannot be denied that the Buddhist precepts look and sound very different from contemporary declarations on human rights. The Buddhist precepts make no reference to 'rights' at all, and are couched instead in the form of undertakings.[61] Let us examine what these undertakings involve. On the basis of our earlier analysis it would seem that 'taking the precepts' in Buddhism is actually the formal acknowledgement of a subsisting duty, a duty which arises from Dharma. The person who takes the precepts is saying in effect 'I hereby recognize my Dharmic duty not to do x, y, and z.' Since duties have their correlative in rights, however, rights must also be implicit in the good the precepts seek to promote. We saw earlier that rights provide a way of talking about what is just and unjust from a special angle. We noted further that a person who has a right has a benefit, a benefit which can be described as either a claim or a liberty. In the context of the precepts, then, the right-holder is the one who suffers from the breach of Dharmic duty when the precepts are broken. In the case of the first precept this would be the person who was unjustly killed. The right the victim has may therefore be defined as a negative claim-right upon the aggressor, namely the right not to be killed. In simple terms we might say that the victim has a right to life which the aggressor has a duty to respect.

That the translation between precepts and rights is accurate, and that the agreement between the two formulations is more than superficial or accidental, is supported by the authenticity with which the Dalai Lama was able to affirm the Global Ethic. Kuschel comments as follows:

> The reason why the Dalai Lama's speech was so convincing, and indeed seized people's hearts, so that it was often interrupted by spontaneous applause, was that this man simply wanted to be an *authentic Buddhist*. His plea for mutual respect, dialogue and collaboration, for understanding between peoples and respect for creation, was not an adaptation to Christian or Western values, but came from the depths of his own Buddhist spirituality.[62]

Further evidence of the linkage between the Buddhist precepts and social justice is found in the Theravāda tradition. Writing on the theme of 'Justice in Buddhism' Vajiragnana states:

> Man is responsible for society. It is he who makes it good or bad through his own actions. Buddhism, therefore, advocates a five-fold disciplinary code for man's training in order to maintain justice in society ... These five ... precepts are extremely important funda-mental principles for promoting and perpetuating human welfare, peace and justice.[63]

I suggest, then, that the apparent differences between the moral teachings of Buddhism and human rights charters is one of form rather than substance. Human rights can be extrapolated from Buddhist moral teachings in the manner described above using the logic of moral relationships to illumine what is due under Dharma. A direct translation of the first four precepts yields a right to life, a right not to have one's property stolen, a right to

73

fidelity in marriage, and a right not to be lied to. Many other human rights, such as the rights to liberty and security can either be deduced from or are extant within the general corpus of Buddhist moral teachings. A right not to be held in slavery, for example, is implicit in the canonical prohibition on trade in living beings.[64] These rights are the extrapolation of what is due under Dharma; they have not been 'imported' into Buddhism but were always implicitly present.

If modern conceptions of human rights and Buddhist moral teachings are related in the way I have suggested, certain conclusions follow for our understanding of the Buddhist precepts. If there are universal and exceptionless rights, as human rights charters affirm, there must be universal and exceptionless duties. If human rights such as a 'right to life' (by which I understand a right not to have one's life taken unjustly) are exceptionless, there must also be an exceptionless duty to abstain from unjustly depriving a human being of life. The First Precept in Buddhism, therefore, should be understood as an exceptionless duty or moral absolute.

Is this reverse translation, from absolute human rights to absolute moral duties, supported by textual sources? There is every reason to think that it is. Such an understanding of the precept is clearly evident in classical Buddhism, which tirelessly reiterates the principle of the sanctity of life found in the pan-Indian teachings on non-harming (*ahiṃsā*), and which gives no reason to suppose that its moral precepts are to be understood as anything other than exceptionless norms. If, on the other hand, it is thought that the precepts are not to be understood as moral absolutes, then it is difficult to see what justification there can be for Buddhists to hold that there are universal and exceptionless human rights. It would be inconsistent to affirm the latter but deny the former.

The above account of human rights in Buddhism has been given entirely within the context of an understanding of human good which has its apex in nirvana-in-this-life. Reference to the transcendent dimension of human good and its ground has been avoided for several reasons. The first is that no reference need be made to transcendent realities in order to ground human rights. That this is so can be seen from the absence of any reference to such realities in contemporary human rights charters, and the fact that many atheists are vigorous defenders of human rights. Where Buddhism is concerned, the vision of human good set out in the third and fourth noble truths provides the necessary basis for a doctrine of human rights. Human rights turn out in essence to be what justice requires if human good is to be fulfilled. The second reason for avoiding reference to transcendent realities is that my aim has been to suggest a basis for human rights acceptable to classical Buddhism as a whole. Since all schools of Buddhism affirm the third and fourth noble truths and the vision of human good they proclaim, the required common ground for a pan-Buddhist doctrine of human rights is present.

The above should not be read as a denial that there can be a transcendent ground for human rights in Buddhism. Because the transcendent dimension of human good is left obscure in Buddhist teachings, however, the transcendent ground for human rights is also obscure. In terms of the account given here, the transcendent ground for human rights would be post-mortem nirvana, not in the sense of an absolute reality (as suggested by Küng) but as the universalization of human good on a transcendent plane. The twin axes of human good are knowledge (*prajñā*) and moral concern (*karuṇā*), and on the graph defined by these axes can be plotted the soteriological coordinates of any individual. Through participation in these twin categories of good, human nature progressively transcends its limitations and becomes saturated with nirvanic goodness. Eventually, in post-mortem nirvana, this goodness attains a magnitude which can no longer be charted. If a transcendent ground for human rights is desired, this is where it should be sought.

To sum up: it is legitimate to speak of both rights and human rights in Buddhism. Modern doctrines of human rights are in harmony with the moral values of classical Buddhism in that they are an explication of what is 'due' under Dharma. The modern idea of human rights has a distinctive cultural origin, but its underlying preoccupation with human good makes it at bottom a moral issue in which Buddhism and other religions have a legitimate stake. The Global Ethic endorses the view that the principles it sets forth on human rights are neither new nor 'Western' when it states: 'We affirm that a common set of core values is found in the teachings of the religions, and that these form the basis of a global ethic.'[65]

A final thought. Above I have spoken only of human rights, and in the context of Buddhism this perspective may be unduly narrow in that it seems to preclude the universe of sentient non-human beings from any entitlement to rights. Buddhists may feel, therefore, that it is less prejudicial in discussions of this kind to revert to the older terminology of 'natural' rights. Whether or not animals have rights, and whether these are the same rights as human beings, is a matter which requires separate discussion. If human rights flow from human nature, as suggested, it may be that rights of different kinds flow from natures of different kinds. Such would seem to be the understanding of classical Buddhism as set out in its hierarchical scheme of the different realms of rebirth.

Notes

1 First published in the *Journal of Buddhist Ethics* 2 1995 pp. 3–27 and reprinted in Damien V. Keown, Charles S. Prebish and Wayne R. Husted (eds) *Buddhism and Human Rights* (London: Curzon Press, 1998). The permission of Curzon Press to republish in the present collection is gratefully acknowledged. This edition contains minor modifications and formatting changes.

2 The text of the Declaration, along with commentaries and supplementary information is available in Hans Küng and Karl-Josef Kuschel, eds *A Global Ethic. The Declaration of the Parliament of the World's Religions* (London: SCM Press, 1993).

3 Küng and Kuschel (eds) (1993) p. 8.

4 For a range of cultural and ideological perspectives on human rights see Adamantia Pollis and Peter Schwab *Human Rights: Cultural and Ideological Perspectives* (New York: Praeger, 1979).

5 On the absence of ethics in Hinduism see Austin B. Creel *Dharma in Hindu Ethics* (Calcutta: Firma KLM, 1977), p. 20ff.

6 In spite of its contemporary importance, however, little appears to have been written on the subject from a specifically Buddhist perspective. The only monograph on the subject appears to be L.P.N. Perera *Buddhism and Human Rights. A Buddhist Commentary on the Universal Declaration of Human Rights* (Colombo: Karunaratne and Sons, 1991).

7 On the analogous question of whether there is an 'African' doctrine of human rights see Rhoda Howard 'Is there an African concept of human rights?' *in Foreign Policy and Human Rights*, ed. R.J. Vincent (Cambridge: Cambridge University Press, 1986), pp. 11–32.

8 For information on these empirical questions see Charles Humana *World Human Rights Guide* (Oxford: Oxford University Press, 1992); James C. Hsiung *Human Rights in East Asia: A Cultural Perspective* (New York: Paragon House, 1985); K.M. de Silva et al eds. *Ethnic Conflict in Buddhist Societies: Sri Lanka, Thailand and Burma* (Boulder, Co: Westview Press, 1988). Also *Human Rights in Developing Countries, Yearbook 1993* (Copenhagen: Nordic Human Rights Publications, 1993).

9 Richard Dagger 'Rights,' in Terence Ball et al. (eds.), *Political Innovation and Conceptual Change* (Cambridge: Cambridge University Press, 1989), pp. 292–308. I am indebted to Dagger's excellent paper throughout this section.

10 Dagger (1989) p. 294. Original emphasis.

11 J.M. Finnis *Natural Law and Natural Rights* (Oxford: Clarendon Press, 1980), p. 206.

12 Max Stackhouse lists five in *Creeds, Society, and Human Rights* (Grand Rapids, Michigan: William B. Eerdmans Publishing Company), p. 435ff. David Little shows the dependency of the modern Western secular and liberal ideology on Christian theology by tracing the historical connection between the Christian concept of conscience and the intellectual framework within which the American doctrines of liberty and religious freedom emerged in the eighteenth century in the writings of Thomas Jefferson and James Madison. He suggests that this Western framework applies relatively unproblematically to Buddhism and Islam, and notes in general: 'Thus, current human rights formulations, along with the important notions that underlie them, are by no means necessarily irrelevant to cultures outside the West.' See David Little, John Kelsay, and Abdulaziz Sachedina, eds *Human Rights and the Conflict of Cultures* (Columbia, S.C.: University of South Carolina Press), p. 31. For perspectives on human rights from the world's religions see Leroy S. Rouner *Human Rights and the World's Religions* (Notre Dame: University of Notre Dame Press, 1988) and Arlene Swidler ed. *Human Rights in Religious Traditions* (New York: Pilgrims Press, 1982). A commentary on the *Universal Declaration* from the perspective of Buddhism, Hinduism, Christianity and Islam may be found in L.H.H. Perera ed. *Human Rights and Religions in Sri Lanka. A Commentary on the Universal Declaration of Human Rights*, published by the Sri Lanka Foundation (Colombo, 1988). The Buddhist commentary by Perera was republished separately in 1991 (see note 6 above).

13 Stackhouse (1984) p. 35.

14 Stackhouse (1984) p. 36.

15 For a survey see R.W. Carlyle and A.J. Carlyle *A History of Medieval Political Theory in the West* (Edinburgh: Blackwood and Sons, 1950).

16 Finnis (1980) p. 208.

17 The most influential modern analysis of rights is that by Wesley Hohfeld *Fundamental Legal Conceptions* (New Haven: Yale University Press, 1964).

18 Finnis (1980) pp. 199–205.

19 Finnis (1980) p. 205, original emphasis.

20 Perera's discussion of Buddhism and human rights does not address these questions, and seems to assume that the concept of rights and human rights as understood in the *Universal Declaration* are directly applicable to canonical Buddhism.

21 For the view that moral values are determined by culture, as maintained by many anthropologists, see John Ladd (ed.) *Ethical Relativism* (Lanham: University Press of America, 1983). The defensibility of a specific cultural custom (female circumcision) from a human rights perspective is discussed by Stephen A. James 'Reconciling International Human Rights and Cultural Relativism: the case of female circumcision,' *Bioethics* 8, 1994 pp. 1–26.

22 *Pali Text Society Pali-English Dictionary, uju* and *ujju.*

23 On the concept of rights in Hinduism and the meaning of *adhikāra*, see Purushottama Bilimoria 'Is "Adhikāra" good enough for "rights",' *Asian Philosophy* 23 1993, pp. 3–13; also Creel (1977) p. 19. In Buddhist languages the notion of rights may be distributed among a variety of terms, as perhaps, in Latin among the words *auctoritas, potestas, dominium, iurisdictio, proprietas, libertas and ius* (Dagger, 1989 p. 291).

24 Quoted in Dagger (1989) p. 286.

25 Finnis (1980) p. 209.

26 Ven Vajiragnana 'Justice in Buddhism,' *Vesak Sirisara* (unpaginated version from the Electronic Buddhist Archive, 1992).

27 See, for example, the *Sigālovādasutta.*

28 Dagger (1989) p. 297.

29 Finnis (1980) p. 209.

30 Finnis (1980) p. 210.

31 Alasdair MacIntyre *After Virtue. A Study in Moral Theory* (London: Duckworth, 1981), p. 69. Cf. Theodore de Bary on the Chinese neologisms which have been coined to express these concepts: 'Neo-Confucianism and Human Rights,' in *Human Rights and the World's Religions*, ed. Leroy S. Rouner, Notre Dame: University of Notre Dame Press, p. 183.

32 The institution of caste is criticized in numerous early discourses, notably the *Soṇadaṇḍasutta.*

33 Michael Carrithers suggests that the Buddhist concept of the 'self' (which he relates to Mauss's concept of the 'moi') is one which is easily transportable across cultural frontiers. This enhances the prospects for a Buddhist doctrine of universal human rights. See 'An alternative social history of the self,' in *The category of the person. Anthropology, philosophy, history*, eds M. Carrithers, S. Collins, and S. Lukes, (Cambridge: Cambridge University Press, 1995), pp. 234–256.

34 Useful discussions of the philosophical basis of human rights may be found in Jack Donnelly *The Concept of Human Rights* (London and Sydney: Croom Helm, 1985) and James W. Nickel *Making Sense of Human Rights* (Berkeley: University of California Press, 1987).

35 On how far the Western concept of human rights is relevant or applicable to other cultures see R. Panikkar 'Is the Notion of Human Rights a Western Concept?' *Diogenes* 120 1982, pp. 75–102; Fernando R. Teson 'International Human Rights and Cultural Relativism,' *Virginia Journal of International Law* 25 1985, pp. 869–898; Yogesh K. Tyagi 'Third World Response to Human Rights,' *Indian Journal of International Law* 21 1981, pp. 119–140. A.J.M. Milne *Human Rights and Human Diversity* (London: Macmillan, 1986); C.E. Welch and V. Leary *Asian Perspectives on Human Rights* (Boulder, Co: Westview Press, 1990).

36 Perera (1991) p. xi.

37 MacIntyre (1981) p. 69.

38 *A Global Ethic*, p. 14.

39 *A Global Ethic*, p. 23, original emphasis.

40 Hans Küng, Josef Van Ess, Heinrich Von Stietencron, and Heinz Bechert *Christianity and the World Religions*, (second ed. London: SCM Press, 1986) p. 383f., original emphasis.

41 *A Global Ethic*, p. 62f.

42 Kenneth K. Inada 'The Buddhist Perspective on Human Rights,' *in Human Rights in Religious Traditions*, ed. Arlene Swidler (New York: Pilgrims Press, 1982 pp. 66–76), p. 71.

43 Inada (1982) p. 70 (paragraphs joined).

44 Ibid.

45 Inada (1982) p. 70f.

46 An earlier attempt to ground Buddhist ethics in dependent-origination can be found in Joanna Rogers Macy 'Dependent Co-Arising: The Distinctiveness of Buddhist Ethics,' *Journal of Religious Ethics* 7 1989, pp. 38–52. Macy offers the Sarvodaya Shramadana, a self-help movement in Sri Lanka, as 'A notable example of the ethics of *paṭicca-samuppāda*,' but, like Inada, fails to explain how a moral imperative arises out of this doctrine. Also drawn to the seemingly magnetic doctrines of no-self and dependent-origination is Taitetsu Unno, whose 1988 article, supposedly about rights, is taken up almost entirely in providing a Pure Land perspective on these two doctrines ('Personal Rights and Contemporary Buddhism,' *in Human Rights in the World's Religions*, ed. Leroy S. Rouner, Notre Dame: University of Notre Dame Press, pp. 129–147). While these doctrines offer a congenial metaphysical backdrop for Buddhist ethics, they cannot provide a *moral* ground for rights. Ian Harris (1994) expresses doubts that dependent-origination can provide a satisfactory basis for Buddhist ecology ('Causation and Telos: The Problem of Buddhist Environmental Ethics,' *Journal of Buddhist Ethics* 1 1994, pp. 45–56).

47 In a second essay on the subject Inada gives much less emphasis to dependent-origination and seems to want to ground human rights in compassion. However, the nature of the argument, and in particular the concluding paragraph, are far from clear. 'A Buddhist Response to the Nature of Human Rights,' *in Asian Perspectives on Human Rights*, eds. Claude E. Welch Jr. and Virginia A. Leary (Boulder, Co: Westview Press, 1990) pp. 91–103.

48 Perera (1991) p. 28 (cf p. 88).

49 Perera (1991) p. 29.

50 A further problem, although I believe it is ultimately a pseudo-problem, is that Buddhism sees desire as the cause of suffering. Desire would therefore seem an unlikely foundation for human rights.

51 Perera (1991) p. 28.

52 Article 1: 'All human beings are born free and equal in dignity and rights. They are endowed with reason and conscience and should act towards one another in a spirit of brotherhood.'

53 Perera (1991) p. 24.

54 A discussion of human nature and human good in Buddhism will be found in part one of my *Buddhism & Bioethics* (London: Macmillan, 1995).

55 A more familiar way of making the same point in Buddhist terminology would be to say that all beings are potential Buddhas or possess the 'Buddha-nature.'

56 Emphasis added.

57 Emphasis added.

58 In the view of Perera: 'From the religious angle, it is possible to state that in this Declaration lie enshrined certain values and norms emphasized by the major religions of the world. Though not directly expressed, the basic principles of the Declaration are

supported and reinforced by these religious traditions, and among them the contribution of the Buddhist tradition, to say the least, is quite outstanding' (1991, p. xiii). Though not wishing to deny that the early teachings support the principles of the Declaration, I do not agree that the contribution of the Buddhist *tradition* to the cause of human rights is in any way 'outstanding.'

59 In certain areas (such as the prohibition on alcohol and matters of sexual morality) the precepts go beyond the more limited aims of human rights charters. This is because Buddhism provides a *particular* vision of human good and also defines the practices required for its fulfilment.

60 Damien Keown *The Nature of Buddhist Ethics* (London: Macmillan, 1992), p. 33.

61 Sometimes a contrast is drawn between the 'voluntary' nature of the Buddhist precepts and the 'commandments' of Christianity. While the format of the Buddhist precepts is certainly more appealing to liberal tastes, the distinction has little real meaning. The precepts apply whether or not they are formally 'undertaken,' and are commandments in all but name.

62 Küng and Kuschel (eds) (1993) p. 104, original emphasis.

63 Vajiragnana (1992).

64 A.iii.208.

65 Küng and Kuschel (eds) (1993) p. 14.

CHAPTER FOUR

Buddhism and Animal Rights

Paul Waldau

'Animal rights' is a complex group of diverse and sometimes very controversial issues centered on the nature and status of nonhuman animals. In considering the relevance of Buddhist claims, insights and approaches to these issues, several complex problems must be faced. These problems are: (1) What does 'animal rights' involve? (2) What are the Buddhist tradition's views of other animals? and (3) How might we relate Buddhist insights to the admittedly modern notions and terminology used when the many versions of 'animal rights' are discussed? Consider first some complexities that arise when trying to address each of these problems.

(1) What does 'animal rights' really involve?

In contemporary societies, 'animal rights' is many different things and movements, and these are by no means internally consistent phenomena. The term itself has come to have many meanings, which, roughly, operate around two poles. First, 'animal rights' acts as a generic term describing a vast universe of concerns for 'other animals.' Such concerns have appeared in many different ways in various cultures, both east and west; they came to limited prominence at the end of the eighteenth century in several countries in Europe. However, as Gold notes, 'it is only in the last twenty years that there has been what can accurately be described as a popular movement for social reform.'[1] Concern for other animals has been a venerable, even if often minor, tradition in all of the major religious traditions and in some philosophical traditions.[2] Further, concern for other animals is a feature of many indigenous societies as well.[3] Nevertheless, the term 'animal rights' is now generally used to designate a range of views in those societies which have seen a serious philosophical, theological and political concern for other animals develop somewhat fitfully since the end of the eighteenth century.

In this broadest use of the term 'animal rights,' the word 'animal' actually means 'animals other than humans.' Of course, one use of the word 'animal' is 'all animals, including humans.' This is the sense of the word we have when we read Aristotle's dictum, 'man is by nature a political animal.'[4] But this inclusivist sense is not the primary sense of the English word 'animal' today. Rather, the most common use is more exclusivist. It appears very widely, as in the translation of Thomas Aquinas' statement that 'there is nothing wrong in a man using plants for the sake of animals or animals for his own sake.'[5] 'Animals' here, of course, means 'all animals other than humans.' The most generic use of 'animal rights' relies on this sense, and thus means a general concern for *other* animals.

There is a far more restrictive sense of 'animal rights' associated with a 'more radical wing' of the broad 'animal liberation movement.'[6] This sense is associated with the claim that some individual animals other than humans possess 'rights.' 'Rights' in this claim often means that the individual animals are conceived to have traits such that there is a *limit of a moral nature* on what human animals can, in good conscience and in the face of alternatives, do to those other animals. The most influential contemporary statement of this position is Regan's *The Case for Animal Rights.*[7] Regan's argument reflects the more radical sense of 'animal rights' in its claim that animal advocates who advance the interests or 'rights' of *species* are guilty of 'environmental fascism' because they ignore the 'rights' of *individual* animals.[8] There is, however, no consensus as to what 'rights' means for other animals even among those who claim that 'rights' language is the best language to express the increasing concern of many late twentieth century humans for other living things,[9] as indeed there is no consensus as to what 'rights' language means for other humans. There are many philosophers who champion the cause of other animals while repudiating reliance on the concept and language of 'rights' as the principal means for doing so.[10]

The term 'animal rights,' then, can be used variously, sometimes as no more than a vague reference to a battery of diverse views about why other animals might be important, and at other times as a reference to very specific claims about the status and importance of individuals. In what follows, the references to the broader use will be referred to as 'the broadest animal rights view' and the narrower use will be denominated 'the more radical animal rights view.' These alternatives are really the opposite ends of a crowded continuum. The broadest animal rights view can involve advocacy of a wide range of alternatives, from complete freedom for other animals as holders of 'rights' to merely improving the conditions under which they are transported to slaughter or held in captivity for human benefit.[11] The more radical animal rights view is typically associated with much more onerous (for humans) demands for the cessation of any instrumental use of any other animals possessing certain traits such as the ability to suffer, large brains, familial and/or social abilities of a relatively complex nature, communication, or relatively high levels of intelligence. The common factor in these two views is that at least *some* other animals are viewed as *more* important than traditional ethical systems have allowed.

(2) What is the Buddhist tradition's view of other animals?

The Pali Canon mentions hundreds of animals. Of course, humans are alluded to frequently, but the diverse texts which comprise this large body of material contain an astonishing array of references to other animals. Even some of the drier, 'scholastic' texts in the long *Abhidhamma Piṭaka* mention other animals surprisingly frequently; for example, the *Puggala Paññatti* alone refers to at least fifteen different kinds of animals.[12] The number of references in this text is, however, dwarfed by the very frequent references to other animals found in the *Vinaya Piṭaka* and the *Sutta Piṭaka*. For example, the short *Suttanipāta* mentions as many as twenty-six different kinds of animals.[13]

Primary texts from other Buddhist traditions similarly include frequent mention of other animals. Given the frequency of these references, it is clear that other animals were an important part of early and later Buddhists' awareness of the world. When this is coupled with the great prominence given to the First Precept, the fundamental undertaking to refrain from killing living beings which is a hallmark of Buddhist teaching, it is clear that other animals were valued by the 'Buddhist tradition.'[14] As is commonly pointed out, the Buddhist tradition is internally quite diverse, such that Gombrich has been moved to comment, 'About *all* Buddhists few valid generalizations are possible.'[15] Attitudes toward other animals, however, may be one of the few areas where generalizations are possible. The Theravāda tradition, as noted above, clearly was concerned with the nature, status and treatment of other living things. Different branches of the Mahāyāna tradition also reflect this, perhaps most distinctively in the elaboration of the role of the bodhisattva and of several kinds of compassion, as well as in the relatively stronger emphasis on the duty of vegetarianism.[16]

Yet of equal significance for the question at hand is the fact that Buddhist materials also reflect *far less positive* attitudes towards other animals. The tension between, on the one hand, views in the tradition which value the lives of other animals, and, on the other hand, views which denigrate them suggests that there is no simple answer to questions about Buddhist views of other animals.[17] The less positive attitudes will be examined below, but suffice it here to mention not only the Buddhist tradition's acquiescence in instrumental uses which were harmful to other animals, but also the tradition's subtle *promotion* of such uses. While this will be examined at the end of this chapter, particularly with regard to acceptance of harmful, instrumental uses of elephants, a frank evaluation of the tradition's less positive attitudes towards other animals is not meant to suggest that the tradition's insights into the value of other animals were insignificant, for they are on any account an achievement of a very high order. Such insights are, however, accompanied by, and indeed often interwoven with, complex and arguably inconsistent attitudes which suggest that serious harm to other animals was acceptable to the tradition from the very beginning.

(3) How might one relate Buddhist insights to animal rights?

If the Buddhist tradition has important insights but is itself mixed in its views, and perhaps even internally contradictory on the significance of other animals, and if modern insights into why other animals should matter are also extremely diverse and subject to radical disagreement, how might one work with the Buddhist insights in relation to the complex of modern notions generally labelled as 'animal rights'? There is an incentive to relate Buddhist insights to different views in the panorama of modern animal rights views, for in many respects the core insights of the modern movement are akin in spirit to the Buddhist respect for life embodied in the First Precept. Yet any attempt at extrapolation entails severe risks, namely those of anachronistic thinking.

In all fairness, it would be naive to criticise the Buddhist tradition for a failure to attain the 'insights' about other living things that are now available because of recent work regarding the complexities of some other animals. Since the 1960s, wide-ranging work has been done in very specialized Western biological sciences (particularly ethology, the cognitive sciences, comparative and developmental psychology, primatology, behavioural ecology, biological anthropology, evolutionary biology, neurosciences, and genetics) which reveals that *some* other animals have biological, mental and social complexities undreamed of by Western philosophers, theologians and scientists even at the mid-point of *this* century. Insensitive application to ancient religious traditions of contemporary views based on information only recently obtained would surely be anachronistic. Further, because any attempt by a contemporary individual to ask ancient traditions for answers to contemporary problems entails risk, perhaps it is inevitable that some anachronistic thinking will take place by virtue of the very effort to use the wisdom of older views to address concerns which (1) have emerged in our culturally distinct circumstances, and (2) are framed in our culturally distinct discourses.

But concern for other beings is now and always has been an integral part of the Buddhist tradition. Attempts to use it, or to be enlightened by it, then, are not fraught with the same risks of anachronism which one faces when attempting to use the tradition's core insights on other, far more modern issues (some of which are addressed in other chapters of this book). Further, leaving Buddhist insights in their original cultural garb and insisting that no adjustment for subsequent changes be allowed runs the opposite risk of antiquarian thinking. The conceptually related problems of anachronism and antiquarian thinking are simply inevitable risks that must be taken if one wants to work with the insights of long-standing traditions.

Thus, although there are some hazards involved in attempts to cross-relate the concerns and concepts of 'animal rights' with the approaches, insights and views of the Buddhist tradition, a concern for other living things is common to both such that the attempt is understandable and, it will be suggested below, productive of valuable insights.

Getting past the problems of extrapolation – the appeal of the First Precept

Since the Buddhist tradition's core insights into the moral nature of killing and harming appear to be precisely the kind of concerns which animate the contemporary animal rights scene, it is worth asking what this ancient tradition can tell us about concerns for other animals. It is surely the case that the profound ethical insights at the heart of the tradition challenge any position that purports to justify the instrumental use of *all* other animals for non-essential human purposes.[18] As noted above, concern for other living things is fundamental to the Buddhist tradition, for the First Precept (which has various formulations, but all of which are against killing) is a primary and arguably 'uncompromisable' part of the tradition.[19] This moral commitment is *first* in several senses. It is regularly listed as the first of the five principal moral commitments or 'undertakings, expressed in the first person'[20] known generally as 'the Five Precepts.' It is also first in the list of eight precepts observed by the Buddhist laity on the four fast (*uposatha*) days of the month, and in the ten precepts observed by novices and fully ordained monks; it is further included as the first in the list of ten good actions.[21] Non-killing is also 'first' in the sense of being an introductory and representative part of the tradition's message. For example, in the *Dīgha* a victorious warlord proclaims the message of the Buddha to the vanquished kings. The message begins, 'Ye shall slay no living thing.'[22] Finally, the First Precept is also 'first' in time, appearing in the oldest parts of the oldest Buddhist scriptures and perhaps even predating them.[23]

Aśoka, a Buddhist emperor who ruled in the third century BCE, is one of the most prominent figures in the entire tradition, and arguably this is so *precisely* because he attempted to integrate the First Precept into his rule. The text of the edicts which he had posted around his large realm testify again and again to the sanctity of the lives of other animals.[24]

The prominence of such a remarkable undertaking to protect life is one of the reasons for statements such as the following:

Buddhism takes into full account the animal's latent capacity for affection, heroism and self-sacrifice. There is in Buddhism more sense of kinship with the animal world, a more intimate feeling of community with all that lives, than is found in Western religious thought. . . . So in Buddhist texts animals are always treated with great sympathy and understanding.[25]

Variations on these themes of the Buddhist tradition (1) taking 'full account' of other animals' important capacities; (2) having 'more sense of kinship, [and] a more intimate feeling of community with all that lives'; and (3) 'always' treating other animals 'with great sympathy, and understanding,' can be found in the claims of both adherents and scholars. Practising Buddhists A. T. Ariyaratne and Joanna Macy claim, 'The healthy rapport between plants, animals and humans, underlined by boundless compassion, was the basis of Buddhist life.'[26] Similarly, Martine Batchelor, a Buddhist nun, says 'Buddhists . . . have never believed humanity superior to the rest of the natural world.'[27] The scholar Damien Keown refers to the 'wider moral horizon' of Buddhism such that 'respect for animal life is a prominent feature of Buddhist ethics.'[28] The historian of ideas John Passmore refers to a slightly different claim, namely that the Buddhist tradition has resources not found in the 'West' for an extension of ethics to include ecosystems.[29] Passmore also notes that the historian Lynn White, notorious for his criticism of Christianity's attitude toward nature, speaks approvingly of Zen Buddhism as a source for those who seek a new man/nature relationship.[30] Finally, Peter Singer, who is no promoter of religious traditions, describes the Buddhist tradition as 'kinder to animals than our own.'[31]

Importantly, it is not only the First Precept which provides a basis for such claims. The Buddhist tradition also asserts an important continuity between humans and all other animals, promotes universal compassion as an ethical absolute,[32] and generally gives animals a very high profile (as in the stories about the previous lives of the historical Buddha known as the *Jātakas*). Of particular interest is the emphasis in the Buddhist tradition on *individuals*, for the First Precept and various formulations of the virtue of compassion are clearly aimed at individuals rather than at species or ecosystems.[33]

The Buddhist attitude toward other animals – the first face

These preliminary observations make it clear that the Buddhist tradition has important perspectives to offer when we consider the issues raised by 'animal rights.' Yet, despite the fact that concern for other animals must be a prominent feature of any account of Buddhist beliefs and ethics, references in Buddhist texts reveal that the underlying conceptuality regarding other animals is *not* consistent with *some* concerns of 'animal rights.' One way of explaining this is to note that in the Pali Canon, there are two different 'faces,' as it were, to the Buddhist attitude toward other animals.

There is the face already presented – the First Precept and other avowals of the importance of animals' lives. This is such an important feature of the tradition, that *at worst*, Buddhism will be a mixed source for 'animal rights' advocates of all kinds. Currently, the systematic killing of animals is a prominent feature of contemporary Western societies due to the rise of factory farming, an idea which had its origins in England in the late eighteenth century but which has rapidly spread through Western societies since the mid-1950s.[34] In brief, factory farming involves technologically advanced but highly unnatural conditions of confinement and treatment which are, to be sure, the source of much suffering both prior to arrival at the slaughterhouse and then at the slaughterhouse.[35] The Buddha was uncompromising with regard to those who participate in the intentional killing of animals, repeatedly describing the awful fate which awaits deer hunters, pig butchers, sheep butchers, and fowlers.[36] The animal tamer is described as having the same fate, though the commentary glosses this by saying that a hellish fate awaits only the tamer who is cruel in his methods.[37] Arguably, even this narrower interpretation applies to the intentional infliction of harm caused by the confinement that is the essence of factory farming and animal experimentation.

Various reasons are given in the tradition for refraining from killing other animals. Schmithausen speculates that the precept of non-killing is 'the heritage of an earlier cultural stratum – a stratum in which killing animals (and even plants, earth and water) was, in a sense at least, as serious as killing people (not of course one's own ethnic group), because animals, too, were believed to take, if possible, revenge on the killer in the yonder world.'[38] Another reason given for the prohibition on killing is the recurring statement that all other beings have at one time been one's own father or mother.[39] This belief is reliant upon the notions of rebirth and the very long time spans during which beings cycle through *saṃsāra*. Keown notes that, even though there is no definitive statement as to which forms of life are valued and why, Buddhists do value other 'karmic' or 'telic' (having a *telos*, or goal) life forms in *saṃsāra*, and that the basis for doing so may simply be an assumption that other living beings, by virtue of being living beings, have an 'intrinsic' value, that is, each being is 'affirmatively valued for its own sake rather than as a means to something else (i.e. its value is not instrumental).'[40] The historically important *Metta Sutta* contains a remarkable passage regarding compassion:

> Just as a mother would protect with her life her own son, her only son, so one should cultivate an unbounded mind towards all beings, and loving kindness towards all the world.[41]

Horner, arguing that no clear picture of early Buddhist monastic life can be obtained if the concern for other life is ignored, notes:

> ... no doubt a mixture of motives operated. Such championship may have seen in non-harming a way to increase the moral welfare of the monks; it may have been part of a disinterested social reform movement; it may have been, as in the case of sacrifice, polemical in nature, anti-brahminical; and it may have been due to the presumption that animals have as much right to their lives, and to compassion, as have human beings.[42]

Whatever the particular reason given, the function of the precept is to broaden the range of beings who are deemed morally considerable. As Schmithausen says, 'in the First Precept, and hence also for a Buddhist lay person, society is not to be taken in the narrow sense of human society, but in a broader sense of a community comprising all living or sentient beings.'[43] It is clear that this valuing of other life is related to Gotama's affirmation that there is an overarching moral order. It is this moral order which itself, apart from the teaching of a Buddha, entails the sanctity of life. This conviction, especially through the compassion which it engenders, creates the first face of the Buddhist attitude toward other animals with which any animal rights advocate would be quite pleased.

The Buddhist attitude toward other animals – the second face

There is another face, however, which is as ancient and central a part of the tradition as is the first face. This is a much less 'friendly' face which coexists with the more favourable face (favourable, that is, for other animals and, therefore, animal rights activists). This less favourable face can be seen in several ways. First, the manner in which early Buddhists talked about other animals reveals that they thought about them in ways which are none too congenial to the concerns of the more radical animal rights view. In the next section, this will be examined in terms of the early Buddhists' generalizations about living things and other animals. Second, the Buddhist tradition's attitude toward instrumental uses of other animals reveals that the hierarchical notions of life which dominate Buddhist thinking are, again, in tension with modern animal rights views.

How early Buddhists thought and spoke about other animals

Several levels of generalization about other animals can be identified in the earliest Buddhist materials. A look at these reveals that the earliest stratum of the tradition, despite the important prohibition on killing, contains views antithetical to some of the core concerns of the modern animal rights movement. Examples are ethical anthropocentrism (recognition of humans alone as morally considerable beings) and speciesism (humans' favouring of their own interests, often very minor in nature, over and against even major interests of all other animals solely on the irrelevant ground of species membership[44]).

In the Pali Canon, the broadest generalizations about living things can be seen in the nouns *satto*, *jīvo*, *bhūto*, and *pāṇo* These are intended to be highly inclusive; they are not strictly defined, but are used rather loosely, overlapping in many ways. *Satto*[45] is sometimes translated as 'beings' and 'living things' but most often as 'creatures,'[46] and this broad term clearly includes other animals. *Bhūto* is another generic term often translated as 'creatures' or 'beings.'[47] Like *satto*, it can include other animals,[48] but it also covers more than just 'living things' in the modern sense. The term can also have more specific referents, such as 'ghosts' or 'goblins.'[49] *Jīvo* (plural, *jīvā*) is a third generalization applying to animals which appears in the Pali Canon, though far less often than *sattā* and *bhūtā*. *Jīvā* can be translated as 'living things,' 'all that lives,' or 'souls (in plants),' or 'all souls.'[50]

The generalization most applicable to other animals is *pāṇo*. This is related to the word for 'breath' or 'breathing,' and is sometimes translated as 'breathers.'[51] It is a central term in the scriptures in the sense that it occurs often and in extremely important passages. For example, it occurs in the *Vinaya* passage dealing with the obligations of monks to other living beings:

> Whatever monk should intentionally deprive a living thing [*pāṇaṃ*] of life [*jīvitā*], there is an offence of expiation.[52]

The succeeding lines narrow down those 'living things' which are covered by the term: '*Living thing* [*pāṇo*] means: it is called a living thing that is an animal [*tiracchānagatapāṇo*].'[53] The word occurs as part of the extremely common injunctions against the taking of life.[54] It also occurs frequently outside First Precept statements[55] and is commonly translated simply as 'living creatures,'[56] 'life' or 'living things.'[57]

The second level of generalization – 'animals'

There is another, narrower level of generalization which is directly applicable to other animals. The most common of these second level generalizations is *tiracchāno* and related compounds. One example from the *Vinaya* has already been given: '*Living thing* [*pāṇo*] means: it is called a living thing that is an animal [*tiracchānagatapāṇo*].' *Tiracchānagatapāṇo* is a very broad notion, encompassing the great diversity of life on the earth which Buddhists clearly noticed.[58] The *-gata* portion of the compound is a past participle form which literally means 'gone away, arrived at'; in applied meaning, its sense is, 'gone in a certain way, i.e., affected, behaved, fared, fated, being in or having come into a state or condition.'[59] Thus, *tiracchānagata* means 'the state or realm of animals.' Importantly, humans are *not* part of this realm, for members of the human species are conceived by the Buddhist tradition to comprise an entirely separate realm. *Tiracchāno*, then, means 'all animals other than humans' and is the equivalent to the most common use of 'animal' in contemporary English. This can be seen in the translations of *tiracchānagata* as 'animal kingdom' by Ñāṇamoli; 'brute creatures' by Mrs. Rhys Davids and Woodward; and 'animal world' by Woodward.[60]

Importantly, this 'realm of other animals' is viewed by Buddhists as one of the three 'states of woe' (*duggati*). Ishigami notes, 'The division of beasts indicates animals and is counted as one of the three evil paths. Beings in this group are stupid, possess no wisdom, and are always killing one another. It is a sphere of much suffering and little happiness. It is where a stupid person would be born through his evil actions.'[61] Thus, *any* other animal, by virtue of being a member of the animal realm, must be 'of miserable existence, poor, unhappy, illfated, gone to the realm of misery.'[62] To the Buddhist mind, then, in a most fundamental way, other animals' existence *must* be unhappy. As it is put in the *Aṅguttara*, humans and other beings (*sattā*) who are

> given to the practice of evil deeds, of evil words, of evil thoughts ... of perverted view and reaping the fruits of their perverted view – these beings, when body broke up, beyond death rose up again in the Waste, the Ill-bourn, the Downfall, in Purgatory.[63]

These places – 'the Waste, the Ill-bourn, the Downfall, in Purgatory' – include the entire animal kingdom, and the English translation conveys clearly that existence as another animal is not in itself prized by the Buddhist tradition, for it is a state of punishment inferior to that of membership in the human species. Thus, in the Buddhist ideal worlds there are no animals ... other than humans.

This view that *all animals other than humans* belong to one realm is a kind of 'conceptual lumping' which can be seen when Gotama says, 'Men are indeed a tangle, whereas animals are a simple matter.'[64] The 'lower,' 'simpler' existence of all other animals is the subject of extraordinary claims in the tradition, as is evident in the following assertion attributed to Gotama: 'I ... comprehend animal birth and the way leading to animal birth and the course leading to animal birth, and that according to how one is faring along one uprises, at the breaking up of the body after dying, in animal birth.'[65] These are 'extraordinary' claims because the Buddhist tradition was demonstrably unconcerned with exploring the realities of other animals.[66] Gotama's statement perhaps reflects a trace of the belief in the equivalence of the human microcosm and the macrocosm – that is, through a human knowing himself or herself, the universe's significant realities are well known. But, as will be suggested by way of references to elephants below, Buddhists did *not* know other animals well. Nonetheless, they held that all non-human animals, from the simplest of karmic forms on up to the most complex such as the large-brained social mammals (elephants, other great apes,[67] and the marine creatures we know as 'whales and dolphins') are *tiracchānā*, and fundamentally inferior to *any* human. This is not an exclusively Buddhist assertion, for it is a pan-Indian assumption that humans are qualitatively distinct from all other animals, who are simple and inferior.[68]

Tiracchāno, which literally means 'horizontal goer,'[69] thus operates as the generic term designating all nonhuman animals, *even if* they are not 'horizontal goers.' The derogatory hint in this, as well as that in the assertion that *all* animals are 'a simple matter,' parallels the view that the animal realm is a place of punishment, woe and viciousness. A related belittling of other animals can be seen in the compounds *tiracchānakathā* (which means, literally, 'animal talk,'[70] but is translated as 'low conversation' or 'unedifying conversation'[71]) and *tiracchāna-vijjā* (translated as 'low arts' by Rhys Davids and 'base arts' by Walshe[72]).

In actual fact, the realm of *tiracchāno* is extremely diverse, a fact which, as noted above, clearly impressed Gotama. Consider the animal groupings described by Gotama in an extended passage; his breakdown reflects several different things, including the classifications of folk taxonomy, the Buddhist penchant for subdivision and classification, and recognition of some of the natural history of different animals.

> There are, monks, animals [*tiracchānagatā*], breathing creatures [*pāṇā*] that are grass eaters. These eat moist and dry grasses, chewing them with their teeth. ... Horses, cattle, asses, sheep, deer, and whatever other.... There are [also] ... creatures that are dung-eaters. ... Cocks, swine, dogs, jackals, and whatever other. ... [There are also creatures that] grow old in the dark and die in the dark [such as] [b]eetles, maggots, earth-worms and whatever other. ... There are [also] ... creatures that are born in water, grow old in water, die in water. ... Fish, turtles, crocodiles, and whatever other. ... There are [also] ... creatures that are born in filth, grow old in filth, and die in filth. [This describes animals living in rotting fish, carcasses and rice, and pools near villages.][73]

The Buddhists' awareness of the diversity of other animals is also reflected in a remarkable passage citing the 'divisions in the kinds [*jāti*] of living things.'[74] Gotama explains that while there is diversity in the many kinds of living things, each of which has its distinctive mark, humans alone are qualitatively different. After listing many different kinds of living beings (*pāṇā*), Gotama notes that they each share in a basic trait or quality of their group, species or kind:

Each after his kind bears
His mark ...[75]

But humans are differentiated from any other animal in this way:

... in man there is not manifold [that is, 'no variety of marks.'[76]]
Not in the hair or head or ears or eyes ... [long list of physical
attributes]
... colour or voice,

Is [there a] mark that forms his kind as in all else [that is, all other
animals].
Nothing unique in men's bodies is found:
The difference in men is nominal.

The passage takes several readings to unpack. It most obviously claims that
humans are not, as are all other animal kinds, characterized by a physical
trait which distinguishes the species. This is the 'mark,' which functions
like the supposed Platonic 'essence' of pre-Darwinian thinking about
species in the West.[77] But the passage also asserts the unity of the human
species through its argument that 'the alleged differences among members
of the human species are merely nominal.' Ñāṇamoli's translation of the
last line makes the point more clearly: 'Distinction among human beings is
purely verbal designation.'[78] Ñāṇamoli paraphrases the commentary's
explanation:

... among [other] animals the diversity in the shape of their bodily
parts is determined by their species (*yoni*), but that (species
differentiation) is not found in the individual bodies of brahmins
and other classes of humans. Such being the case, the distinctions
between brahmins, *khattiyas*, etc., is purely a verbal designation; it is
spoken of as mere conventional designation.[79]

Gotama's assertion of the unity of the human species was an important
claim because it challenged the culturally significant assumption that
ontological differences existed among the four *varṇa*s or estates (sometimes, though misleadingly, referred to as 'castes').[80] Gotama's claim relies,
then, on a universalism within the class of humans. It *also* relies on two
other assumptions. First, the claim assumes that members of each other
species are, within their distinctive species, like each other because they
share a unique, defining set of physical (morphological) traits. Members of
other animal species, then, have, as members of their respective species, a
kind of uniqueness, but this is a different kind or level of uniqueness than
that characterizing members of the human species. Another assumption
operating in this passage is that all other animals are alike in the sense of
being distinguished by their *physical* mark, while members of the human

species, by virtue of that membership, possess a special ability which is mental or psychological rather than merely physical. Seeing all other animals as alike, that is, as having natures characterized only by physical 'marks,' is the product of the lumping tendency alluded to above. Gotama goes on to explain what it is that distinguishes one human from another:

I call none brahmana from mere parentage,
... the man ... who grasps not, brahman I call him.[81]

The claim that only humans can be aware of their 'grasping' (which here has the characteristically Buddhist sense of desiring, craving or being attached to something) is by no means a problem for the animal rights position. The fact that members of the human species possess distinctive characteristics or abilities is no more troubling than would be a finding that members of some other species possessed distinctive mental lives or characteristics. Further, that the trait which humans alone are said to possess is a moral sensibility is, again, not a problem for animal rights advocates, for possession of such a trait, though not necessarily exclusive possession of it, is the pre-condition for having the sensibilities which animal rights advocates seek to develop in other humans.

A problem arises, however, *if* the claim that humans are unique is transmuted into the logically distinct claim that *only* humans have mental, social and intelligence-related complexity. Such complexity contributes to the development of distinctive 'individuality' or 'personality,' and this adds to any being's moral considerability, for the termination of the life of a unique individual linked to other individuals through a social history creates suffering of the distinctive kinds with which humans are quite familiar. That humans have distinct kinds of intelligence and individuality does not imply that other animals cannot have these traits. To paraphrase Porphyry, to argue that other animals lack important abilities because humans have more of those abilities, or have them in special degree, is like arguing that partridges cannot be said to fly because hawks fly higher.[82]

In the Buddhist tradition, this transmutation (that is, a metamorphosis of the claim that human are distinct into the different claim that *only* humans have special abilities or individuality), or something very much like it, arguably did occur. Humans *alone*, held to be different from *tiracchānā* and like each other by virtue of species membership, were seen as having the only important mental dimensions, one of which involves the potential to perceive and then act in harmony with the 'normative' in the universe. Of course, humans might not do this, but only they could. It may be implied in the claim that, because other animals can eventually move out of the *tiracchāno* category, they, too, must be able to act in conformity with this norm, but this latter theme, namely what it means for a non-human animal to act well, is neither emphasized nor explored in the Buddhist tradition. It occurs more as a background assumption than a conclusion drawn after systematic exploration of the realities of other animals' lives. Other animals' ability to conform to the moral norm, and thereby advance in the hierarchy towards human status, apparently entailed only a conformity of lower abilities with lower possibilities; if an animal behaved properly (the standard not being explicitly identified), the result would be a move 'up' the hierarchy. As Story says, 'Animals, being without moral discrimination, are more or less passive sufferers of the results of past bad *karma*. In this respect they are in the same position as morally irresponsible human beings, such as congenital idiots and imbeciles.'[83] Humans conforming to the normative in the universe is qualitatively different from nonhumans conforming, requiring an engagement with morality, mindfulness and *paññā* (a complex notion which is essentially cognitive, traditionally translated as 'wisdom'[84]) in ways which are, to the Buddhist mind, totally foreign to any other biologically identifiable being. The upshot of this assertion of a fundamental division is a failure to consider the possibility that some nonhuman individuals have abilities or traits which, though not shared by humans, are morally considerable.

So, while it is accurate to say that in the Buddhist conception of the order of beings '[m]en are somewhere in the middle' of a universe in which there are 'hierarchically ordered strata,'[85] it is also accurate to note that, in *this* world, humans are considered to be supreme *and* qualitatively more important than all other living things. Schmithausen makes a related point in his comments that there is in the tradition a 'certain inborn anthropocentricity of man, reinforced by the "pro-civilization strand" of Buddhist tradition.'[86] The reality that undergirds these comments – humans promoting even minor human interests to the exclusion of major interests of any other animals – is the alleged speciesism of the tradition.

The problem with lumping

That *all* other animals are thought to be 'of a kind,' that is, that they are all conceived of as belonging to the same realm, is, from the animal rights standpoint, problematic simply because all other living things are not alike. The philosopher Stephen Clark has noted that one's ethics, as well as one's theory of the basic make up of the universe (ontology), 'is determined by what entities one is prepared to notice or take seriously.'[87] Indeed, part of the animal rights agenda is to discern which living things have which traits and to take those traits seriously. This process allows meaningful assessments of suffering to be made, whereas under a lumping mentality all other animals are equated with each other such that one example (say, a domestic animal bred to be subservient) suffices to represent all other animals' possibilities. This radically disadvantages the more complicated animals. For example, the suffering of animals with large brains, familial and social dimensions, intelligence, and individuality of the kind with which humans are familiar (because we possess these faculties) is, according to *any* animal rights view, different than the suffering of other animals which don't have these traits. In other words, 'animal rights' is most often *not* a position which seeks 'rights' for *all* other living things – consider the living organisms on the skin killed by daily washing, or plants eaten, or viruses which are killed because they cause virulent diseases. Rather, animal rights in even its broadest forms involves a concern for only *some* living things. These living things are typically the larger, more 'complex' animals which are described as 'higher' in the phylogenetic scale, and these are generally the later and more complex products of evolution.[88] Another simple example of this is the ordinary distinction made between mammals and birds, on the one hand, and insects, on the other. There are only about 4400 species of mammals, while there may be as many as 30,000,000 species of insects.[89] Thus, humans who are 'animal rights' advocates are most typically advocates of rights for only some forms of life, and typically these are identified on the basis of a criterion such as 'sentience' (by which animal rights activists mean the ability to suffer or, even more simply, to experience pain). The classic statement of the problem is Bentham's dictum, '[T]he question is not, Can they *reason*? nor Can they *talk*? but, Can they *suffer?*'[90] There are other criteria such as intelligence, self-awareness, and distinctive individualities or personalities which have been used to establish moral considerability, but the point remains that animal rights in any form presents only *some* kinds of animate life as morally considerable.

The Buddhist tradition does have something like a vague hierarchy among other animals (that is, among *tiracchāna*). Elephants, for example, are more respected by Buddhists than are 'creeping things'(*sirimsapā*). Gombrich in speaking about Sinhalese values, notes, 'Animals require only a few words. They too are vaguely considered to form some kind of hierarchy, with the elephant, hero of Sinhalese folklore, at the top.'[91] Spiro also notes that, 'In general, despite the absolute prohibition on taking of life, the Burmese view the demerit acquired from killing as falling along the following moral gradient: pious man, impious man, mammal, vertebrate, invertebrate.'[92] Consistent with this valuing of some animals more than others is the prohibition on only certain animals' flesh: elephants, horses, dogs, serpents, lions, tigers, leopards, bears or hyenas.[93]

Yet, when it comes to protecting the essential interests of other animals (that is, their interest in their lives going well, freedom from captivity and intentional infliction of pain or other suffering), the vague hierarchy among other animals has relatively little significance in the Buddhist tradition. This is evidenced by the fact that, generally, ethical insights about the differences between the many kinds of other animals are not systematically worked out. Buddhaghosa noted that, according to the *Vinaya*, there is no difference in offence when a monk kills a small or a big animal, but that nonetheless killing a big animal is worse because more intention, effort and aggressiveness are required.[94] Importantly, it is *not* differences in the life taken which make a difference. Instead, crucial ethical injunctions are formulated at the level of *pāṇā* (other than humans) and *tiracchānā*, rather than according to the diverse, inherent traits of the living victims. At the level of the most important ethical rules, then, all other animals are 'lumped' together. This can be seen in the penalties provided by the *Vinaya*, which clearly reflect the division 'humans on one side, all other living things on the other side.' Killing a human was a fundamentally different kind of offence than killing any other animal. The penalties for a monk who intentionally killed a human were the most severe possible,[95] while the penalty for the intentional killing of any other animal was far less drastic. This is not to imply that killing other living things was not considered a serious matter, for, to be sure, as noted above the *Vinaya* does mention in several places that intentionally, and even negligently, killing other living things is an offence. Yet *intentionally* killing an elephant merits no more punishment than does (1) intentionally killing vegetable growth or earthworms, or (2) the negligently caused destruction of life caused by sprinkling of water containing 'living things.' Further, in the passage discussing levels of intention when acting so as to deprive a living thing of life, there is a difference between penalties as well. For example, if a pit is dug, and a human falls in and dies, the offence is of the highest type (a *pārājika*, or defeat) which requires expulsion from the order; if one of the imaginary *yakkha* or *peta* beings is killed, or an 'animal in human form' (*tiracchānagata-manussaviggaho*), this is a lesser but still serious offence known as a *thullaccaya*. If some other, real-world animal (*tiracchānagato*) falls in and is killed, there is an offence, but it is a still lower level offence requiring only expiation.[96]

Deprecation of 'animals'

In the Buddhist hierarchical view, any being's current position is the just consequence of past acts; in other words, the karma system is exact and moral. A being in a low position is there because of wrong acts; a being in a high position is there because of good acts. This provides a rationalization for negative views of those beings considered to be lower in the hierarchy. This deprecation is closely allied with the conceptual lumping which takes place throughout the Buddhist texts. Schmithausen, having identified in the tradition's attitude toward nature a dominant 'pro-civilization' strand (relative to an important but less influential 'hermit' strand which is more positive about nature), concludes that there is a 'one-sidedly depreciative view of animals and wild nature' in the dominant, pro-civilization attitude.[97]

It turns out, then, that both deprecation and lumping are reflected in the general features of the Buddhists' thinking about and evaluation of other animals.

(1) There is a negative view of the very fact of birth as an(other) animal.

(2) The product of bad conduct is existence as an(other) animal. Those who act immorally risk birth in the animal realm. A telling example is the fate of the hunter who kills animals; his fate, ironically, is to reborn in an animal womb.[98] The realm of rebirth for one who lives properly is 'either those heaven-worlds that are utter bliss' (and contain no animals other than humans) or rebirth in 'whatsoever [human] families are exalted, such as the families of nobles or brāhmins, or housefathers of a great household....'[99] Thus, it is not only nonhumans who are deprecated, but those humans who are non-'standard,' that is, impoverished, ugly, or handicapped in some way. On the basis of this depreciation of some other humans, one might argue that the karma/rebirth realities claimed by the tradition are *not* speciesist, although there remain speciesist overtones given the great divide between humans and all other animals and the implication that even the lowest human is better than the best of other animals.[100]

(3) To be another animal is to have previously led a less than appropriate series of lives or existences. There is, then, in the Buddhist view a kind of culpability in being any other animal.

(4) Other animals are simple and easily understood by humans, for, as noted above, Gotama says, though 'Humankind is a tangle, ... the animal is open enough.'[101] The lumping here disadvantages the more complex animals.

(5) Other animals are less important in the moral scheme of the universe, as reflected in the *Vinaya's* penalties for killing. The relative value of the two groups – creatures inside the species line (humans), on the one hand, and all other real world, living creatures lumped together on the other hand – is also evident when Gotama says to Ānanda:

> ... when a gift has been given to an animal [*tiracchānagato*], it is expected that the offering (yields) a hundredfold; when a gift has been given to an ordinary person of poor moral habit ... a thousandfold. When ... to an ordinary person of moral habit, ... a hundred thousandfold. When ... to one who is beyond and without attachment to sense-pleasures [a hundred thousandfold times one hundred thousandfold].[102]

The increase in benefit continues as gifts are given to monks who are further and further along the path to enlightenment; the point is that giving to any nonhuman is not even remotely as valuable as giving to the 'lowest' human who is immoral. Yet, it is true that giving to other animals, even if dwarfed by giving to humans, is recognized as within the moral universe. Continuity, then, exists, but, again, it is overwhelmed, so to speak, by a deep conviction of an essential discontinuity.

All of these factors lead to descriptions of other animals which are fundamentally negative. Of course, such descriptions are meant to be, as with the *Jātakas*, teaching devices, but they are nonetheless reliant on a negative view of the relative status of any other animal. Further, in the *Jātakas* while some animals are pictured in a positive way, it is almost always the bodhisattva reborn as the king of some animal group who is so pictured, not the other, ordinary animals. This feature subtly reflects that it is *not* real-world animals which are positively pictured in the *Jātakas*. Consistent with this is the way that, to the Buddhist mind, failure to see the inferior side of other animals' state results in grave consequences. This is evident in the story of ascetics who thought that living as a dog or cow would lead to a rebirth among the *devas*; on the contrary, Gotama notes, these are 'wrong views' and '...there is one of two bourns for one of wrong view: either Niraya Hell or animal rebirth.'[103]

Another upshot of the lumping and deprecation is that abilities and traits of other animals are ignored in a wholesale manner (an example regarding elephants is given below). The dominance of this negative view of other living things in the natural world is counterbalanced somewhat by occasional positive images and implications about the natural world such as occur in Gotama's exhortations to the monks to resort to natural habitats, where they can, undisturbed by human activity, meditate.[104] One possible implication of this exhortation is that natural places away from humans are not troubled in the way humans and their places are troubled and troubling. Yet, there are many negative views of natural places, such as those suggesting that the wilderness is unsafe and that civilization is where humans belong.[105] In the end, however, these occasional, positive implications do not effectively challenge the recurring negative views of other animals generally as a realm 'lower' than the privileged realm of humans.

Comments on the second face and what the early Buddhists knew about other animals

It can be argued that the Buddhist 'second face' is unfair because it is not based on extensive knowledge of other animals. Given that the early Buddhists were unconcerned with exploring the actual realities of other animals, their comments about other animals merely reflect the dominant 'ideology'[106] of the times regarding the complete inferiority of all other animals. An elephant example will have to suffice to show just how this is so, although the same could be done for their knowledge of other 'more complex' animals such as great apes (that is, other great apes) or cetaceans (whales and dolphins).

The elephant example is actually a surprising error. What is arguably the most important feature of elephants' existence, namely family and social grouping, is seriously misrepresented in the animal stories which abound in the tradition. In summary, the Buddhist storytellers simply got the most significant reality of elephant social structure wrong. The misrepresented fact is the dominance of males in the elephant groups, for elephants are *eminently* matriarchal in their social groupings. This patent reality is missing from the Buddhist tales, and while perhaps being the product of patriarchal values,[107] it is so wrong as to positively mislead. In fact, matriarchy is more than central to the lives of elephants; it is constitutive. It is through the matriarch that formative experiences are created, seen, regulated, and passed from generation to generation. The matriarchs in a group lead it, make decisions and communicate them in signals understood by the others, pass on traditions of knowledge and experience, and defend other individuals. Mature bulls are solitary, and wander in and out of different groups; they are by no means the leaders. They are simply not social in the same way as elephants in the matriarchal groups are, though there may be some commerce among bulls about which we do not yet know. The matriarchs give crucial signals which initiate and control the whole group's movements, and these are obvious to any sympathetic observer. That the Buddhists always portray the elephant groups as being led by a male, usually a king, is doubly strange, since in reality it is the matriarch who carries the burden of leadership and Indian female elephants are easier to differentiate from Indian males than are African females from African males because the Indian females typically have no tusks. In other words, matriarchy is an especially obvious phenomenon among Indian elephants. In fairness, it must be observed that Western science was woefully ignorant of this feature, as well as many others, until the mid-1970s when Iain Douglas Hamilton observed it and published details.[108]

So while Story's claim that, 'The stories of animals in the canonical books and commentaries are often very faithful to the nature of the beasts they deal with'[109] may in some instances be true, it is not correct regarding elephants. The inevitable conclusion is that Buddhist references to elephants are not very helpful in understanding the realities of real-world elephants. The same kind of argument could be made about other animals which are socially complex, large-brained and intelligent individuals, but this really is not necessary given a second argument about the less-kind face of the Buddhist evaluation of other animals.

The second argument is that Buddhist claims that *all* other animals are inferior to humans and of a limited, simple nature were unnecessary on the grounds asserted by Gotama himself. Such claims violate some of the very principles which Buddhists brought to bear in their critiques of existing claims of competing religious traditions. For example, Buddhists ridiculed the brahmins for making claims about the divine *Brahmā*, analogizing them to the claims of a man who wants to marry an unseen princess despite knowing nothing about her. This was referred to as *appāṭihīrakata-bhāsita*, 'irresponsible talk' or 'talk ... without a good ground.'[110] This kind of observation limiting human claims to 'know' the universe is also featured in many other stories in the tradition which illustrate the priority of working on one's liberation (soteriology) over the possession of factual knowledge. One well-known series of questions in the tradition is the ten *avyākatāni*, 'the indeterminates, points not determined.'[111] Rhys Davids says of them, 'The position taken by the primitive Buddhists as to these Indeterminates is so often referred to that it undoubtedly was an important item in the Buddha's actual belief.'[112] While none of these has to do with other animals (dealing, instead, with the determinateness and finitude of the world, the relation of soul and body, and existence after death), they do exemplify the principle that what really matters is liberation, not pointless and unprovable claims about the realities around us. The logic which makes humility on such subjects a significant issue also applies to claims about both (1) the status of humans relative to other animals, and (2) the realities of other animals. Arguably, the Buddhists' pretence to talk about *all* other animals provides a classic example of talk which tends not to edification or liberation but which, instead, reflects a tendency to the kind of self-affirmation and pride which so many other Buddhist insights repudiate. Buddhist talk about other animals often does have the ring of 'talk ... without a good ground.'

For personal liberation, then, there is generally no need to make claims about other animals' abilities. There is such a need, however, *if* one wishes to have knowledge of the impact of one's intentional actions. For example, what *is* the impact if one removes a young elephant from its matriarchal social group? Is the impact different than keeping a dog as a domestic pet? Are the consequences of pulling a fish from the sea different than those of pulling a dolphin which is a member of a social group with a different kind of social complexity? A desire to be informed so as to act responsibly leads one to assess the consequences of one's actions, and this could in turn have led to inquiries about the nature and complexities of the living beings affected by any human action. But this is precisely what did *not* happen. The Buddhist position on other animals has relatively little to commend it as a program for discerning what effect one's actions have on the radically different kinds of individuals in the diverse universe of living beings. In this regard, Buddhism is quite different than the modern animal rights movement, in that the latter has as one of its underlying principles a commitment to understanding the realities of other animals' real-world lives.

Acceptance of instrumental uses of other animals – the case of elephants

An examination of the Buddhist tradition's acceptance of the instrumental uses of elephants helps reveal some of these tensions with the animal rights movement which are carried within the Buddhist tradition. The significance of such acceptance is at first difficult to see, for the captivity of elephants is a complicated matter. It will help to point out two aspects of elephants' lives which are the basis for challenging the Buddhist tradition's acceptance of the use of elephants by humans. First, elephants are very complex individuals who grow and develop slowly and richly in distinctive social systems which are essential parts of their lives. They possess very distinctive personalities (relative to one another, and relative to other kinds of animals, including humans). They have very large brains, a capacity to communicate with one another, and remarkable intelligences very unlike those that 'animals' are caricatured as possessing by anthropocentric views which accord only individual members of the human species ethical significance. All of these traits cooperate in producing lives which are neither simple nor unadorned by play and care for others. Their lives are, thus, the lives of truly complex individuals. Second, holding such large, powerful and complex creatures captive involves a great deal of work on the part of the humans who 'own' them.

In order to convey why the acceptance of instrumental uses of elephants is contrary to the more radical view of animal rights, and arguably the broader view as well, consider what captivity *necessarily* entails. Apart from an abridgment of the extraordinary connections which the rich elephant social envelope makes available to the individuals of each group, captivity entails elephants living lives directed to *human* purposes. This results in curtailment of the elephants' own interests in favour of some human's interest. It is important to note that captivity can change an elephant from a potential member of an elephant society to a creature unfit for either human or elephant society. Chadwick has noted how ownership by one man of one elephant makes it unsocial and a psychological misfit,[113] and this reveals how human intervention distorts the animal's reality – its interests are eclipsed in favour of human interests.

With the complexity of elephants in mind, consider the following description of contemporary Thais breaking a young wild elephant:

> After tying it to a tree, men would poke and prod and beat it with sticks for days on end – singing traditional songs the whole time they tortured it – until the youngster quit lashing out at its tormentors and stood dazed and exhausted and wholly subdued. Once the animal stopped reacting, the men would start touching it with their hands rather than sticks, and, rather quickly, the animal accepted their

dominion and became receptive to their demands. If it did not, it might have wounds inflicted in its neck and salt rubbed into them, then a rattan collar with embedded thorns placed around the neck to make the animal more responsive.[114]

The pain and torment do not stop once dominion has been established, for as the following account shows so graphically, the dominion is maintained by ongoing, intentional infliction of pain:

Some of the traditional methods of handling elephants in India are extremely harsh. To restrain a newly captured, willful, or musth animal, its leg may be clamped in an iron hoop with inward-pointing spikes. The harder the animal strains against the device, the deeper the points bite. A long pole, called a *valia kole*, is used to prod the giant in the sensitive ankle and wrist joint while the handler keeps out of reach of the trunk and tusks. Some of these goads have blunt ends and are thrust so as to bruise the small bones that protrude near the surface of the lower foot. Others are actual spears but have a hilt on the blade to limit penetration.

Mahouts usually carry a *cherya kole*, a short rod with a blunt metal end, also used for walloping joints or, when mounted, the top of the skull. Close to the Nepal border, I rode on several occasions behind mahouts who whacked the top of the elephants head with the dull edge of the large, curved *kukri* daggers men carry in that country. Crueler yet is the technique I saw of incising a wound atop the elephant's head and worrying it with a knife blade to get the animal to respond. One Nepali mahout carried a hammer for pounding on his elephant's head. Whether the weapon was a hammer, knife, or *cherya kole*, the giants would stagger with a loud groan when struck.[115]

The captivity of elephants, then, involves at least two ethically significant problems: intentional curtailment of another being's interest for the purpose of advancing one's own interests, and intentional infliction of harm (pain) for the same self-interested (or, more generally, human-interested) reasons.

These problems were recognized in the Buddhist materials. For example, in the *Jātakas* there is recognition that (1) elephants are possessed of interests and can be subjected to non-lethal harms which have moral dimensions, (2) elephants prefer freedom to captivity by humans; and (3) elephants suffer when in captivity. Consider, for example, a description of an elephant which has broken away from its trainers:

And they tied the elephant up fast to a post, and with goads in their hands set about training the animal. Unable to bear the pain whilst he was made to do their bidding, the elephant broke the post down, put the trainers to flight, and made off to the Himalayas. ... [T]he elephant lived in the Himalayas in constant fear of death. A breath of wind sufficed to fill him with fear and to start him off at full speed, shaking his trunk to and fro. And it was with him as though he was still tied to the post to be trained. All happiness of mind and body was gone, he wandered up and down in constant dread.[116]

Additionally, the harsh, pain-oriented treatment of elephants in captivity was clearly recognized. In one story, this description appears: '... racked through and through like a goad-stricken elephant, poor wretch, he roars amain.'[117] In addition, other negative consequences of captivity were recognized, including the danger of captive elephants, as opposed to wild elephants, causing death[118] and the failure of some elephants to thrive in captivity despite being given food and shelter.[119] Several passages in the *Jātakas* reflect recognition that the interests of individual elephants were overridden, even eclipsed, in captive situations.[120]

Another example of an elephant's interests being eclipsed for human purposes appears in the story in which the Buddha in a previous life is born as the son of an elephant trainer, learning his father's trade. In battle, when an elephant is afraid, the words of the Buddha encourage the elephant, who then fights and wins. Here, the animal's emotions, perhaps akin to human fears in battle, are recognized and overridden for solely human purposes.[121] This matter of fact acceptance of elephants as tools for human warfare is common in the Pali Canon.[122]

The issue of intentional harm

The Buddhist tradition began with Gotama's revolutionary understanding that the goodness or badness of an act was not a matter of doing acts in the proper form (as was emphasized by the then contemporary brahminical religion). As Gombrich points out, Gotama ethicized the notion of karma, making it a matter of *intention* rather than ritual correctness.[123] Gotama's insight is relevant to the contemporary animal rights claims that it is a moral matter to challenge human choices which override the major interests of other animals for the mere benefit of humans' minor interests (non-essential needs).

The various animal rights positions focus heavily on the fact that modern consumers have access to alternatives to many of the products which involve the most harm to other animals. It is often argued that consumer choices which promote the miseries of factory farming should be seen as *intentional* choices which promote *unnecessary* harm. Further, because zoos are not necessary for education or conservation (other means being available), some argue that patronizing them means the intentional infliction of unnecessary harm on innocent creatures.[124] Similarly, because many animal experiments are conducted for the purpose of testing non-essential items (such as cosmetics), patronizing businesses which create and market such products can be seen to involve an intentional, even if indirect, infliction of unnecessary harm. Even more radically, the intentional infliction of harm in animal experiments, even if perpetrated by someone who believes that such acts will advance *essential* human needs, can be challenged on the ground that the individual subjects of the experiments are as innocent as the victims of the hunters and butchers whom Gotama condemned.

Acts patronizing, supporting, or even legitimating these practices are intentional ones. Even when they are based on ignorance, they may still be the result of culpable moral blindness given the fact that information about the processes of factory farming and the nature and purpose of animal experimentation is widely available. This insight provides a basis from within the core values of the tradition itself for challenging the Buddhists' acceptance of the instrumental uses of other animals. Captivity of elephants is eminently an intentional act which clearly involves harms. Since these harms were recognized by the Buddhists, it might at first seem baffling why instrumental uses were not condemned by someone who had the extraordinary insights which Gotama surely had. The answer lies in the Buddhist view of the relative value of humans, on the one hand, and all other animals, on the other hand.

The acceptance of instrumental uses is so widespread in the Pali Canon that it could fairly be called a 'background' view which was simply assumed, much as many educated Westerners today automatically assume that no other animal could *possibly* have any of the traits which the Western traditions have for so long claimed as their exclusive possession (such as rational souls, language, culture, tool-making abilities, and morality). In fact, in the Pali Canon there occasionally appears something more than mere acceptance of instrumental uses. Consider the story in which Gotama sees fishermen who have caught fish and are selling them. He asks the monks if 'as a result of such deeds, of that way of living [that is, killing the fish]' the fishermen have then been seen 'going about on an elephant or on horseback ... or living in the abundance of great wealth.'[125] He clearly is condemning the killing of living things, and pointing out that there are negative karmic consequences to such intentional acts. His comparison, though, reveals that there were not negative consequences to riding around on a captive elephant. Rather, that is seen as a *reward* for good acts: 'Indeed, monks, he who gloats evilly on creatures being slaughtered ... shall not go about on elephants...'[126] The existence of an assumption regarding the propriety of the instrumental use of elephants could not be clearer, for the story reflects that, at times, humans' use of elephants was not merely condoned but actually seen as part of the fabric of the moral universe which the tradition asserts with such stridency.

This acceptance of harmful instrumental uses of elephants may seem to be contradicted by the many passages in the Buddhist scriptures which make it clear that elephants were deemed important. They were honoured with the name *nāgas*, understood to be presences or at least images to which a Buddha could be compared, and held to be possessions fit for a human king. Further, they are one of the seven treasures.[127] But, clearly, *elephants were not valued for their individual selves or for the complexity of their lives*, but rather as property and thus valuable possessions. What is significant from the animal rights point of view is that the Buddhists' peculiar way of 'valuing' elephants was seen to be *without ethical problems*. Thus, while the Buddhist ethical sense was engaged on behalf of other animals at times, it was conditioned to an ethical blindness when it came to the instrumental use of animals such as that evidenced by the subordination of the interests of elephant individuals. It is precisely the ethical dimensions of such an overriding of other animals' interests which forms the key point in any view of animal rights.

Conclusion

Given that the tradition has both the kinder, first face and the harsher, hierarchically-based second face, and given that animal rights issues are expressed in modern discourse, it is perhaps inevitable that the tradition would have some tensions with the aims and concepts which drive activists in the contemporary animal rights movement. While in this chapter more attention has been paid to the second face, this should not obscure the fact that the first face and the related core insights of the tradition regarding compassion, the significance of intention in ethics, and the inherent value of life itself offer rich possibilities to those who seek insights relevant to the modern animal rights movement. The Buddhist tradition confirms the ancient nature of a concern for living things, a concern which has been dominated in the other major religious and philosophical traditions by a tendency to ethical anthropocentrism. Even though the claims of the tradition regarding the 'simple' and limited abilities of all other animals may not be particularly perceptive regarding the unique, nonhuman traits of some other animals, the insights and approaches which Buddhism offers for respecting other animals as real world entities entitled to the privilege of life without human interference do justify some of the optimistic statements made about the tradition and other animals. For example, the tradition is capable of accepting the radical program of animal advocates, from the relatively conservative Great Ape Project which seeks limited rights or their functional equivalents for the other great apes (chimpanzees, gorillas, and orangutans),[128] to the ambitious creation theologies which, going well beyond protecting large-brained, social animals, condemn avoidable harms to all creatures capable of suffering in any way.[129] The Buddhist tradition also has room to accept and respect some *nonhumans*' ability to live complex lives which are different from, independent of, and even in competition with humans' modes of living. It also has great potential for a contribution to environmental ethics and to the benefits which increased environmental awareness entails for other animals' lives. Of course, important caveats regarding the tradition's acceptance of certain negative assumptions about all other animals, and the resultant shortcomings in its claims about the realities of their lives, are in order, but, in summary, the Buddhist tradition offers a profound understanding of the moral agent's responsibility for his or her own intentional actions. This is pertinent to humans' ability to choose between alternatives to harmful uses of animals, human or otherwise. The emphasis on compassion alone, which pervades the tradition so thoroughly, makes the Buddhist tradition a fertile source for insights regarding the shortcomings and even immorality of many contemporary practices with regard to other animals.

Notes

1 Mark Gold, *Animal Rights: Extending the Circle of Compassion* (Oxford: Jon Carpenter, 1995), p. 5.

2 The debate in Western intellectual history is addressed in Richard Sorabji, *Animals Minds and Human Morals: The Origins of the Western Debate* (London: Duckworth, 1993).

3 Interesting examples appear in David Suzuki and Peter Knudtson, *Wisdom of the Elders: Honoring Sacred Native Visions of Nature* (New York: Bantam Books, 1992), and Tim Ingold ed., *What is an Animal?* (London and New York: Routledge, 1994).

4 Aristotle, *Politics* I, 2, 1253a, p. 1987 of *The Complete Works of Aristotle: The Revised Oxford Translation*, ed. by J. Barnes, 2 vols (Guildford, Surrey, and Princeton: Princeton University Press, 1984).

5 Aquinas, *Summa Theologiae* (London: Eyre & Spottiswoode, and New York: McGraw Hill) Blackfriars Edition 2a, 2ae, q. 64, art. 1 (Volume 38, p. 21).

6 Use of the term 'radical' here is *not* meant to suggest association with the violent wing of the animal liberation movement which has committed acts of harm. In the opinion of the vast majority of animal activists, such violence is not only wrong but also morally contradictory.

7 Tom Regan, *The Case for Animal Rights*, 2nd edn (London: Routledge, 1988).

8 Regan (1988) pp. 361–2, p. 396.

9 See, for example, the radically different senses of 'rights' used by Regan (1988), and the Christian theologian Andrew Linzey in *Christianity and the Rights of Animals* (London: SPCK and New York: Crossroad, 1987) and *Animal Theology* (London: SCM Press and Chicago: University of Illinois, 1994).

10 The most famous of these is Peter Singer, whose influential *Animal Liberation: A New Ethics for Our Treatment of Animals* (London: Jonathan Cape, 1976) was originally published in 1975 (New York: New York Review Book/Random House). This book is sometimes referred to as the 'bible' of the animal protection movement, as in Deborah Blum, *The Monkey Wars* (New York: Oxford University Press, 1994), p. 115. A second edition was published in 1990 (New York: Avon Books). Other prominent advocates of greater concern for nonhuman animals who nonetheless oppose use of 'rights' language include the English philosopher Mary Midgley in *Animals and Why They Matter* (Athens, Georgia: University of Georgia Press, 1984) and *Beast and Man: The Roots of Human*

Nature, revised edn (London and New York: Routledge, 1995); the American environmental ethicist Holmes Rolston in *Environmental Ethics: Duties to and Values in the Natural World* (Philadelphia: Temple University Press, 1988); and the American feminist theologian Rosemary Radford Ruether in *Gaia & God: An Ecofeminist Theology of Earth Healing* (London: SCM Press, 1993). A thorough discussion of the philosophical issues appears in *The Monist* 70, No. 1 (1987).

11 The latter approach is sometimes referred to as 'welfarism.'

12 Counting species or higher-level taxonomic groups conservatively, these are serpents, mice, dogs, flies, fish, antelope/deer, cows/bulls/oxen, horses, owls, fowl, birds generally, sheep/rams, goats, pigs/boars, elephants, and mules.

13 Again, counting conservatively; the domestic animals mentioned are cows/bulls/bullocks/ oxen; elephants; dogs; and horses. The larger wild animals mentioned are snakes, fish, rhinoceroses (references to horn as an image); lions; antelope/deer; jackals; wolves; tigers; monkeys or apes. The birds include peacocks, geese (or swan), ravens, vultures, and crows. Smaller, non-mammals include gadflies or mosquitoes; worms, beetles, moths, ants and termites. The twentieth-sixth kind mentioned is the human species.

14 The notion 'religious tradition' is inherently cumulative; it is a helpful tool when addressing the complex problems which arise when dealing with any of the older religions. The concept of 'cumulative tradition' was proposed in a very thorough and imaginative manner by Wilfred Cantwell Smith, *The Meaning and End of Religion: A New Approach to the Religious Traditions of Mankind* (New York: The Macmillan Company, 1962).

15 Richard Gombrich, *Theravada Buddhism: A Social History from Ancient Benares to Modern Colombo* (London and New York: Routledge, 1988), p. 2. The emphasis is in the original.

16 A good example is the influential eighth chapter of the early *Laṅkāvatāra Sūtra*, which Chapple has called 'perhaps the strongest advocacy of vegetarianism in the Buddhist tradition.' Christopher Key Chapple, *Nonviolence to Animals, Earth, and Self in Asian Traditions* (Albany, New York: State University of New York Press, 1993), p. 27. See, generally, D. Seyforth Ruegg, '*Ahiṃsā* and Vegetarianism in the History of Buddhism,' in *Buddhist Studies in Honour of Walpola Rahula* (London: Gordon Fraser, 1980).

17 No book-length, systematic evaluation of the Buddhist tradition's view of other animals has been published as of the writing of this essay. Forthcoming in 2000 from The American Academy of Religion is Paul Waldau, *The Specter of Speciesism: Early Buddhist and Christian Views of Animals*. For some evaluation, see Francis Story, *The Place of Animals in Buddhism* (Kandy, Ceylon: Buddhist Publication Society, 1964) (this may also be found in Volume II, Publication No. B 23, in the *Bodhi Leaves* series by the same publisher [n.d.]); Zenno Ishigami, 'Animals,' in *Encyclopaedia of Buddhism* edited by G.O. Malalasekera (Colombo, Ceylon: Government Press, 1961–1993), Fascicle 4 (1965), pp. 667–672; I.B. Horner, *Early Buddhism and the Taking of Life* (Kandy, Ceylon: Buddhist Publication Society, 1967) (also in The Wheel Publication, No. 104); Jack Austin, 'Buddhist Attitudes Towards Animal Life,' in *Animal Rights. A Symposium*, ed. by David Patterson and Richard Ryder (London: Centaur Press, 1979), pp. 25–33; James P. McDermott, 'Animals and Humans in Early Buddhism,' *Indo-Iranian Journal* Vol. 32, No. 4 (1989), pp. 269–280; Lambert Schmithausen, *Buddhism and Nature: The Lecture delivered on the Occasion of the EXPO 1990. An Enlarged Version with Notes* (Tokyo: The International Institute for Buddhist Studies, 1991) (referred to below as Schmithausen 1991a); and Chapple (1993).

18 Not *all* instrumental uses of other beings are harmful. For example, our use of a messenger is in some sense *instrumental*, but rarely, if ever, harmful. In this chapter, however, the term 'instrumental' is meant to include only *harmful* instrumental uses.

19 In the multi-faceted Buddhist tradition, there are always exceptions. Shigeo Kamata reports that the Korean monk Cha-jang has interpreted the First Precept as having only

limited application to the killing of other animals. Lambert Schmithausen, *Buddhism and Nature: Proceedings of an International Symposium on the Occasion of EXPO 1990* (Tokyo: The International Institute for Buddhist Studies, 1991)[this version includes the text of Schimithausen 1991a but also has additional comments by others and Schmithausen's reply], pp. 46–7. Similarly, Gombrich (1988 p. 141) quotes an argument made by monks to a Sinhalese king to the effect that killing men of wrong views in battle was not a problem.

20 Gombrich (1988) p. 65.

21 McDermott (1989) p. 27, lists the scriptural sources.

22 *Dīgha-Nikāya* (referred to below as D.) III, 63. The translation used in the text is *The Dialogues of the Buddha: Translated from the Pali of the Dīgha Nikāya*, 3 volumes, called Parts I-III, edited by T.W. Rhys Davids and, second and third volumes only, C.A.F. Rhys Davids; these are volumes II-IV of the *Sacred Books of the Buddhists* (SBB) series (first volume, London: Henry Frowde, 1899; second volume, Henry Frowde, 1910; third volume, London: Humphrey Milford, 1921).

23 Damien Keown, *The Nature of Buddhist Ethics* (London: Macmillan, 1992), p. 25f.

24 See Naresh Prasad Rastogi, *Inscriptions of Aśoka* (Varanasi: Chowkhamba Sanskrit Series Office, 1990), and in particular, Rock Edicts I-IV, VI, IX, XI, and XIII, and Pillar Edicts II, V, and VII.

25 Story (1964) pp. 6–7.

26 A.T. Ariyaratne and Joanna Macy, 'The Island of Temple and Tank: Sarvodaya: self-help in Sri Lanka,' in in *Buddhism and Ecology*, ed. by Martine Batchelor and Kerry Brown (London and New York: Cassell, 1992), pp. 78–86, p. 80.

27 Martine Batchelor, 'Even the Stones Smile,' in Batchelor and Brown 1992, pp. 2–17, p. 12.

28 Damien Keown, *Buddhism and Bioethics* (London and New York: Macmillan and St. Martin's Press, 1995), p. 22.

29 John Passmore, *Man's Responsibility for Nature* (London: Duckworth, 1974), p. 4. See also John Passmore, 'The Treatment of Animals,' *Journal of the History of Ideas* 36 (1975), p. 195 ff.

30 Passmore (1974) p. 4, referring to Lynn White Jr., 'The Historic Roots of Our Ecologic Crisis,' *Science* 155 (1967), pp. 1203–1207.

31 Peter Singer, *How Are We to Live? Ethics in an age of self-interest* (London: Mandarin Paperbacks, 1993), p. 221.

32 See Paul Williams, *Mahayana Buddhism: The Doctrinal Foundations* (London and New York: Routledge, 1994), p. 198, where he notes that while there are no ontological absolutes in Mahāyāna, compassion does function as 'an ethical absolute.'

33 See Schmithausen (1991a) p. 8 and p. 32f.

34 Roberta Kalechofsky, *Autobiography of a Revolutionary:Essays on Animal and Human Rights* (Marblehead, Massachussetts: Micah Publications, 1991), pp. 51–2. See, also Andrew Linzey, Jonathan Webber, and Paul Waldau, 'Farming' in *Dictionary of Ethics, Theology and Society* (London and New York: Routledge, 1996), pp. 375–377.

35 A summary of these and references to other sources appear in Singer (1990).

36 See, for example, *Saṃyutta-Nikāya* (referred to below as S.) II, 171. The translation used is that by Mrs. Rhys Davids (assisted on the first volume by Sūriyagoḥa Sumangala Thera, and on the second volume by Woodward), and F.L. Woodward (last three volumes), *The Book of the Kindred Sayings (Saṃyutta-Nikāya) or Grouped Suttas*; five volumes in PTS translation series, Nos. 7, 10, 13, 14, and 16 (London: Oxford University Press, the first volume has no date, but the preface is dated 1917; the date on the last volume is 1930).

37 Cited by Mrs. Rhys Davids at S. II, 172, Footnote 1.

38 Schmithausen (1991a) pp. 38–9, Paragraph 42. See, also, McDermott (1989) p. 274, as to the self-interested as well as moral reasons for not eating the flesh of other animals. Snakes, for example, were thought to take offence that snake flesh was eaten, retaliating

against the perpetrator. Other animals were thought to sense the odor of flesh eaten, this odor encouraging an attack by that kind of animal.

39 This appears in a wide range of Buddhist sources, such as S. II, 128; the *Laṅkāvatāra Sūtra*; the *Fan-wang-ching* (*Brahmajāla Sūtra*; and the *Nihon ryōiki of the Monk Kyōkai*. The last three are cited by Chapple (1993) pp. 27, 29, 40.

40 Keown (1995) p. 36 ff.

41 *Suttanipāta* 149–150. The translation used is *The Group of Discourses (Sutta-Nipāta)*, Volume I, translated by K.R. Norman, with alternative translations by I.B. Horner and Walpola Rahula (London and Boston: Pali Text Society/Routledge and Kegan Paul, 1984), Pali Text Society Translation Series No. 44. This text is referred to as Sn.

42 Horner (1967) p. 27.

43 Schmithausen (1991a) p. 40. See also Lambert Schmithausen *The Problem of the Sentience of Plants in Earliest Buddhism* (Tokyo: The International Institute for Buddhist Studies, 1991).

44 See, generally, Richard Ryder, *Animal Revolution: Changing Attitudes towards Speciesism* (Oxford: Basil Blackwell, 1989); Singer (1990); and Linzey, Andrew, and Paul Waldau, 'Speciesism' in *Dictionary of Ethics, Theology and Society* (London and New York: Routledge, 1995), pp. 788–792.

45 The plural form is *sattā*.

46 For the first two, see, respectively, the translation of the *Dīgha Nikāya* by Maurice Walshe, *Thus Have I Heard: The Long Discourses of the Buddha (Dīgha Nikāya)* (London, Wisdom, 1987), p. 95 (this translation is referred to below as DW); and *Aṅguttara-Nikāya* III, 153. The translation of the latter used is F.L. Woodward, (Volumes I, II, and V), and E.M. Hare (Volumes III and IV), *The Book of the Gradual Sayings (Aṅguttara-Nikāya)*, 5 vols, Pali Text Society Translation Series, Nos. 22 and 24–27 (London: Oxford University Press, 1932–1936). This is referred to below as A. The translation of the *Majjhima-Nikāya* used is I.B. Horner, *The Collection of the Middle Length Sayings (Majjhima-Nikāya)*, 3 vols, Pali Text Society Translation Series, Nos. 29–31 (London: Luzac & Company, 1954, 1957, and 1959). This is abbreviated M. For other translations using 'creatures,' see, M. II, 406–7; A. V, 16; A. II, 82; Sn. 24, vv. 145 and 147; Chalmers' translation of *Suttanipāta* (*Buddha's Teaching being the Sutta-Nipāta or Discourse-Collection*, with original text and English translation by Lord Chalmers (Cambridge, Massachusetts: Harvard University Press, 1932) Harvard Oriental Series, Vol. XXXVII), p. 37; and *The Minor Readings (Khuddakapāṭha)*, translated by Bhikkhu Ñāṇamoli (London: The Pali Text Society/Luzac & Company, 1960), Translation Series No. 32 (this includes the commentary by Buddhaghosa called *Paramatthajotikā* Part I, and is referred to below as KhpA), p. 92.

47 Respectively, pp. 156f. and p. 146f. of *The Minor Anthologies of the Pali Canon: Part I Dhammapada: Verses on Dhamma, and Khuddaka-Pāṭha: The Text of the Minor Sayings*, re-edited and translated by Mrs. Rhys Davids, Volume VII of SBB series (London: Humphrey Milford/Oxford University Press, 1931) (this also contains the Pali).

48 Buddhaghosa gives some examples: sons and daughters, sheep and goats, cocks and swine, elephants, cows, horses, and mares. Cited and translated by Horner at M. I, 5, Footnote 1.

49 See, for example, D. II, 52.

50 Respectively, Horner at M. II, 406–7; Walshe at DW. p. 95; Rhys Davids at D. I, 71; and Bhikkhu Ñāṇamoli (original translator) and Bhikkhu Bodhi (editor and revising translator), *The Middle Length Discourses of the Buddha* (Boston: Wisdom Publications, 1995), p. 513 (this is abbreviated MNB).

51 See, for example, Horner's comment at M. II, 76, Footnote 2.

52 *Vinaya Piṭaka* [Vin.] III, 1. Expiation here simply means an act of atonement. The translation used is Horner, I.B., *The Book of the Discipline (Vinaya-Piṭaka)*, six volumes in SBB series vols X, XI, XIII (London: Humphrey Milford, 1938–1942), vols XIV, XX,

XXV (London: 1951–1966). Regarding citation format, Vin. I is a reference to SBB Volume X, Vin. II is a reference to SBB Volume XI, and so on. The citation format includes volume and page, for example, Vin. V, 193, means the fifth volume of this translation series, p. 193.

53 Vin. III, 2. The word *tiracchānagata* will be explained below.

54 See, for example, D. I, 3–4.; A. I, 171–4; A. II, 107; and *The Book of Analysis (Vibhaṅga)*, translated by Paṭhamakyaw Ashin Thiṭṭila (Seṭṭhila) (London: Pali Text Society/Luzac & Company, 1969), pp. 376, 473, 489.

55 See, for example, A. III, 156; A. IV, 129; and M. III, 250.

56 See, for example, Sn. 20, v. 117; Sn. 35, v. 220; Sn. 66, v. 400; Sn. 104, v. 600.

57 Chalmers Sn. at 33, v. 117, uses the English 'living things'; at p. 53, v. 220, he translates this as 'life,' and again as 'living things' at p. 148, v. 600. *The Path of Discrimination (Paṭisambhidāmagga)*, translated by Bhikkhu Ñāṇamoli (London: The Pali Text Society/ distributed by Routledge Kegan Paul, 1982), Translation Series No. 43, at pp. 245, 264–5, uses 'living things.'

58 Gotama says, 'Brethren, I see not any single group so diverse as the creatures of the animal world.' S. III, 128.

59 *The Pali Text Society's Pali-English Dictionary*, ed. by T.W. Rhys-Davids and William Stede (London: Pali Text Society, first published 1921–25, reprinted 1952), p. 71 (this source is referred to below as PED).

60 At, respectively, KhpA. V 171, VI 138 and 96, and VII 30; S. V, 203; A. II, 36; and S. III, 128.

61 Ishigami (1965) p. 669.

62 The definition of *duggati* at PED II, 72, which is variously translated as 'state of woe,' 'evil path' or 'unhappy bourn.'

63 A. V, 25.

64 Lord R. Chalmers, *Further Dialogues of the Buddha (Translated from the Pali of The Majjhima Nikāya)*, 2 volumes, V and VI in the SBB series (London: Humphrey Milford/ Oxford University Press, 1926–7) (this is referred to below as MSBB), p. 247.

65 M. I, 98 f.

66 See Richard Gombrich, 'The Buddhist Way,' in *The World of Buddhism: Buddhist Monks and Nuns in Society and Culture*, edited by Heinz Bechert and Richard Gombrich (London: Thames and Hudson, 1991), pp. 9–14, p. 10: 'Buddhism as such is not about this world. Such spheres of human activity as the arts and sciences are not part of its concerns.'

67 Humans are, biologically, great apes. Richard Dawkins, 'Gaps in the Mind,' in *The Great Ape Project: Equality Beyond Humanity* ed. by Paola Cavalieri and Peter Singer (London: Fourth Estate, 1993), pp. 80–87, pp. 82–5.

68 This is, of course, an assumption that is dominant in other parts of the world.

69 PED IV, 137.

70 PED IV, 1.

71 At, respectively, D. I. 13, and DW. 70. Buddhaghosa's commentary on the *Dīgha* explains the reasoning behind this description, noting that as other animals walk parallel to the earth ('horizontal goer'), so this kind of talk does not lead upward. Cited in DW. 70, Footnote 33 at DW. 539.

72 Respectively, D. I, 19, and DW. 73. The same translation is given at PED IV, p. 137.

73 M. III, 213–4. Other passages which reflect the Buddhist awareness that there was important internal differentiation among other animals include M. I, 97 where four modes of life are described: 'The mode of life born from an egg, the mode of life born from a womb, the mode of life born from moisture, the mode of life of spontaneous uprising.'

74 This important passage appears at M. II, 381 ff. and Sn. 104, vv. 600 ff.

75 M. II, 382.

76   Horner's Footnote 1 at M. II, 382.
77   The history of the species concept is summarized at Ernst Mayr, *The Growth of Biological Thought: Diversity, Evolution, and Inheritance* (London and New York: Belknap Press, 1982), pp. 251 ff.
78   MNB 801.
79   MNB 1298, footnote 902.
80   See Gombrich (1988) p. 39f.
81   Brahman here is the term more familiarly spelled brahmin, a member of the hereditary priestly class.
82   Cited by Stephen R.L. Clark, *The Moral Status of Animals* (Oxford: Clarendon Press, 1977), p. 18.
83   Story (1964) p. 21.
84   Keown (1992) p. 80.
85   Richard F. Gombrich, *Precept and Practice: Traditional Buddhism in the Rural Highlands of Ceylon* (Oxford: Clarendon Press, 1971), p. 68.
86   Schmithausen (1991a) p. 49.
87   Clark (1977) p. 7.
88   'Complexity' here and elsewhere in this chapter must be understood as a reference to various features of mental lives and nervous system structures, and not to mere physical complexity.
89   Terry L. Erwin, 'Tropical Forest Canopies: The Last Biotic Frontier,' *Bulletin of the Entomological Society of America* 29:14–19 (1983).
90   Jeremy Bentham, *An Introduction to the Principles of Morals and Legislation*, ed. by J.H. Burns and H.L.A. Hart (London: The Athlone Press, 1970), Footnote 2, p. 283. In this intellectual lineage are thinkers as diverse as Regan, Singer, and Linzey.
91   Gombrich (1971) p. 167.
92   Melford E. Spiro, *Buddhism and Society: A Great Tradition and Its Burmese Vicissitudes* (London: George Allen & Unwin, 1971), p. 99.
93   Vin. IV, 298–300. But, compare Edward Conze, *Buddhism: Its Essence and Development* (London, New York and San Francisco: Harper Colophon/Harper and Row, 1975), p. 195, describing certain Tantric practices that deliberately violate these taboos on elephant and other flesh.
94   Cited by Schmithausen (1991a) p. 49.
95   Vin. I, 125–6.
96   Vin. VI, 63.
97   Schmithausen (1991a) p. 21.
98   A. V, 187. Other examples: misers are born '[i]n purgatory, or as animals, in Yama's kingdom they come back to life.' S. I, 47; and, one of perverted view has two paths, either purgatory or rebirth as an animal. S. IV, 217. See, also, M. III, 72.
99   A. V, 188.
100   This implication also appears in the gifts passage analysed below (M. III, 303).
101   This is Ñāṇamoli's translation at MNB 445. Horner's is, 'For this . . . is a tangle, that is to say human beings. But this . . . is an open clearing, that is to say animals.' M. II, 5; Chalmers translates, 'Men are indeed a tangle, whereas animals are a simple matter.' MSBB 247.
102   M. III, 303.
103   M. II, 55. So the canine ascetic will, if he prospers, end up with dogs, or, if he fails, in Niraya Hell. And at M. II, 56, Gotama says the same thing about the bovine ascetic.
104   See, for example, S. IV, 264, cited by Batchelor and Brown (1992) p. 24.
105   See Schmithausen (1991a) p. 14f.
106   'Ideology' is used here in the narrow sense of a prejudiced view not subject to change by evidentiary means.

107 A full account of the Buddhist tradition's patriarchal features, together with argument
     that the tradition is *not* at its core patriarchal, can be found in Rita M. Gross, *Buddhism
     After Patriarchy: A Feminist History, Analysis, and Reconstruction of Buddhism*
     (Albany: State University of New York Press, 1993).
108 See, for example, Iain Douglas-Hamilton and Oria Douglas-Hamilton, *Among the
     Elephants* (New York: Viking, 1975). The other facts in this paragraph, as well as those
     mentioned below regarding harmful instrumental uses, can be found in Douglas H.
     Chadwick, *The Fate of the Elephant* (San Francisco: Sierra Club Books, 1994); Cynthia
     Moss, *Elephant Memories: Thirteen Years in the Life of an Elephant Family* (New York:
     William Morrow and Company, 1988); R. Sukamar, *The Asian Elephant: Ecology and
     Management* (Cambridge: Cambridge University Press, 1989); and Katherine Payne,
     'Elephant Talk,' *National Geographic*, Vol. 176, No. 2 (August 1989), pp. 265–277.
109 Story (1964) p. 7.
110 M. II, 230 and 237; see, also, D. I, 259 where the phrase is translated at 'witless talk' and
     'talk ... without a good ground.' Walshe translates it 'talk [which is] stupid.' DW p. 166.
111 Rhys David's translation at D. I, 187.
112 Ibid.
113 Chadwick (1994) p. 311.
114 Chadwick (1994) p. 378.
115 Chadwick (1994) p. 297.
116 *Jātaka*s, story number 105 at p. 456 of E.B. Cowell, (principal editor, different
     translators for each volume), *The Jātakas or Stories of the Buddha's Former Births*
     (Cambridge: University Press, 1895 for vol I and 1907 for vol VI). Referred to generally
     as J. Each of the stories is numbered. References in the text are to story number; any
     second number is a page number. Thus, the reference J. 123/456 means story number
     123, at page 456.
117 J. 530/134 and 138.
118 See, for example, J. 161/28, where the bodhisattva advises against keeping an elephant
     because kept elephants cause death. See, also, J. 26/67 where a captive elephant turns
     violent.
119 See, for example, J. 410/235 where an orphaned elephant calf is taken to a hermitage by
     an ascetic, but, despite being given care and food, does not survive.
120 See, for example, J. 409/233.
121 J. 182/63.
122 See, especially, A. II, 120, and III, 117–120.
123 Gombrich (1988) p. 46.
124 See, for example, Dale Jamieson, 'Against Zoos,' in *In Defence of Animals*, ed. by Peter
     Singer (Oxford: Blackwell, 1985), pp. 108–17.
125 A. III, 216–7.
126 A. III, 217.
127 Or five treasures, as at A. III, 126.
128 See Paola Cavalieri and Peter Singer, eds, *The Great Ape Project: Equality Beyond
     Humanity* (London: Fourth Estate, 1993).
129 See, for example, Linzey (1994).

CHAPTER FIVE

Buddhism and Ecology

Ian Harris

There is after all an order to which man belongs by nature though
some mistaken quirk of patronage has elevated him beyond it.
William Golding (after Aristotle)

It is only with great ingenuity that one can identify approximate Buddhist
equivalents to the terms, such as 'environment,' 'eco-system,' 'ecology' or
indeed 'nature' itself, that are central to the contemporary discourse of
environmental concern. This observation applies to all of the major
canonical writings of Buddhism be they in Sanskrit, Pāli, or Chinese. If
readers will forgive the author's juvenile sense of humour, nothing remotely
resembling a *Tractatus Ecologico-Philosophicus* exists in any of the three
great epochs, namely the canonical, classical and modern, of Buddhist
history. This is hardly surprising for ecological concerns are quintessentially
modern concerns with origins that can be traced to the collapse of
traditional Western cosmological certainties under the impact of science.
Indeed, there may be some justification for the view that the eco-
catastophist outlook is the contemporary inheritor of Judaeo-Christian
eschatology with its great emphasis on the events leading up to the 'end of
history.' If this geneaology is accepted, the lack of any explicit discussion of
environmental ethics in the foundational documents of Buddhism is
understandable. We simply should not expect to find coherent discussion
of a topic that, strictly speaking, is not crucial to the Buddhist
understanding of reality.

In our attempt to establish 'the authentic position' on any issue we
should also remember that Buddhism, in common with all other world-
historical traditions, is not a monolithic entity. It has a history covering
some two and a half millenia and, owing to its missionary character, a
geographical spread throughout most of Asia. Since the late nineteenth
century, a significant and growing toehold has also developed in Europe and

North America. Given the fact that Buddhism has continually adapted itself to new cultural contexts, in most cases already endowed with vigorous ethico-philosophical worldviews, it is rather unsurprising that variety is the hallmark in most aspects of subsequent Buddhist thought. Indeed, Buddhism does not possess the authoritarian structures necessary to enforce unanimity in any aspect of doctrine or practice. This principle applies to the traditional areas of Buddhist ethical concern.

We have already noted that [an explicit environmental ethic is not an obvious feature of the foundational documents of Buddhism in any of its traditional cultural forms. If we proceed from the assumption that the development of a Buddhist-based ethic of environmental concern has significant value, an assumption endorsed by many contemporary representatives of the modernist Engaged Buddhist movement, the most fruitful way forward will be a two-pronged approach to the evidence.] The first line of attack will involve consideration of authoritative Buddhist literary materials to discover how far implicit ideas and notions can be worked up into an explicit ethic. Our problem here is that the vast bulk of Buddhist literary activity has its locus amongst an urbanised, educated and monastic élite – hardly the milieu in which rustic concerns are likely to make a significant impression. The difficulties associated with the archaeology of literary evidence are further compounded by the fact that it is impossible to know how far these materials actually influenced the behaviour of individual Buddhist monastics and laity in the past.

This brings us to our second approach for, alongside the élite tradition, generally regarded as dominant from the perspective of western scholars with a philological persuasion – Tambiah's 'Pāli text puritans' – there have always existed other Buddhisms whose influence has waxed and waned depending on a variety of circumstances. These are the forms of Buddhism observed amongst the rural peasantry and forest-dwelling monks. It is to this milieu, particularly in its Indic and Southeast Asian Theravāda context, that some sympathetic scholars have turned to find hints of ideas and practices that run parallel to the concerns of contemporary eco-activism.

Again, problems are associated with the anthropological approach. In the first place, the method cannot take us back before the nineteenth century. The fact that practices of a broadly eco-friendly character are observed in recent times tells us next to nothing about Buddhist practice in earlier periods, particularly where such practices have no obvious support in the textual record. The more obvious difficulty associated with the study of 'popular Buddhism' with its focus on the propitiation of nature dieties, *nats*, *yakkhas*, and the like, is how far it represents an authentic expression of Buddhism at all, rather than a simple recrudescence of autochthonous cults overlaid by a veneer of orthodoxy. Given these and related methodological uncertainties, such as the difficulty in deciding whether to privilege textual or anthropological evidence, it will be impossible to construct a definitive Buddhist position on ecological matters. Rather, we shall confine ourselves to an appraisal of the evidence for and against Buddhism as an ecologically aware tradition.

Positive evidence

Buddhism, in common with all significant renunciant traditions of ancient India such as Jainism and Yoga, certainly makes a virtue of contentment. Thus, Buddhist monks are expected, on the authority of the Buddha, to have few possessions, to make full use of those things that they do possess and to avoid luxury and wastefulness. For example, monastic robes are to be repeatedly repaired. Once the robe deteriorates beyond a condition in which it may be worn with decorum, it must be recycled and employed in other ways, such as as a floor mop.[1] Likewise lay people, through the application of the five precepts and by attending to the example of devout monks, are unlikely to make a virtue of untrammeled consumerism. As such, Buddhism may be said to endorse the kind of anti-materialist outlook that leads to low-environmental impact that is, at least in part, in tune with modern ecological concerns.

The first precept, observed by monks and lay people alike, states 'I undertake the precept to abstain from the taking of life.' This, at least theoretically, applies to all form of life ranging from human beings to insects and beyond, though in reality the situation is more complex. We would expect, for instance, that adherence to the first precept would entail the observance of a fully vegetarian diet. In actual fact, the Buddha himself accepted meat. Why is this? It seems that Buddhism from its inception, and contrary to the teachings of its rivals – the Jains – only regarded intentional killing as wrong. In general, then, only intentional acts may be judged karmically right or wrong in the Buddhist scheme of things. Bearing this in mind, the Buddha deemed it acceptable to receive meat[2] from lay donors assuming only that the meat was pure in three respects, i.e. that a monk had neither heard or seen the slaughter, nor suspected that the animal had been killed on his behalf. This is the famous *tikoṭiparisuddha* rule.

Vegetarianism as a fully articulated ethic only manifests itself at a comparatively late stage in Buddhist history, probably appearing for the first time in connection with the Mahayanist 'embryo of the *Tathāgata*' (*Tathāgatagarbha*) theory. This theory in turn becomes the basis for the East Asian notion that all things are receptacles for the Buddha-nature. We shall have to examine this doctrine in more detail at an appropriate point. However, on the broader topic of intentionality and ethics, we might note that much that is presently characterised as environmental pollution is, strictly speaking, the unintentional by product of industrial activity, etc. Does this mean that the general degradation of the environment should be regarded as a necessary evil from the Buddhist perspective, particularly when we hold in mind the Buddha's continually reiterated teachings on the structural impermanence of all conditioned things? It would clearly be misrepresentation to suggest that Buddhists are in favour of pollution and environmental decay. The correct application of right mindfulness (*sammā sati*), for instance, would presumably instill a greater awareness of the unintentional consequences of their actions in the minds of potential polluters. Nevertheless, from the ultimate perspective both the black rhino and the oil slick are subject to the same inexorable law of decay. It could be argued, then, that the correct Buddhist response to inevitable environmental flux is a mindful equanimity that steers a middle path between the extremes of inaction (i.e. support for late capitalist modes of production) on the one hand and action (ie. a social activist programme of intervention designed to re-establish untainted 'nature') on the other.

Now, while monks and lay people are expected to adhere to the first precept, the manner of adherence may be markedly different. We have already noted the stress placed on intentionality in Buddhist ethics. Suppose, for example, that a Buddhist peasant ploughs a field prior to sowing seed. It is inevitable that worms and other small creatures will be killed and injured in very large numbers. This, at least on the surface, seems contrary to the spirit of non-injury (*ahiṃsā*) of which the first precept is the most obvious expression. Nevertheless, because the action is devoid, at least theoretically, of the intention to kill, and because food production is essential to the maintenance of society, and of course to the continuity of the *saṅgha* whose members rely on food donations from their lay supporters, the ploughing of land is permitted. The situation is not the same for monks who are forbidden from engaging in all agricultural pursuits.[3] In this way the concept of non-injury (*ahiṃsā*) is open to differing strata of interpretation. Monks must avoid injury to animals and to plants[4] whether intentioned or otherwise, while quasi-intentional injury (for what farmer could fail to notice the holocaust that follows the plough) is permitted to the laity. In this manner, monks may remain recipients of physical nourishment and the laity in their turn benefit from the ultimate donation, the gift of the *Buddhadharma*. Through this casuistical chain of reasoning the adverse karmic (and environmental) effects associated with lay farming activity are deemed to be compensated.

None of this seems closely tied to an explicitly ecological ethic, particularly when we note that monks are allowed to eat meat, in contrast to their more ascetic rivals the Jains. Indeed, in some parts of the Asian Buddhist heartlands, most notably in Tibet where the terrain prevents significant arable farming, meat plays an important role in the sustenance of monk and lay person alike. Nevertheless, there are occasions in the canonical literature where the practice of *ahiṃsā* could be compared to environmentalist activity. For instance, on one occasion Mahā Moggallāna, one of the two chief disciples of the Buddha and the foremost possessor of *iddhi*-power, planned to turn the world upside down in order to combat the adverse circumstances of a drought. In this way the world's fertile underbelly would be revealed and beings would prosper once more. The Buddha, learning of this intention dissuades Mahā Moggallāna on the grounds that animals will be thrown about and injured in the process.[5] As Schmithausen observes:

> Such cases show that there was, albeit only sporadically, an awareness of the fact that animals may also be killed or injured in an indirect way, by destroying their habitat, and that this too ought to be avoided.'[6]

We should also note that this 'sporadic awareness' is largely confined to the unforeseen result of supernatural, as opposed to natural, activity. As such, the story does not serve as a very useful analogy for the modern environmental 'crisis.'

The danger of indirect injury to small creatures may also be one of the factors behind the occasional injunctions found in the canonical writings against harm to plants and seeds.[7] As we shall see in a later discussion of East Asian Buddhism, plants occupy an ambiguous position within the Buddhist cosmological scheme being neither fully sentient, though they are said to possess the faculty of touch, nor merely unfeeling matter. They are, nevertheless, the abode for many beings – the larger they are, the more potential injury will be caused to those depending upon them. This makes trees, in particular, of especial concern to rural, and more recently, urban dwelling Buddhists. Of course, the idea of the sacred tree is archaic and pre-dates the development of Buddhism. Nevertheless, the Buddha is said to have achieved his enlightenment underneath a certain tree (*bodhirukka* – the tree of enlightenment) and since that time the tree has provided a focus for a number of symbolic and ritual functions within Buddhism. Not only is it the abode of animals, but deities whose activities may be beneficial to the Buddhist religion may also dwell therein. Vessavaṇa, the king of the *yakkhas* (a class of non-human beings) and a devoted follower of the Buddha, for instance, is said to reside in a mango-tree called Atulamba whose magical character is sufficient to prevent all creatures from drawing near.[8]

The fact that trees have been regarded as the abode of both gods and animals seems to have protected them from destruction in traditional Buddhist cultures. However, with the rise of modernity and the consequent demands of industrial production, many forests are under threat in Buddhist Asia. Indeed, many have already been destroyed. Under these circumstances it is understandable that the issue has become a focus of concern, particularly within South-East Asian Theravāda modernist circles as part of the general broadening out of a longstanding social-activist agenda in an ecological direction. The rationale for this development is based on the idea that matters of social justice may no longer be considered in isolation from wider global and environmental contexts. Since the late 1980s the influential Thai monk Bhikkhu Buddhadasa[9] (shortly before his death) and Sulak Sivaraksa,[10] a prominent critic of some aspects of Thai government policy, have both written about and encouraged positive environmental activity as a means of building a more sustainable and just society founded on fundamental Buddhist principles. The reformers' perception is that contemporary Thai culture, with the connivance of international capital, has become less egalitarian and more positively inclined to exploit the natural world for resources to fuel the demand for unlimited consumption of consumer products. The call, then, is for a Buddhist ethic of wealth creation combined with practical programmes to mitigate the adverse effects of industrialization, with particular emphasis on the protection of forests and forest ecosystems.[11]

In this connection, the practice of ordaining trees[12] as a means to ensure their protection has recently been employed by some well-known Thai monks who include, or have included, Pongsak Tejadhammo – Abbot of Wat Palad and Wat Tam Tu Poo, Chiang Mai Province and a number of monks in the line of the charismatic teacher Ajaan Man, most notably Ajaan In (Wat Paa Kham Noi, Udornthaanii) and Ajaan Thui (Wat Paa Daan Wiwek, Norngkhaai). A specifically Buddhist precedent for the tree-ordination ceremony, in which an engangered tree is 'dressed' in the robe of a Buddhist monk thus making it inviolable to the chainsaw (presumably wielded by a Buddhist logger), is difficult to obtain and questionable on strict *vinaya* principles. This may partly explain the difficulties that some conservation monks have found themselves in with other, more conservative, members of the *sangha*. Indeed, it seems that a number of prominent tree-ordainers have disrobed of late although it has been impossible to determine whether this was a positive decision on their part or the result of pressure from the monastic authorities.

Additional resources for the construction of an authentically Buddhist environmental ethic may be drawn from the related doctrines of *karma* and *saṃsāra*. The Buddhist wheel of existences, at least as far as sentient beings are concerned (we shall deal with plants later), is divided into five (sometimes six) rebirth realms or *gatis*, namely those of the gods (subdivided into the realms of the *devas* and *asuras*), humans, ghosts, animals and hell beings. Now, the number of rebirths experienced by beings is theoretically without number and promotion or relegation from one *gati* to another is accepted doctrine in all traditional forms of Buddhism. Under such circumstances, the standard view is that we must have been in a close kinship relation with all other beings at some stage in our peregrinations through the beginningless cycle of births and deaths. In the words of the Buddha: 'Bhikkhus, it is not easy to find a being who has not formerly been your mother, or your father, or your brother, your sister or your son or daughter.'[13]

The resulting notion of extensive kinship extends to the entire animal realm and beyond to all other spheres of existence not, of course, excepting fellow humans. This way of thinking undoubtedly builds a sense of solidarity between Buddhists and other forms of sentient life. It is also believed to be particularly conducive to the arising of the important Buddhist virtue of loving-kindness (*mettā*).[14] *Mettā* is the first of the four divine-abidings (*brahmavihāra*), a series of meditative exercises culminating in *upekkhā* or equanimity, '...an even-minded serenity towards beings which balances concern for others with a realization that suffering is an inevitable part of being alive.'[15] Theravādin commentators, such as Buddhaghosa, hold that eleven blessings or advantages accrue to the successful *mettā*-practitioner. These blessings include a peaceful death and rebirth as a god. Buddhaghosa tells us that the initial stages of the practice involve the direction of loving-kindness towards oneself. When this has been successfully accomplished the circle of loving-kindness may be sequentially extended towards an honoured teacher, a friend, a neutral person, a foe, a dead person, a member of the opposite sex, etc. The intention, then, is to avoid the extension of *mettā* towards those with whom emotional engagement may cause disturbance. Although it is not explicitly stated in the texts, animals may be included in the list of beings in evil states of existence (*vinipātika*) who should be avoided in the initial stages of the practice, although we must also note that the general injunction 'May all beings be happy and secure, may they be happy-minded. Whatever living beings there are – feeble or strong, long, stout or medium, short, small or large, seen or unseen, those dwelling far or near, those who are born or those who await rebirth – may all beings, without exception, be happy-minded'[16] could be taken to include animals in a rather non-specific manner.

On the odd occasion when a specific animal is mentioned in the context of *mettā*, this is often so that the apotropaic character of the practice may be illustrated. Thus, when the schismatic Devadatta attempts to destroy the Buddha by sending the enraged and intoxicated elephant Nālāgiri to trample him underfoot, the Buddha employs *mettā*, to subdue the beast.[17] In recent times, the practice of *mettā* has been invoked as an important pillar in the construction of a Buddhist environmental ethic. It should be clear from the foregoing discussion that, both theoretically and practically, *mettā* may not provide the unambiguous support that it seems to offer on casual scrutiny. In the first place, practitioners are positively dissuaded from extending *mettā* towards specific animals who, it can be convincingly argued, should be worthy recipients from the environmentalist perspective. Secondly, and perhaps more importantly, the introspective nature of the meditation on loving-kindness is not easily reconciled with the sort of activism normally associated with the contemporary ecological movement. Indeed, the goal of the practice is the cultivation of wholesome mental states by the meditator himself. Its impact within the sphere of ethics is a welcome – though subsidiary – byproduct of this primary motivating factor. The example of the Buddha's pacification of Nālāgiri is a good case in point for here *mettā* is employed to eliminate danger to the Buddha himself. The welfare of the elephant, though not entirely irrelevant, is not at all central to the story.

Let us note, once again, the ambiguous support that the Buddhist doctrine of rebirth provides for an environmental ethic. On the one hand it is bound to instill a fellow feeling for all sentient beings caught in the beginningless circle of *saṃsāra*. This general ethical principle is clearly connected with *mettā*-practice. However, more detailed analysis reveals a significant level of instrumentality in the sense that the practice aims, at least in part, towards the enhancement of the practitioner's own spiritual status rather than the alleviation of the suffering of others. A final problematic feature of the practice is that loving-kindness is crucially directed towards individuals rather than to particular species. Indeed, canonical Buddhism does not seem to have developed a classificatory framework that makes sense of the concept of species, a notion generally considered to be indispensable to the application of ecological ideas. Thus, in the context of a discussion of the Buddhist virtues of non-injury and benevolence, Schmithausen concludes:

> ... it seems doubtful that this idea was ... at any point developed in such a way as to take classes or species of animals not merely as groups of individuals but as something to be *valued* (or at least accorded a right of existence) *as species*.[18]

Nevertheless, it is a fact that organised Buddhism has accorded protection to certain groups of animals, though not necessarily for specifically Buddhist reasons. Thus, the ideal king of the *Cakkavattisīhanāda Sutta*, a long discourse on kingship within the Theravāda canon, is expected to ensure the safety of his people along with that of wild animals of the forest and birds (*migapakkhī*). We also know that the seminal historical Buddhist king, Asoka (c.268–239 BCE), took responsibility for the protection of many kinds of wild and domesticated animals for he tells us this in the surviving edicts (notably 5th Pillar Edict and Rock Edict 1) that he had placed around his extensive empire. Having said this, it is worth noting that very similar restrictions on the harming of animals are to be found in the non-Buddhist *Arthaśāstra* of Kauṭilya, a Brahmanical writer of the late 4th century BCE. It seems, then, that a concern for the welfare of animals was considered a generalised duty in most of the variations on the theme of kingship in ancient India. We are unable to conclude that this was a feature of Buddhist polity alone.

The spiritual and moral status of animals in Buddhism is, on detailed scrutiny, rather ambiguous, perhaps relating to differences between the popular and élite strata of the tradition. In the former, particularly as reflected in the *Jātaka* stories, animals are viewed in a very positive light. They are shown to be capable of tender feelings to one another, they perform acts of extreme altruism and, on occasions, live together in harmonious relations premised on the virtues of courtesy, politeness and deference as in the famous story of the partridge, monkey and bull elephant.[19] As such they may provide guides to the proper conduct of humans. However, it should be noted that the often highly anthropo-morphic character of the essentially pre-Buddhist folk-tradition of the *Jātakas* may be said to empty the stories of any 'naturalistic' content, thus defeating the intention of those who bring them forward as evidence in support of an authentic Buddhist environmentalist ethic. Indeed, in the *Jātaka* context the animals are not animals at all in any accepted sense of the term, for at the end of each story the Buddha reveals that the central character was none other than himself, the *bodhisatta*, in a former life.

The élite tradition takes a rather different line. Monks, for instance, are prohibited from imitating the behaviour of animals. Thus, the Buddha condemned the monk who, as part of his ascetic regimen, grazed like a cow (*Vin*.ii.132) while elsewhere a canine ascetic (M.i.387–9) is soundly castigated for his activities. The standard line seems to be that, although animals are part of *saṃsāra* like ourselves, they are more unfavourably disposed to the possiblility of liberation for three basic reasons; they are inferior to humans existentially, morally and intellectually. On the existential side the level of suffering endured by animals is of an especially gross kind. All suffer exceedingly through their position in the 'natural order' where the weak are at the mercy of the strong[20] – early Buddhism seems to endorse the notion of the 'survival of the fittest' – while some must endure the additional burden of ill-treatment meted out to them by humans. From the moral perspective, animals are constitutionally disposed to acts of violence and sexual misconduct. They are inclined to disregard the taboos that bind human society together and this propensity, on occasion, may result in the crimes of cannibalism or incest. Goats, sheep, chickens, pigs, dogs and jackals are particularly blameworthy in the latter respect.[21] In is customary for the *Vinaya* to classify animals of all kinds alongside human matricides, parricides, hermaphrodites, thieves, and, perhaps most ser-iously, slayers of a Buddha.[22] The intellectual inferiority of animals is no doubt associated with the great difficulty that beings living in a state of perpetual insecurity must have in making their minds calm. Animals patently possess the capacity for mentation though not, in the majority of cases, the ability to achieve insight (*prajñā*). For this, amongst other reasons, they may not seek admittance to the monastic order (*saṅgha*) and cannot easily act upon the teachings of a Buddha. In this way, rebirth as an animal is regarded in a deeply unfavourable light. Indeed, the heavenly paradises of early Mahāyānist piety, such as Sukhāvatī – the Pure Land of the West and the abode of the Buddha Amitābha – are paradises at least in part because they are devoid of animal inhabitants though, for the purposes of balance, it should also be noted that females are likewise excluded from rebirth in these happy lands!

Evidence against

Urge and urge and urge,
Always the procreant urge of the world.
Walt Whitman *Song of Myself*

From the ultimate perspective, Buddhism teaches that all things within *saṃsāra* are impermanent. The first of the four noble truths states all things to be *duḥkha*, or unsatisfactory, and this position is reiterated in the Buddha's last recorded words to the effect that 'All conditioned things are subject to decay. Strive diligently for salvation' (D.ii.156). This assessment of existence is, at the very least, less than wholeheartedly positive and we shall be justified in assuming that this characterisation applies to the whole of the natural world. As such, it provides a rather unsatisfactory basis from which to develop an environmental ethic. In this sense, we may describe the teachings of this particular didactic strand within Buddhism as fundamentally dysteleologic for, on this basis, it is very difficult to maintain the ultimate value, meaning or purpose of anything. We are a good distance away from the teleological frameworks associated with the major theistic religious traditions of the world such as Christianity and Islam in which an omnipotent and omniscient supreme being brings existence into being for some as yet inscrutable but ultimately positive purpose.

The overall thrust of traditional Buddhist cosmology also does little to enhance the environmentalist credentials of early Buddhism. In an important text like the Pali *Aggañña Sutta* (D.iii.80ff), the realm of desire (*kāmaloka*), the lowest part of the Buddhist triple-decker universe and the closest one is likely to come to a Buddhist equivalent to the 'natural world' of contemporary parlance, is said to undergo periodic origination and dissolution. This process is without beginning and without end, with each epoch following the last in a more or less identical fashion. In the initial stages of world production we hear that beings possess a luminous character, being immaterial and without distinguishing marks. However, as the period progresses material bodies emerge, and distinctions – such as those between men and women and perhaps also those between humans and animals (although this is not specified in the text) – emerge as the result of a highly predictable rise in the general levels of desire (*kāma*). We are after all in *kāmaloka*! As the moral conduct of beings degenerates in this highly deterministic manner, so the environment is degraded leading in turn to the disappearance of wild animals (who are reborn as humans at the completion of their karmic debt), the rebirth of humans in the luminous realm of form (*rūpaloka*) and ultimately to a universal conflagration in which the physical structure of the world itself is turned to ash. Interestingly, the highly influential *Abhidharmakośa*[23] gives a variation on the story insisting that domesticated animals survive the destruction of their wilder relatives and are obliged to share the same fate as humans. Whatever the variations, the message of all traditions of interpretation of the root text is clear. Ultimacy is not located within the natural realm, for the world with its inhabitants both human and animal, its forests, vegetation, mountains, and rivers is subject to an inexorable law of impermanency. Perhaps rather unsurprisingly, Buddhist writers have shown little interest in detailed analysis of the stages in this cyclic degradation of the natural world, although the topic of the deterioration of the Buddhist religion and its final disappearance (before the cycle is repeated once again) has provided a regular focus for debate throughout Buddhist history.[24] This seems to suggest that the destiny of the *Buddhadharma* itself has generally been of far more interest and concern than the fate of nature. Liberation, then, comes through escape from the bonds that tie us to *saṃsāra*, not through some fundamental restructuring of existence. In this light the environmentalist agenda of restoration, though well-intentioned, misses the fundamental point.

A short excurcus into the fate of traditional Buddhist cosmology in the modern period may be in order at this point. One of the factors that is said to characterise Buddhist modernism is its tendency to underplay, and in some cases, disregard the Buddha's canonical teachings on the structure of the universe. A good example of this is provided by the attitudes of Thai intellectuals from the middle of the nineteenth century towards the classical triple world (*traibhūmi*) arrangement which, while not exclusively Buddhist (it contains both Hindu and Jaina influences), has its origins in Indic culture. We can see that as Thailand opened itself to the wider world, and particularly to the influence of a modern scientific world view, élite *saṅgha* members, such as kings Mongkut (1851–68) and his son Chulalongkorn (1868–1910), became increasingly uncomfortable with the mythological elements of the *Traibhūmi* cosmology replete with its plethora of heavenly and infernal regions. Mongkut and his circle pushed their demythologisation to the point that they came to repudiate the existence of heavens and hells. Aetiological theories traditionally advanced to account for natural phenomena such as rain, wind, earthquakes, the planetary realm and the like were also attacked and gradually superceded by explanations based on the empirical principles of Western science. Thus, in 1913, when Rama I's edition of the *Traibhūmi* was commercially published for the first time, the preface noted that:

> When the *Traibhūmi*, composed by sages in ancient times more than one thousand years ago, is compared with the writings of geography today, (we can see that) investigations made in the arts and other branches of knowledge have progressed much farther. For these reasons some statements in the *Traibhūmi tend to be not quite correct*. (my italics)[25]

However, it should be noted that while the thought universe of educated circles in Thailand underwent something of a Copernican revolution, though without the gnashing of teeth experienced in early modern Europe, popular Buddhist thought and practice continued to be dominated by the mythological powers acknowledged in the traditional cosmological treatises. The same process seems to have been at work in other regions of the Asian Buddhist homelands although, in Japan, the reception of scientific, particularly astronomical, knowledge in the early nineteenth century seems to have elicited very robust defences from the supporters of the *Traibhūmi* cosmology, of whom the most prominent proponent was Entsū (1754–1834).[26] Nevertheless, Entsū was a rather isolated case. Certainly, the dysteleologic outlook of ancient Buddhism does not appear to have encouraged scientific examination of and speculation about the universe yet, paradoxically, while Christianity did much to open up such possibilities, it was science that ultimately provided the most serious challenge to the authority of the Christian revelation. The reason for this may be that, in the Buddhist context, the adoption of a modern scientific cosmology failed to challenge humanity's place in the natural order for traditional teachings make it clear that we are already decentred in a universe of vast size and scope. In fact, despite the arguments of Entsū and a few others, the rise of science failed to traumatise Buddhism in any significant way.

Some recent commentators, most notably Joanna Macy an American Engaged Buddhist and eco-activist, have argued for a close congruence between the Buddhist doctrine of dependent origination (*pratītyasamut-pāda*) on the one hand, and the modern conception of ecology, on the other. In the early Buddhist period *pratītyasamutpāda* appears to have described the universally applicable rule of causation in which all things are held to come into being in dependence upon specific causes. Yet in Macy's hands the interpretation of the canonical notion of conditionality undergoes a marked transformation. The idea that all entities depend on specific causes and conditions is extended and reworked into a position in which a mutual interdependence, interpenetration, and interrelatedness of all things is upheld. Now, there is no evidence that this way of construing causal processes was ever envisaged within the Indic tradition, although it did become an important strand in the interpretation of the doctrine of *pratītyasamutpāda* in China, particularly amongst those Buddhists influenced by the teachings of the Hua-Yen (*Japanese*: Kegon) school based on the teachings of the highly influential Mahāyānist *Avataṃsaka Sūtra*.

Macy is probably guilty of anachronism in her reading of early Indic sources. However, even if we allow that she has a significant point to make, the consequences of her position are not as she would wish. The doctrine of extreme holism expressed in the Hua-Yen teaching on the mutual identity and interpenetration of all entities cannot easily be employed as the basis of an environmental ethic. In this picture of reality the universe is described as the totality of interdependent elements with each entity understood as the cause of all others. The problem with this ontological model, at least from the environmentalist perspective, can be appreciated if we concretize things a little. Let us take the examples of nuclear waste and an endangered plant species. Everything in the universe depends on the plant as its cause. Conversely, everything depends on the nuclear waste for, without nuclear waste, there could be no totality of interdependent entities. Again, if the plant exerts complete causal power over all other things, it must contain all other things and, consequently, all things are contained, from the causal perspective, within nuclear waste. Another related problem, which I merely mention in passing, is that the Hua-Yen model of existence cannot easily deal with the passage of time. If everything depends on everything else there must be complete identity of entities both spatially and temporally. There can be no differentiation in terms of past, present and future so, returning to our example, nuclear waste must be eternal. Here, then, is the fundamental objection to the invocation of extreme holism in the field of environmental ethics – it leads to absurd conclusions! One will fare little better by employing the doctrine of dependent origination (*pratītyasamut-pāda*) in its temporal form as found in traditional Indic texts. As the important Mahāyāna philosopher Nāgārjuna points out, the temporal flux of causal relations renders all conditioned entities devoid of any self-nature or substantiality. This is the fundamental meaning of the doctrine of emptiness (*śūnyatā*). This is clearly a reiteration of the point made at the beginning of this section; everything within the realm of nature is marked by unsatisfactoriness, impermanence, and lack of self or substantiality (*anātman*).

Despite propagating a teaching that, from the ultimate perspective, seems to transcend the customary dichotomy between nature and culture, there are many occasions in the canon, where texts adopt an uncompromis-ingly pro-civilization position. This is perhaps unsurprisinging given the urban and suburban milieu in which the Buddha and his disciples moved. Living conditions of this kind are perhaps the most likely factors to instill a feeling that the natural world, particularly those areas untamed by human artifice, possesses a rather menacing character. Buddhist texts often characterise the wilderness as a place associated with the presence of malign and uncontrollable forces. As such it is unproductive to the cultivation of the Buddha's teaching. Indeed the Theravāda *Upālisutta* (M.i.378) tells us of some cultivated land that is transformed back into dense forest though the agency of wicked persons. The context of the story makes it clear that wickedness is the human counterpart of wilderness while moral goodness corresponds to a physical environment under the management of human agency. Elsewhere, in the *Vessantara Jātaka*, we hear that the wilderness may be tamed through the practice of the *dharma*.[27] Many stories of this sort can be isolated from Indic sources. Perhaps the most elegant in this regard concerns a quasi-utopian description of the future in which all the conditions for the return of a wheel-turning king (*cakkavati*) have been fulfilled. At this time, Jambudīpa, the most southerly of the great continents of classical Buddhist cosmology 'will be mighty and prosperous, the villages, towns and royal cities will be so close that a cock could fly from each one to the next ... (Jambudīpa) will be pervaded by mankind even as a jungle is by reeds and rushes ... (and) there will be 84,000 towns, with Ketumatī (the royal city) at their head.'[28] To the modern mind, particularly to that attuned to the discourse of environmental concern, this vision of hyper-urbanisation and overpopulation (incidentally, the humans destined to dwell at this time will live to the age of 80,000 years – a major problem for the health and welfare services of the time!) has more in common with a nightmare than a dream of an ideal society.

Of course we may be inclined to emphasise the mythic elements of the story and disregard its prophetic character, but in doing so we must bear in mind the wealth of evidence present in the early sources that speaks encouragingly of cultivated surroundings in all their forms. A case in point is the regularity with which artificial reconstructions of nature, as opposed to nature itself 'red in tooth and claw,' are praised in the texts. A good example of this concerns the merit supposedly earned by lay followers from the laying out of pleasure parks and groves[29] in an early echo of the activities of Capability Brown and others during the European age of improvement. Indeed, some scientific ecologists have recently concluded, and the same may possibly be true of the *āramas* of the ancient period, that contemporary Buddhist temple compounds provide an environment in which species diversity and protection may be far richer than in the surrounding areas.[30] Nevertheless, we should note that while animals and plants may flourish more richly in the confines of places such as temples, these are largely artificial environments leaning more in the direction of culture than towards nature. Perhaps the best way of summing this up is to suggest that Buddhists from all periods, particularly those of an eremitical inclination, seem to have been attracted to the liminal zone[31] that exists on the boundaries between culture and nature.

The foregoing discussion has perhaps given the impression that early Buddhism was thorough-going in its pro-civilization bias. This would be quite incorrect for, since its inception a pro-nature, or 'hermit strand' has been in existence waxing and waning as social, political, and economic conditions change. Never as vigorous as the urbanised monastic élites, at least in terms of numbers, its influence has been extraordinarily pervasive. An early hint of this strain may be traced to the story of the Buddha in the third week after enlightenment when, during a great storm, the Nāga-king Mucalinda emerged from his tree and protected the Buddha by wrapping his coils seven times round the sage's body with his hood held over the head. A similar feeling of identity with the natural is heard in the Pāli *Therīgāthā* and *Theragāthā*, the songs of female and male *arahants*. In some of these verses a plangent strain of nature mysticism feels just as fresh today as it must have seemed some two thousand years ago. Thus, Sāriputta:

> Forests are delightful, where (ordinary) people find no delight. Those rid of desire will delight here; they are not seekers after sensual pleasures.[32]

The plangency is achieved through an emphasis on the sense of detachment that conveys a tone quite alien to the more romantic quest for union with nature found in the work of Wordsworth and his fellow romantic poets. The Buddhist poet recognises the dangers of the forest. These are sufficient to keep the ordinary person at home. But of all the dangers that the forests hold – wild animals, venomous snakes and the like – the most potent is attachment, for in the Buddhist scheme of things this must inevitably lead to greater suffering. It is perhaps unfortunate, at least from the perspective of environmental ethics, that the voices of the early *arahants* and their spiritual ancestors, forest-dwelling monks, never became the dominant voice of organised Buddhism. Indeed, perusal of the scholastic debates within the great universities of northern India contained in the voluminous works of Mahāyānist *śāstra*-writers, like Nāgārjuna, reveals little trace of these considerations.

Nevertheless, for the religious virtuoso the wilderness provides the ideal environment in which to bring about the transformation of consciousness so necessary in the quest for liberation. In the first place, the solitude available here is an indispensable concomitant in the quest. Secondly, untamed nature provides a continual and obvious illustration of the impermanence of all things. Writers as varied as Buddhaghosa[33] and Candrakīrti,[34] for instance, both recommend the forest with its continual fall of leaves as a practical metaphor for impermanence. In a sense, this may be seen as a straightforward recapitulation of the Buddha's realization under the tree of enlightenment. The forest monk must overcome his fear in the face of the very real danger represented by the many wild and poisonous creatures in this place. A sort of metaphysical dread engendered by folk beliefs in the forest as dwelling place of malign spirits must also be conquered. The therapeutic nature of the process is well attested in

Buddhist sources.[35] By conquering fear the forest-dwelling monk achieves supernatural powers. This is undoubtedly an archaic notion and plenty of contemporary evidence exists to support the view that the charismatic monk[36] must overcome fear through the realization of the insubstantiality of all customary sources of that fear, be they demons or the wilderness itself.

East Asian Buddhism and the plant kingdom

According to the Abhidharma, existence in its fullest sense may be differentiated into two basic categories. The first is the realm of karmically determined rebirth, namely the five (or six) destinies (*gatis*) already treated above. The second category is the receptacle world (*bhājanaloka*) into which sentient beings are thrown as a result of their past actions, consisting of rocks, rivers, plants, planets, stars, interstellar space, etc. The receptacle world is, at least in Buddhism's early period, held to be entirely devoid of sentiency, an interesting contrast to the views of ancient Hindu and Jaina philosophers who held all levels of existence to be characterised by greater or lesser degrees of sentiency. The former view extends throughout the Indic period and is, for instance, vigorously defended by Bhāvaviveka (6th century CE) in his *Madhyamakahṛdayakārikā* and its auto-commentary *Tarkajvāla*.[37] Now, we know that both the Abhidharma and the later writings of Mahāyānist masters are essentially scholastic in tone and scope. An important question relates to how far these works may be regarded as articulating the views of Buddhism in its earliest period. The view of many scholars is that the early canonical period of the four *Nikāyas*, the *Prātimokṣasūtra* and verse collections such as the *Suttanipāta* represents a more pragmatic and flexible outlook that that found in the rather doctrinaire stages of development represented by later authors. It has been argued, for instance, that the earliest period represents one in which the formal doctrines of the *gatis,* with their associated notions of *sattva* and *bhājana-lokas,* have not yet crystallized. In this incipient stage in the development of Buddhism, *saṅgha* members, though personally unwilling to admit the sentiency of plants, may have been prepared to tolerate the animistic, pre-Buddhist, beliefs of their lay supporters who clearly did regard trees and plants (and perhaps the earth as well) as the abodes of divine beings and the like.

The distinctive character of East Asian Buddhism, particularly in its Hua-Yen form, has already been noted, even though its putative ecological credentials fail to stand up to any rigorous analysis. Nevertheless, this cultural and geographical domain is the source of one further Buddhist doctrine that merits consideration. This is the idea that all things, including those within the vegetable kingdom, are capable of reaching *nirvāṇa*. The idea that trees and grasses, indeed the land itself, are destined for enlightenment is probably not found in Indic sources although, as noted above, a belief in the sentience of plants may have been a feature of popular Buddhism from the earliest times. Supporters of the doctrine hold that its source is to be found in the Mahāyānist *Mahāparinirvāṇa Sūtra*. This text was translated into Chinese in about 417 CE by Fa-hsien and Buddhabhadra though no Sanskrit version is known. This fact has led some scholars to believe that it may be a uniquely Chinese work without an Indian counterpart. The principal teaching of the *Sūtra* is that all beings are possessed of an embryo of the *Tathāgata (Tathāgatagarbha)* – an idea that we have already had cause to mention in our discussion of the origins of Buddhist vegetarianism.

Now, while the origin of the idea of the 'attainment of Buddhahood by non-sentient beings' (Jap: *hijo jobutsu*) may plausibly be traced to the *Mahāparinirvāṇa Sūtra*, the first explicit reference to the doctrine is found in disputations between masters of the Sui period (581–617 CE) such as Hui-yuan and Chih-i. These debates were further developed by Chan-jan, a T'ien-t'ai writer of the T'ang (624–907 CE). Saicho (767–822) and Kukai (774–835) seem to have imported the doctrine into Japan, although it is to Annan (latter half of ninth century), a prominent Tendai esotericist, that we should look in order to find full systematization and defence of the doctrine of the innate enlightenment (*hongaku shiso*) of all things. His *Private Notes on Discussions of Theories on the Realization of Buddhahood by Grasses and Trees (Shinjo somoku jobutsu shiki)*[38] provides the most detailed presentation of the notion, with a defense undergirded by appeal to the esoteric teaching that 'this phenomenal world is nothing but the world of Buddhas.' The idea is nicely expressed in the *haiku*:

All I pick up
At the ebb tide
Is alive!   (Kaga no Chiyo, 1701–1775 CE)

Tendai is not the only school of Japanese Buddhism to have adopted this kind of attitude towards the natural world. The natural imagery of Zen, expressed through landscape painting, *haiku* and *kōan*, is now quite familiar to us in the West. Indeed, the initial exposure of late nineteenth century European artists to Zen-inspired fine arts appears to have caused significant changes in the way that that nature was characterised in western painting. Two important Japanese terms much used in the context of the Zen attitude to the natural world are *sabi* and *wabi*. The former is employed in Japanese art appreciation to denote rusticity, unpretentiousness and archaic imperfection, although its primary meaning is connected with ideas of loneliness and solitude. The second is more to do with a feeling of contentment, simplicity, and poverty in the sense of 'independence from worldly things.' In Suzuki's opinion, *wabi* denotes 'an appreciation of transcendental aloofness in the midst of multiplicities.'[39]

Of course, both terms are not confined to the language of art criticism, they also indicate existential goals. Their complementarity is demonstrated by the fact that, while *sabi* is concerned with an aesthetic involvement in a nature uncontaminated by human activity, *wabi* articulates an ethical response of contentment with this state of affairs. Aesthetics and morality come together in a mutually supporting relationship.

In recent times it has become something of a commonplace to assume that Buddhism is eco-friendly. In this respect it has sometimes been contrasted favourably with the Judaeo-Christian tradition which, so the argument goes, is a major culprit in the present eco-crisis. D.T. Suzuki, an important figure in the transmission of Buddhism to a western audience, seems to be one of the earliest writers to have articulated this position. Contrasting the western desire to climb and therefore 'conquer' mountains with the significance of Mt. Fuji in Japanese arts and culture, he writes:

> The idea of the so-called 'conquest of nature' comes from Hellenism, I imagine, in which the earth is made to be man's servant, and the winds and the sea are to obey him. Hebraism concurs with this view, too. In the East, however, this idea of subjecting Nature to the commands or service of man according to his selfish desires has never been cherished. For Nature to us has never been uncharitable, it is not a kind of enemy to be brought under man's power. We of the Orient have never conceived Nature in the form of an opposing power. On the contrary, Nature has been our constant friend and companion, who is to be absolutely trusted in spite of the frequent earthquakes assailing this land of ours. The idea of conquest is abhorrent.[40]

Here, then, is an early though tangible demonstration of the way in which Zen 'naturalism' came to affect the initial stages of the ecological discourse. We find plenty of variations on this basic theme. Thus, in a discussion of Buddhism as a positive resource in the fight against commercialism and materialism, Whitehill points out that *wabi* is a key concept for it implies a life:

> manifested in art and ecologically appropriate technologies, graceful and full humanity, and a quest for self-awakening and for participation in the harmony of the world and in the miracle of simple things.[41]

This attitude towards nature is summed up by the famous *haiku* of the poetess Kaga no Chiyo, composed after her discovery early one morning of a morning glory plant twined around the handle of her bucket. Rather than disturb the plant she opts to fetch water elsewhere:

130

The well-pole taken by a morning glory
I went to a neighbour for water.

Zen 'naturalism,' then, may be the most fruitful direction from which to develop an authentically Buddhist ecological ethic. However, a word of warning is necessary. In the first place, the claim that Zen provides the undergirding principle of all Japanese art is highly dubious from the critico-historical perspective. Many more influences are at work here than are admitted by propagandists like D.T. Suzuki. More importantly, analysis of the situation of Buddhism in Japan during the period of Suzuki's literary activity reveals that his ideas have a clear socio-historical context.

In the early part of Suzuki's life Buddhists were still coming to terms with the trauma invoked by the Meiji (1868–1912) persecution of Buddhism. In order to reassert itself in the face of official hostility a modernist, New Buddhism (*shin bukkyō*) emerged that placed great emphasis on the essential dissimilarities between 'Oriental' and 'Occidental' ways of thinking. The fundamental uniqueness of the Japanese character (*nihonjinron*) came to be stressed, particularly by members of the influential Kyoto school of thought such as Nishida Kitaro (1870–1945). In a recent discussion of these *nihonjinron* thinkers, Scharf observes that they 'would assert that the Japanese are racially and/or culturally inclined to experience the world more directly than are the peoples of other nations.'[42]

It is clear from our earlier quotation that Suzuki eagerly embraced this style of thinking. His significance, particularly for the reception of Buddhist ideas in the West, is twofold. In the first place, he was an active propagandist of the notion that the Japanese uniquely respond to nature along holistic lines and, secondly, he identified Zen as the prime factor in this attitude. Echoes of his ideas are still found in the scholarly literature. Social scientists, for instance, regularly claim that Japanese culture, in contradistinction to that of the West, tends to debase the idea of the subject. For instance, in the Japanese visual arts, there is said to be a 'relative minimization of the importance of the subject as against the environment...'[43] and this in turn results in a valorization of nature. Or, as Berque observes:

> ... Japanese culture ... persistently placed nature and the natural at the acme of culturalness ... a sense of place (*bashosei*) is particularly pronounced in cultures which, as in the Japanese case, do not enhance the subject's pre-eminence to the degree that European culture has done.[44]

However, the impact of Suzuki's thought is probably more profound on the level of popular perceptions of Buddhism where it seems to have conditioned the thought of influential figures in the western environmentalist movement. Lynn White,[45] an early advocate of the idea that the problem of eco-degradation must be addressed by turning away from its cause in the Judaeo-Christian thought-universe to embrace Eastern and particularly Zen-like orientations to the natural world, is a case in point. Despite the fact that this romanticised and nostalgic vision of a timeless and paradisiacal Buddhist past rests on dubious historical foundations, it has become quite common in recent times and is no longer confined to perceptions of Japanese and Far Eastern forms. Tibetan Buddhism has also been co-opted as support in the discourse of environmental concern, again on rather flimsy and anachronistic evidence.[46] Protagonists of the Lynn White thesis tend to argue that, if Buddhism was enabled to flourish, the natural expression of the cultivation of the wholesome mental states recommended in the Buddha's teaching would result in the establishment of ecological harmony. This utopian vision claims to rest on the evidence of previous Buddhist culture and practice, even though no real evidence of the kind exists. Indeed, it is doubtful that the practice of meditation was ever as widespread in the Buddhist world as many western observers have fondly imagined.[47] In fact, much that masquerades under the label of ecoBuddhism – a neologism employed to denote the contemporary Buddhist response to the challenge of ecological degradation premised on the prioritisation of 'mental states' – on analysis, turns out to be an uneasy partnership between Spinozism, New Age religiosity and highly selective Buddhism.[48]

Notes

1 *Vin*.ii.29f.
2 For a variety of reasons too complex to enter into here, monks are forbidden to partake in ten kinds of meat. The ten include human flesh, elephant, lion, etc. See *Vin*.i.218ff.
3 *Vin*.iv.32–33.
4 The eleventh expiatory offence in the Theravāda monastic code is directed towards the destruction of vegetable growth (*bhūtagāma*). See *Vin*.iv.34.
5 *Vin*.iii.76.
6 Lambert Schmithausen, 'The Early Buddhist Tradition and Ecological Ethics. How can Ecological Ethics be Established in Early Buddhism' *Journal of Buddhist Ethics* 4 1997:1–74, p. 13.
7 D.i.5.
8 J.iv.324.
9 Bhikkhu Buddhadasa *Buddhasasanik Kap Kan Anurak Thamachat* (Buddhists and the Conservation of Nature) (Bangkok, Kamol Kimthong Foundation, 1990); and 'A Notion of Buddhist Ecology' *Seeds of Peace* 3/2 (1987) pp. 22–27.
10 Sivaraksa's 'True Development' in Alan Hunt-Badiner (ed.) *Dharma-Gaia: A Harvest of Essays in Buddhism and Ecology* (Berkeley: Parallax Press, 1990) pp. 169–177 (adapted from a paper delivered to the World Conference on Religion and Peace, Melbourne, Australia, 1989) merely notes the existence of a growing emphasis on ecology within Buddhism but fails to develop any significant connections with social justice.
11 Ecological considerations are beginning to manifest themselves within the practice of Buddhist monks, particularly in the north-east of the country. See J.L. Taylor, *Forest*

Monks and the Nation State: An Anthropological and Historical Study in North Eastern Thailand (Singapore: ISEAS, 1993). Also Leslie E. Sponsel and Poranee Natadecha 'Buddhism, Ecology and Forests in Thailand' in J.K. Dargavel, K. Dixon and N. Semple (eds) *Changing Tropical Forests: Historical Perspectives on Today's Challenges in Asia, Australasia and Oceania* (Canberra, ANU/CRES, 1988), pp. 305–325; Leslie E. Sponsel and Poranee Natadecha-Sponsel *The Role of Buddhism in Creating a More Sustainable Society in Thailand* (London: School of Oriental and African Studies, 1994); and Phra Thepvedi *Phra Kap Pa* (Monks and the Forest) (Bangkok, Khrongkan Vanaphitdak, 1992).

12 The practice may well have its origin in a wide-spread revival of tree-planting in Thailand in the wake of the Bangkok Bicentennial of 1982, see Kasetsart University *Invitation to Tree Planting at Buddhamonton* Bangkok, Public Relations Office, 1987.

13 S.ii.189.

14 See *Vism.* IX. 36 & 47.

15 Peter Harvey, *An Introduction to Buddhism: Teachings, History and Practices* (Cambridge, Cambridge University Press, 1990), p. 209.

16 *Karaṇīya-mettā Sutta* cf. also *Mettā Sutta* (A.ii.129).

17 *Vin.*ii.194.

18 op cit p. 12.

19 *Vin.*ii.161.

20 M.iii.169.

21 D.iii.72.

22 *Vin.*i.320.

23 *Kośa.*178.11f.

24 Cf. David Chappell, 'Early Forebodings of the Death of Buddhism' *Numen* XXVII/1 (1980) pp. 122–154, and Jan Nattier, *Once Upon a Future Time: Studies in a Buddhist Prophecy of Decline* (Berkeley, Asian Humanities Press, 1991).

25 Quoted from Craig J. Reynolds, 'Buddhist Cosmology in Thai History, with Special Reference to Nineteenth-Century Culture Change' *Journal of Asian Studies* XXXV/2 (1976) p. 212. Also see Lithai, King of Sukhothai *Three Worlds According to King Ruang: A Thai Buddhist Cosmology* translated by Frank and Mani B. Reynolds (Berkeley, Asian Humanities Press, 1982. Berkeley Buddhist Studies Series No. 4); and G. Coedès, 'The Traibhumikatha Buddhist Cosmology and Treaty on Ethics' *East and West* VII/4 (1957) pp. 349–52.

26 Entsū's most important work is *Bukkoku rekishōhen* (On the Astronomy and the Calendrical Theory of Buddha's Country; 5 vols., 1810). See Shigeru Nakayama *A History of Japanese Astronomy: Chinese Background and Western Impact* (Cambridge, Mass., Harvard University Press, 1969), particularly chapter 15, pp. 203–215.

27 Cf. M. Cone and R. Gombrich (trans.) *The Perfect Generosity of Prince Vessantara* (Oxford, Oxford University Press, 1977), p. 28f.

28 D.iii.75 (T.W. Rhys Davids translation).

29 S.i.33.

30 The fullest ethnobotanical study of the impact of Buddhist temples on the dispersal of certain plant species is Sheng-ji Pei,'Some Effects of the Dai People's Cultural Beliefs and Practices on the Plant Environment of Xishuangbanna, Yunnan Province, Southwest China' in Karl L. Hutterer, A.T. Rambo and G. Lovelace (eds.) *Cultural Values and Human Ecology in Southeast Asia* (Ann Arbor, Center for South and Southeast Asian Studies, University of Michigan, 1985. Michigan Papers on Southeast Asia No. 24), pp. 321–39.

31 On the importance of topographical liminality in the lives on early Christian saints see Peter Brown, *The Cult of the Saints: Its Rise and Function in Latin Christianity* (Chicago: University of Chicago Press, 1982).

32 *Thag.* 992. A similar tone is adopted by Mahānāma (115), Sappaka (307–10), and Mahā Kassapa (1069–70).

33 *Vism.*ii.58.

34 *Pras.* 246, 13 & 299, 9f.

35 A good example here is the *Yogāvacara's Manual* (T.W. Rhys Davids ed, London, Pali Text Society, 1896) translated by F.L. Woodward, as *Manual of a Mystic, Being a Translation from the Pali and Sinhalese Work Entitled the Yogavachara's Manual* (London: Pali Text Society, 1916).

36 On the charisma of successful forest-dwelling monks see S.J. Tambiah, *Buddhism and the Spirit Cults in Northeast Thailand* (Cambridge: Cambridge University Press, 1970. Cambridge Studies in Social Anthropology. Also his *The Buddhist Saints of the Forest and the Cult of Amulets* (Cambridge: Cambridge University Press, 1984. Cambridge Studies in Social Anthropology) and M. Carrithers, *The Forest Monks of Sri Lanka: An Anthropological and Historical Study* (Delhi: Oxford University Press, 1983).

37 For a detailed discussion of the relevant sections of these works see Kawasaki Shinjo 'Principle of Life According to Bhavya' in R.K. Sharma, (ed.) *Researches in Indian Buddhist Philosophy: Essays in Honour of Professor Alex Wayman* (Delhi: Motilal Banarsidass, n.d.), pp. 69–81.

38 Recently published for the first time in moveable type, together with modern Japanese translation and notes, by Sueki Fumihiko *Heian shoki Bukkyo shiso-shi no kenkyu* Shunju sha, 1995. Also Sueki Fumihiko 'Annen: The Philosopher who Japanized Buddhism,' *Acta Asiatica* 66 (1994).

39 D.T. Suzuki, *Zen and Japanese Culture* (London: Routledge and Kegan Paul, 1959), p. 22f. On *wabi* and *sabi* also see James D. Whitehill, 'Ecological Consciousness and Values: Japanese Perspectives' in Schultz, Robert C. and J. Donald Hughes (eds) *Ecological Consciousness: Essays from the Earthday X Colloquium University of Denver, April 21–24, 1980* (Washington: University Press of America, 1981), pp. 165–182.

40 D.T. Suzuki 'Love of Nature' *Eastern Buddhist* VII/1 (1936) reprinted in *Zen and Japanese Culture, op cit.* p. 334.

41 *Op cit* p. 177.

42 Robert H. Scharf, 'The Zen of Japanese Nationalism' in Donald S. Lopez, Jr. (ed.) *Curators of the Buddha: The Study of Buddhism under Colonialism* (Chicago and London: University of Chicago Press, 1995), p. 124. For a detailed analysis of *nihonjinron* thought see Peter Dale, *The Myth of Japanese Uniqueness* (London: Routledge, 1986).

43 S.N. Eisenstadt, 'The Japanese Attitude to Nature: A Framework of Basic Ontological Conceptions' in Bruun, Ole and Arne Kalland (eds) *Asian Perceptions of Nature: A Critical Approach* (London: Curzon Press, 1995 pp. 189–214), p. 190.

44 Augustin Berque, 'The Sense of Nature and its Relation to Space in Japan' in Hendry, Joy and Jonathan Weber (eds) *Interpreting Japanese Society: Anthropological Approaches* (Oxford: JASO, 1986. JASO Occasional Papers No. 5, p. 100–110), p. 103.

45 Lynn White, 'The Historical Roots of Our Ecological Crisis' *Science* 155 (1967) pp. 1203–1207. White's thesis has been extraordinarily influential and is repeated in most of its essential features by John Passmore who considers environmentalism to be a form of 'anti-scientific nature mysticism' with no basis in the history of Western civilization. See John Passmore, *Man's Responsibility for Nature: Ecological Problems and Western Traditions* (London: Duckworth,1974), p. 123. Peter Beyer, *Religion and Globalisation* (London: Sage, 994), p. 207 argues that the sociological treatment of religious environmentalism has generally proceeded as if White were correct.

46 See Toni Huber, 'Traditional Environmental Protectionism in Tibet Reconsidered' *Tibet Journal* 16/3 (1991) pp. 63–77: p. 72.

47 On the magnification of the significance of meditation in the modern period see Robert H. Sharf, 'Buddhist Modernism and the Rhetoric of Meditative Experience' *Numen* 42 (1995) pp. 228–283.

48 See my 'Getting to Grips with Buddhist Environmentalism: A Provisional Typology' *Journal of Buddhist Ethics* 2 (1995) pp. 173–190; and 'Buddhist Environmental Ethics and Detraditionalisation: The Case of EcoBuddhism' *Religion* 25 (1995) pp. 199–211.

CHAPTER SIX

Buddhism and Abortion

Robert Florida

At one level, the Buddhist approach to abortion is very simple. Ancient teachings and current religious teachers agree that abortion is a wrong act, that it has grievous consequences for those who do it, and that it should be avoided purely and simply. Of course, at other levels, the issue is neither pure nor simple. This chapter will review some basic Buddhist teachings on the ethics of abortion, then will discuss the situation in Thailand, Korea, and Japan, all of which are countries with both strong Buddhist traditions and high rates of abortion.

In contrast to the situation in Western countries, there has been relatively little serious discussion of abortion as a religious and ethical issue in Buddhist countries. The debate in the West has been carried on to a very high level of learned philosophical and theological reflection alongside a lively political and popular debate with religious leaders, politicians, and ordinary citizens making strong declarations. In Thailand, Japan, and Korea the Buddhist establishment – that is, the leaders of the Buddhist *saṅgha* have said very little indeed on the issue. Some contemporary Buddhist thinkers and scholars of Buddhism in the West and a much smaller number in the East, mostly laymen and laywomen, are beginning to address bioethical issues systematically, but the field is relatively new and open. It is worth noting that nearly all of the writers in this field are either Westerners or Asians educated in the West. Politicians and medical people have mainly carried on the public debates in Asia. Buddhist organisations and leaders have said very little; and theological issues have very little weight in the public debates. In fact, the local Roman Catholic Churches in Thailand, Japan, and Korea, though representing small minorities, have probably had more public impact than the much larger Buddhist organisations.

Some Buddhist ethical principles[1]

The Buddhist religious path[2] aims to liberate all sentient beings from a continuous cycle of painful existence (*saṃsāra*). We are trapped by our own selfish impulses of passion, aggression, and ignorance, which cause us to be reborn again and again only to suffer, decay, and die. Buddha taught a way of life involving morality, contemplation, and ultimately wisdom, which was so deep that it resulted in liberation from the cycle of rebirth and suffering. Such wisdom involves understanding that all beings are contingent and interdependent (*pratītyasamutpāda*) and leads directly to compassion because the wise know that the suffering of self and others is driven by selfish and deluded grasping, which can be overcome.

Practically, wisdom leads to selfless action for the sake of others. Thus *prajñā*, or wisdom, and *karuṇā*, or compassion, are the two major Buddhist ideals, the first relating to the realm of ultimacy and the second to the world of day to day existence. Without ultimate wisdom one will be defective in *upāya* or skilful means for helping others. Moral behaviour in Buddhist systems then, is not an absolute in itself; it is a means towards a religious end, the transcendence of those selfish cravings, which bind all beings to an unending round of suffering. Accordingly all moral acts are understood either to be *kuśala karma*, skilful deeds which are beneficial to self and others, or *akuśala karma*, unskilful deeds which harm self and others. In popular Buddhism *kuśala karma* is 'making merit' which can be achieved through ethical behaviour, generosity (especially to the *saṅgha*), and rituals.

One's deeds or karma obey fixed laws of causality, and the resultant karma determines a person's destiny. Basically the moral consequences of an act are determined by the will or motivation (*cetanā*) of the actor. If the will behind an act is driven by greed, hatred, or delusion, which Buddhists understand as the three poisonous roots of selfish craving, then the act is *akuśala* or unskilful. Every act involves body, speech, and mind working in conjunction. Mind starts a train of activity, and if greed, hatred, or delusion motivates mind, then the speech and bodily activity which follow are doomed to be unskilful. Unskilful acts always have negative consequences for the actor and generally for the recipient of the act. This is not a fatalistic or pessimistic teaching as the Buddhist path provides practical ways to replace unskilful with skilful acts.

Buddhist precepts are designed to provide guidelines for skilful activity. When the guidelines are followed negative karmic consequences are avoided and good results accrue. From the Buddhist vantagepoint of the middle way, there are two basic errors one could fall into on this issue. If one denies the reality of karmic consequences, one has adopted the nihilistic extreme view, which tends towards antinomianism and the abandonment of the precepts. The eternalistic extreme view takes moral rules as absolute, resulting in inflexible dogmatic positions.

138

Thus even the precepts of morality laid down by the Buddha are not absolute commandments. They are clearly understood as 'rules of training,' which the individual undertakes in order to advance along the religious path. In fact, so little are they absolute commandments, that the precepts have been used since the earliest days of the Buddhist community as temporary vows, freely assumed by individuals for specified lengths of time. A lay meditator, for example, might undertake to follow the rule of training to abstain from the misuse of sensual pleasures for the period of a retreat. The relativity of the precepts is further demonstrated by the fact that there are traditionally five for the ordinary person, eight for the advanced laity, and more than two hundred for monks and nuns.

Dr. Hema Goonatilake, a Theravadin Buddhist from Sri Lanka makes this point very well:

> It is ... to be understood that precepts are rules of training and not commandments from God, the Buddha or anyone else. It is only an undertaking by one, to oneself, if one is convinced that it is a good practice to observe.[3]

This fundamental difference of attitude towards the nature of the basic religious laws of human life underlies and helps to explain, in my opinion, many of the differences and misunderstandings that arise between Eastern and Western people.

Buddhist embryology[4]

Interestingly enough, there are several places where Buddha himself discussed conception and fetal development.[5] He taught that there are three factors necessary for rebirth into a new life: (1) intercourse must take place (2) when the woman is in her fertile period and (3) there must be an 'intermediate being' or *vijñāna* present and ready for rebirth. From the very earliest days, the theory of co-conditioned causality, or *pratītyasamutpāda*, the teaching that every thing in the universe is interrelated with every other thing, was interpreted in terms of the details of the process of rebirth, providing a Buddhist embryology.[6] The basic idea is that ignorant, selfishly motivated, acts in our past lives establish the karmic foundations or preconditions that give rise to our rebirth in another life. The third link in this process (*vijñāna*) was described by Vasubandhu, a great Buddhist commentator of the fourth or fifth century CE, as the physical and mental components of a living being at the moment of conception, that is, the moment of reincarnation.[7]

What all this boils down to is that traditionally Buddhists have understood that the human being begins at the instant of conception, when sperm, egg and *vijñāna* come together. Contemporary Buddhist ethicists, such as Taniguchi, maintain this point of view: 'there is no qualitative difference between an unborn fetus and a born individual.'[8] R.H.B. Exell of the Siam Institute of Technology, in a recent article, attempts to understand modern science and technology from the point of view of Buddha's original teachings. After considering the quality of life of the human fetus from the modern scientific view, he concludes: 'These observations suggest that abortion should be regarded as killing a separate human being, not just removing a part of the mother.'[9] All of this fits very well with the fundamental Buddhist insight that all living beings are interdependent, which is most obvious in the case of the fetus. This point is reinforced, I think, by the Buddha's canonical description of childbearing as being divided into four stages: the fertile period, pregnancy, birth and nursing.[10] There seems to be no distinction in kind made between the prenatal child and the newborn.

Indeed, modern embryological research confirms the Buddhist teaching that a separate, co-dependent human life begins at the moment of conception. The first sentence of K.L. Moore's *The Developing Human: Clinically Oriented Embryology* clearly and succinctly makes the point: '*Development is a continuous process* that begins when an ovum is fertilized by a sperm and ends at death.'[11] As Keown puts it, 'Although the basic Buddhist position on how and when individual life begins was formulated over two thousand years ago, the conclusions reached are in some respects remarkably modern.'[12]

On the other hand, the traditional Buddhist belief about the nature of the environment and the quality of the life of the fetus is very different from the prevailing modern western view. Most of us westerners seem to imagine that the fetus lives a peaceful, blissful life, floating without a care in the warm protective environment of the womb. The Buddhist idea is quite the opposite. I quote from *Three Worlds According to King Ruang*, written by a great king of the Sukhothai era in the fourteenth century. It closely follows the Pali scriptures and their commentaries and is an extremely influential source for traditional Thai thought.[13]

> The baby has great trouble while it is in the mother's abdomen: the place is extremely revolting and disgusting; it is damp and full of bad smells caused by the eighty broods of worms and parasites that live there. . . . [T]hese worms and parasites are all mixed up in the mother's abdomen and cover the body of the fetus like a skin disease. . . . [B]lood and lymph run down all over its body, dripping at all times; the baby is like a monkey who, when it rains, sits in the hollow of a tree clutching its fists in a sluggish and dejected way.[14]

Furthermore, it suffers greatly from being confined as though in a narrow jar and is burnt by the digestive juices of the mother. In short, its entire existence in the womb, from conception to birth, is characterised by relentless pain and disgusting filth.

The Buddhist attitude towards human life is profoundly ambivalent. On one hand, to be born at all in any of the six realms of existence, including the human, is regarded as the result of unresolved karmic problems from past lives.[15] Thus the human fetus is not particularly a blameless being, and its miserable state of existence is a very direct manifestation of the first holy truth that Lord Buddha proclaimed: that all of life is ill, unsatisfactory, and subject to suffering. On the other hand, to be born as a human being is to be born in one of the two fortunate realms; the other is the world of the gods. There are six realms altogether, four unfortunate and two fortunate. To be a human offers a rare opportunity to take up the holy path of Buddha dharma, the only way to escape the endless wheel of existence.[16]

Buddhist ethical views on abortion

We will now consider how the basic precepts of Buddhist morality apply to the question of abortion. The first five precepts which all Buddhists, whether monk, nun or lay person, are encouraged to follow are the following:

> I undertake to observe the rule
> > to abstain from taking life;
> > to abstain from taking what is not given;
> > to abstain from sensuous misconduct;
> > to abstain from false speech;
> > to abstain from intoxicants as tending to cloud the mind.[17]

Although the first precept against taking life includes all sentient life, the taking of human life was a much more serious offence.

Note that the form of these precepts shows that they are understood to be personal commitments or practical guidelines to be undertaken provisionally as steps on a religious path. All Buddhist practitioners are expected to try to follow the first five, and their violation involves karmic consequences for anyone, Buddhist or not. Nonetheless, they are not absolute commandments.

As we have seen, Buddhists understand the fetus to be a human being; therefore, abortion obviously should be covered under the first precept. Indeed it is. The *Vinaya* section of the Pali Canon, which is the most ancient of the Theravāda scriptures, contains a passage, which makes this point very clearly.

> An ordained monk should not intentionally deprive a living thing of life even if it is only an ant. A monk who deliberately deprives a human being of life, even to the extent of causing an abortion, is no longer a follower of the Buddha. As a flat stone broken asunder

cannot be put back together again, a monk who deliberately deprives a human being of life is no longer a follower of the Buddha.[18]

In other words, such a monk will receive the maximum penalty; he will be expelled from the order and may never be readmitted in his present lifetime. The text continues to give a useful gloss on the term 'human being': 'A human being [exists] in the interval between the first moment when mind arises in the mother's womb [that is to say] the first manifestation of ... *vijñāna*, and death.' There are also seven *Vinaya* cases where Lord Buddha makes rulings concerning monks who were involved with abortions.[19] In all cases, it is clear that they were treated like any other homicide, and the penalties were proportioned in accord with the intent of the monk and the result of the procedure. When there was no intent to kill, as in the case where the abortifacient that the monk prescribed failed to kill the unborn child but killed the mother, the penalty was grave, but less than the maximum. Similarly, when both the mother and fetus survived, the monk was strongly condemned, but not permanently expelled since no one was killed even though fetal death had been intended.

Buddhaghosa, a fifth century Theravāda commentator, who is still very influential today, in commenting on a *Vinaya* passage, made it very clear that taking fetal life was as serious an offence as killing an adult. In the case of digging a trap with the intent to kill someone, he concluded the following:

> If a pregnant woman falls in and dies along with her child, this counts as two breaches of the precept against taking life. If the child [alone] dies there is one [breach], and if the child does not die but the mother dies there is also one.[20]

The early scriptures and commentators are clear and consistent. Human life begins very early in the womb, and killing a fetus is equally as grave an unskilful act as killing an adult person.

Tibetan sources, which are considerably later, support the early Theravādin view. Tibetan Buddhists early and contemporary, drawing on their *Vinaya* tradition, uniformly condemn abortion on the same scale of offensiveness as any other taking of life.[21] Tibetan medical texts, which were passed on through the monastic system, also are very clear in their embryology that the fetus is fully human at a very early stage, as soon as the *vijñāna* joins with the female and male physical components that are united through sexual intercourse. 'From the moment of conception, through karma, the embryo's mind spreads the breath of life.'[22] It is not at all suprising to find Tibetan Buddhist leaders, from long ago to the current Dalai Lama, condemning the practice of abortion.[23] Tibetan Buddhists, then, agree that abortion is a serious unskilful act as it involves violence, with the intent to kill, against a fetal human being.

A very recent article by Michael G. Barnhart attempts to make a Buddhist argument to justify abortion. He focuses on Damien Keown's work primarily and argues that Keown has reified the *vijñāna* into something akin to the Christian soul or pan-Indian *ātman*, a fatal error for a Buddhist. More particularly Barnhart takes issue with Keown's account of the timing of the appearance of the *vijñāna* in human prenatal development.

> Buddhism need not take *vijñāna* to be present at any particular point in the process of embryonic development. That is, *vijñāna* or consciousness is present whenever one would customarily say it is and that could be just as well at viability as at conception.[24]

On both accounts, in my view, Barnhart is wrong. Keown's presentation of the nature of *vijñāna* stays close to the tradition and avoids the error of reification. On the second point, Keown concludes after a very careful consideration of both Buddhist textual evidence and contemporary medical research[25] that it is impossible to know precisely when in the process of prenatal development that a fully human life is present. Nonetheless, it is very clear from all sources that the *vijñāna* is present very early indeed in the process of human development. The most common view of Buddhists today is that there is a fully human being present from the moment of conception.

There is some controversy about whether or not, from the Buddhist point of view, a late term abortion is a more unskilful act than one performed early on in the pregnancy. Trevor Ling and Peter Harvey both report that some Buddhists believe that the bad karma for aborting a large fetus is proportionally greater than the bad karma for aborting a small one.[26] In an earlier paper,[27] I took the same line and quoted the following passage from Buddhaghosa in support.

> 'I undertake to observe the rule to abstain from taking life.' ... 'Taking life,' means to murder anything that lives. It refers to the striking and killing of living beings ... 'Taking life' is then the will to kill anything that one perceives as having life, to act so as to terminate the life-force in it, in so far as the will finds expression in bodily action or in speech. With regard to animals it is worse to kill large ones than small. Because a more extensive effort is involved. Even where the effort is the same, the difference in substance must be considered. In the case of humans the killing is the more blameworthy the more virtuous they are. Apart from that, the extent of the offence is proportionate to the intensity of the wish to kill.[28]

In discussing a very similar passage from Buddhaghosa, Keown makes the point that the moral distinction based on relative size applies only in regard to animals, and that in all cases treated in scripture and by the classical commentators, the size of the fetus is not taken into account.[29] All abortions are treated equally, regardless of the stage of fetal development, as culpable homicide.

Stott independently comes to the same conclusion as Keown, that size does not matter, maintaining the classical view that the *vijñāna* joins with the sperm and egg at the moment of conception thus:

> It is not a 'partially souled' individual nor a 'potential' being but an embodied sentient being, however small. It would thus be difficult for any Western Buddhist to make the claim that the smaller the fetus, the less serious the abortion.[30]

While Keown and Stott are right on this issue, I would nonetheless argue that a good Buddhist case could be made for saying that late term abortions are worse than early ones. 'If the criterion of causing suffering is to be taken as a measure of how bad the karma is, then killing a young embryo would appear to be less bad than killing a well developed fetus.'[31] This contemporary common-sense comment by Exell fits in very well with basic Buddhist ethical principles. There are good clinical reasons to agree, and morally it is somehow intuitively obvious that the earlier an abortion the less bad, which is also what contemporary Thai Buddhists maintain.[32] The physical and mental harm done to the mother, and to the abortionists, is less the earlier that the deed is done. Buddhaghosa's comments about the effort involved and the intensity of the wish to kill also seem pertinent. My view is that although all abortions are condemned by Buddhists as the taking of human life, as the pregnancy progresses, the ensuing suffering and bad karma of an abortion increase.

There are no scriptural or authoritative commentaries on abortions performed for therapeutic reasons.[33] Perhaps such were beyond the capacities of ancient Asian medicine. It would seem to me that there is no clear guidance at all for a Buddhist caught in the medically rare situation of a conflict between the life of the mother and of the fetus. Buddhaghosa's reasoning from relative size, as Keown points out, would not apply. Buddhaghosa did say that killing a more virtuous person was more blameworthy than killing someone of lesser virtue, but how could this principle possibly be applied in such a case? It would seem that the people involved are left to rely on their wisdom and compassion to make a very difficult decision.

It seems clear that in cases of pregnancies, which harm the health of the mother but do not endanger her life, abortion would generally be ruled out. Procuring the death of the fetus would be a grave violation of the first precept. Perhaps if it were certain that the harm done to the mother and to the community as a whole would be very much greater if she had the child than if she had the abortion, it might be possible to justify the abortion as a form of justifiable homicide. However, since there is no reliable way to make such a measure, and since the killing of the unborn child is an unskilful act, the abortion should be foregone. All of the abortions discussed in the ancient texts were done to terminate unwanted pregnancies that would have resulted in socio-economic hardships for the mother.[34] As we have seen, they were all strongly condemned. Furthermore, as discussed more fully below, bearing and raising a child as an act of selfless compassion for others, exemplifies living the Buddhist path.

So far we have looked at abortion primarily from the outside, as an objective act, so to speak. However, from the Buddhist view, it is the internal motivation of an act that primarily determines its karmic or moral nature. It would seem that abortion involves several grievous errors.[35] Greed, hatred, and delusion, the three root drives of unskilful men and women, seem to apply all too well to abortion decisions. Greed, or passionate attachment, would lie behind persons' considering only their own interests or pleasures in the situation. It would also solidify the notion that an 'I' owned the fetus and could do with it what 'I' would. Hatred would motivate one to strike out to eliminate the perceived cause of discomfort, the fetus. Delusion might cloud one's understanding and lead to denial that the fetus is a living being. It also could result in a condition of apathy where one, avoiding responsibility for oneself, blindly followed advice to terminate the pregnancy. Underlying these three 'poisons' of greed, hatred, and delusion are even more fundamental errors. The three poisons arise through lack of insight into the interconnectedness of all beings, a misguided sense of difference between I and other. When *prajñā* is so lacking, then so too *karuṇā* or compassion will also fall short, and *upāya* or skilful means will not be conspicuous.

In the light of co-conditioned causality, the moral consequences of abortion do not only concern the death of the fetus. Abortion also entails physical and mental trauma to the woman who chooses to abort and has karmic consequences for the technicians, advisors, friends, and family involved. Somewhat surprisingly, Buddhists also consider the karmic effect of an abortion on the fetus itself:

> Having just experienced the trauma of death and the terrifying uncertainty of the intermediate state, at last he has found a point upon which his energies can focus. When the consciousness is abruptly cut loose again, the effect may well be to accentuate feelings of fear and insecurity which will make an unfavourable rebirth more likely.[36]

Thus the unskilfulness of an abortion is increased because it steals away a rare opportunity for another living being to be reborn as a human, the only status where one can advance spiritually.

The seriousness karmic consequences of abortion are illustrated in the *Three Worlds According to King Ruang*, where a special variety of female hungry ghost, a very unfortunate rebirth, is described:

[They] are generally naked and have a strong and revolting odor coming from every part of their bodies. There are lots of flies swarming all over them and eating them, making holes in their bodies. Their bodies are very skinny ... and [they] cannot find anything to eat.[37]

Twice a day they give birth to seven babies and each time, driven by their terrible hunger, gobble them down. They find themselves in this woeful state as a result of having been abortionists in past lives and having uttered a falsified oath of innocence.[38] Abortion is also mentioned in other Thai texts as one of the three special offences for women that lead to unfortunate rebirths. The other two are to treat her husband or her husband's relatives with contempt.[39]

Sexual impropriety is often a factor in the situation where one might consider abortion as a solution. The precept concerning sexuality, is explained by Buddhaghosa in this way:

'I undertake to observe the rule to abstain from sensuous misconduct.' ... The offence is the more serious, the more moral and virtuous the person transgressed against. Four factors are involved: someone who should not be gone into, the thought of cohabiting with that one, the actions, which lead to such cohabitation, and its actual performance. There is only one way of carrying it out: with one's own body.[40]

Sensuous misconduct leads to an awkward pregnancy, which leads to thoughts of abortion, which may then lead to killing the fetus, resulting in so much unfortunate karma to bear. One unskilful act generates another as long as one lives unmindfully.

This leads us back to the religious context of this discussion. What Buddhists aim to do is to perfect themselves by following the path that the Buddha blazed for them. It involves replacing unwholesome roots of action, namely the selfish drives of greed, hatred, and delusion with wholesome motives: loving-kindness, compassion, joy for others, and equanimity. Similarly, the first precept, which is expressed negatively as abstention from taking life, has a positive form as well: 'With deeds of loving kindness, I purify my body.'[41] The application to abortion is obvious.

Steven Aung, MD describes how *mettā* or loving-kindness should pervade a Theravāda Buddhist physician's practice. What he says about loving-kindness in his profession, also can serve as a guide to everyone's day to day life.

It should be given with ... selflessness, signifying that one must serve others without any expectation of reward; karuna (compassion), implying gentle, warm, open, and intelligent communication; [and] ... pure joy at the good fortune of others.

Pinit Ratanakul, one of Thailand's leading bioethicists, also places compassion at the centre of Buddhist ethical thought. 'Compassion is self-giving and self-denial – the voluntary sacrifice of one's rights beyond that which is socially obligated.'[42] Thus any pregnancy, even if very inconvenient, is an opportunity for the woman and the other people involved to practice loving-kindness and compassion, by selflessly nurturing and protecting the developing person. Abortion, on the other hand, seems to cultivate the opposite of these virtues. At any rate, whatever one does, one's acts will ripen, with those skilful acts that are beneficial to self and others bearing good fruit, and while those unskilful acts that harm self and others yielding bad fruit.

David Stott stresses a similar point that is made by Mahāyāna Buddhists. 'The mother's care for her child from conception to adulthood is held up as an embodiment of the selfless compassion toward which we should aspire in order to repay our debt to all our mothers, that is to say, all sentient beings.'[43] This imagery of the mother's unselfish love is, in fact, a central part of one of the most widespread meditative exercises used to nurture loving-kindness and compassion in the Mahāyāna tradition. Needless to say, abortion does not sit very well with this; it seems fundamentally out of step with the Mahāyāna emphasis on the mindful sacrifice of oneself for the good of others.

Finally, it should be noted that the Buddhist tradition is not at all pro-natalist.[44] While Buddhists do not scorn the procreative life of the householder, the way of the celibate monk, who abstains from the pleasures and entanglements of sex and family, is understood to be the better way. Similarly, it should also be mentioned that contraception, if the methods used do no harm to fetus or lovers, is considered to be skilful means. As the contemporary Tibetan leader, Kenchen Thrangu Rinpoche, put it:

> Personally I see no great fault in preventing conception. But of course once conception has occurred, to kill the unborn child would be to destroy a sentient being, to commit an act of killing and would therefore be an unvirtuous act.[45]

Obviously, then, from the Buddhist point of view, preventing unwanted pregnancies is far better than terminating them.

Abortion and Buddhism in Thailand[46]

Thailand is one of the most devout Theravāda Buddhist countries, and the people there are very well aware of their tradition's condemnation of abortion. Nonetheless, abortion is quite widespread. In January 1994, the Bangkok authorities were scandalised by the discovery of thirty-four aborted fetuses beside a main road leading from Bangkok to Ayutthya.[47] They were presumed to come from one of the estimated one hundred illegal abortion clinics found along that route. Abortion, as we will see later, is legal only under certain controlled circumstances in Thailand. However, in this case, as in so many aspects of life in Thailand, what the law prescribes is not necessarily what actually is the practice. In this case, the authorities announced their resolve to see that the law would be enforced, and some arrests and convictions of abortionists were made from 1994 to 1996.[48] In 1997 authorities raided the family planning clinics of the Population and Community Development Association,[49] a highly respected non-governmental agency, through which abortions could be obtained.

In Thailand most of the research on abortion has been in the social sciences or medicine[50] with a few works by scholars of religion. I have found only a very few scattered statements in publications by monks and official religious spokesmen on the issue. In large part, I believe this is a reflection of the Thai traditional attitude that monks as world renouncers should be above the ordinary earthy concerns of those who remain enmeshed in day to day life. Monks are to serve as exemplars and as purified fields of merit for individuals and the nation by devoting themselves to studying the Buddhist scriptures, performing rites and public service such as education, and (for a few) dedicating themselves to meditation. Thus most monks have little reason to pay close attention to contemporary social issues; indeed, such concerns can lead to difficulties with government and *saṅgha* officials. Furthermore, their form of intellectual discipline, the minute study and memorisation of ancient texts, does not encourage critical reflection on the modern world.

One of the things that impresses me about the learned books and sermons produced by the official *saṅgha* today is that they hardly seem aware of the twentieth century. Take, for example, the recent book, *Plan of Life*, which was written by a leading monk, dedicated to Her Majesty Queen Sirikit on her sixtieth birthday in 1992, commended by the Supreme Patriarch of Thailand, and published jointly by a prestigious foundation, an Air Chief Marshal, and a Buddhist university.[51] This book is an inspirational review of Pali texts and traditional commentaries, but almost completely ignores the modern realities of Thai life. Abortion is not mentioned.

It is very interesting that a plan of life published in 1992, for all practical purposes, could have appeared in 1792. Please note that this is not particularly meant as a criticism of the Thai Buddhist establishment. Perhaps the greatest service that Thai Buddhism can provide to the modern world is to preserve its pure traditions. Of course, there is a real danger that if the *saṅgha* does not effectively address current concerns, Thai youth and the modernised section of the population, which is increasingly in charge of the country's development, will simply find Buddhism irrelevant. Indeed, sometimes it is already difficult to discern traditional religious ideals in contemporary practices, and one hears constant complaints that the young know very little about their own religion. This dilemma of Thai Buddhists, how to maintain their ancient and noble tradition while also being relevant and effective as Buddhists today, is obvious in the issue of abortion.

One high *saṅgha* official, in an oral communication to one of my informants, said that abortion clearly entails a violation of the first precept against the taking of life, and is therefore always a sin and out of the question for those who live as monks in the religious world. However, most of us live in another world, the ordinary secular realm, which has different requirements. For example, in the secular world we think that capital punishment is necessary, and the monks will accept it to the extent that they will sermonise and comfort the condemned person and the executioner, but would never do the actual killing. Similarly, the monks will eat food prepared from living beings, but will never act as a butcher, and will consecrate soldiers but never go to war. Thus the *saṅgha* may tolerate abortion while never encouraging it.

Indeed, the *Vinaya* rules that govern the life of the Thai monk are very clear that any monk who arranges or encourages an abortion is subject to expulsion from the order with no chance of return in his current lifetime. The Thai handbook of monastic rules makes it very clear that the rule against taking human life applies in this case: 'By the body of a human being is meant that which appears in the womb of the mother at the time of conception, lasting until the time of death.'[52] Acharn Passano, the Abbot of Wat Pah Nanachat, noted that there really was no reason for the *saṅgha* leadership to make special public statements about abortion as what they must say is covered in this *Vinaya* teaching. It is both cut and dried and well known by everyone. He went on to add that Buddhist morality is a personal undertaking, not something imposed from without, and that abortion is therefore a personal moral dilemma which every one must decide for her or himself. What monks must uphold in these matters, he said, is very clear, but standards for monks and for lay people are very different. Nonetheless, abortion is 'basically unskilful action.'

Professor Siralee Sirilai of the Faculty of Social Sciences and Humanities at Mahidol University, Bangkok, points out that the main Buddhist criterion for moral decision-making is whether or not the act has wholesome motivation.

> A skilful deed should work against greed, hatred, and delusion, and thus will be for the good of self and others. However, there are also secondary criteria such as 'wholesome-unwholesome, usefulness-unusefulness, trouble-untrouble, admirability-blameworthiness.'[53]

She thinks that for the world renouncers, only the first criterion can be taken into account, but that for the Buddhist layperson the secondary can also come into play. Therefore, in some circumstances, abortion could perhaps be morally permissible.

While Thailand has enshrined religious toleration in its constitution and in the hearts of its people, over ninety per cent of Thais are Theravāda Buddhists; and the laws and customs of the country are both consciously and unconsciously informed by Buddhist principles. Since these principles recognise the fetus as a human being from the moment of conception and take the precept against killing as the primary one, one would not expect to find abortion on demand permitted in Thai law. In fact the current law, the Penal Code of 1956, specifies strict penalties: three years in prison or a fine of 3000 baht or both, for a woman who causes an abortion for herself or who procures one from another party. The penalty for the abortionist is greater, five years or 5000 baht or both. If the woman is injured or killed in the process, the penalties are much more severe.[54]

However, therapeutic abortions, those performed by qualified medical practitioners, are permitted in two circumstances: first, if 'it is necessary for the sake of the woman's health' and, second, if the pregnancy is the result of rape.[55] Since 'woman's health' is not defined, the medical practitioner has a great deal of freedom in deciding when to perform therapeutic abortions. As to rape, the second circumstance under Thai law that legitimates abortion, it would seem to me that, strictly speaking, even though the outrage of rape involves both violence and sexual misconduct, there are not adequate dharmic grounds for an abortion, since abortion always involves the taking of human life. One unskilful act does not justify another. The point is to break the chain.

If one looks at official figures, abortion would appear to be a very rare phenomenon in Thailand. Only five therapeutic abortions per year were reported in the 1960s.[56] However, as so often is true in Thailand, what is officially reported is not necessarily what is actually happening. There have been several major studies that attempt to determine the scope of abortion practice in the Kingdom.[57] While the numbers do not exactly coincide from study to study, they all confirm that the abortion rate in Thailand is rather high, probably in the range of around 300,000 per year, or at a rate of 37 abortions per 1000 women of childbearing age.[58] To compare with other countries, some other rates for the same period were: Canada 11.1, Hungary 35.3, Japan 22.6 officially but probably between 65 and 90, Singapore 44.5, USA 24.2, and the USSR an incredible 181.[59]

In a hospital study done in Thailand, published in 1987, 17 per cent of the abortions surveyed were therapeutic, that is, performed by physicians in hospitals, and the remainder were illegal abortions.[60] However, in fact, the proportion of medically performed abortions done under good clinical conditions is probably greater than this study shows because many are done in private clinics, government and NGO clinics, and doctors' offices. Since private services are expensive and public services are concentrated in Bangkok and other major cities, 'The majority of abortion-seeking women are still economically forced to choose low cost services from unqualified practitioners.'[61] Some of the illegal abortionists offer relatively clean and safe services, but many of them are appalling, resulting in many deaths and severe complications in one third of the cases.[62] The two most popular methods for illegal abortions are uterine massage and the introduction of a fluid into the cervical canal.

Judging from many conversations with Thais including some in medical fields, it would seem that most believe abortion is primarily a problem for single women who have misbehaved and who wish to conceal their sexual activity because premarital virginity is highly valued and unwed mothers are disgraced. Furthermore, it is thought that abortion is an urban problem primarily because traditional morality is said to be weaker in the cities than in the country. However, the reality is far different. A study done in 1987 shows that 'the majority of illegal abortion clients were married women employed in agricultural work.'[63] 91 per cent of the therapeutic abortions and 85 per cent of the illegal ones were obtained by married women.[64] A study published in 1975 found a high degree of acceptance of abortion amongst countrywomen 'because it has been the traditional means to birth control in rural areas.'[65] This was born out in a study done in northeastern Thailand, published in 1981, which found a very high illegal abortion rate there of 107 per 1000 rural women between the ages of fifteen and forty-four.[66]

Cleo Odzer, who did field research for her doctorate in the Patpong community of Bangkok prostitutes, noted that many of the women she knew, even though they were well-versed in contraceptive techniques, became pregnant. Perhaps a little surprisingly, none of them chose to have abortions. She advances several reasons to explain this.[67] First, the group of prostitutes she studied was financially very well off indeed in that they worked for well-established businesses that specialised in Western males as clients. On average a Thai prostitute earns twenty-five times the average female wage in the country,[68] and Patpong women make far more than most. Additionally, most of them came from the northeastern province of Isan, and sent much of their money to support their family. Their families generally were quite happy to take the children to raise. Thus the women were able to keep and support their children without much difficulty and could enjoy the pleasures of motherhood.

Socially, Patpong women had three strikes against them. They were female, Isan, and prostitutes, all markers of low status in Thailand. One way that a woman can gain merit or improve her karma is to bear children. Child bearing itself is seen as a manifestation of compassion and loving-kindness. Furthermore, one of the most highly meritorious acts in Thai Buddhism is for a man to become a monk. There is no order of nuns. The mother of a monk, however, attains the merit of his world-renunciation. Thus one of the best ways for a prostitute to accrue merit is through having sons. Finally, as a good Buddhist, she would shrink from inflicting suffering

151

on an unborn child, and would wish to avoid the considerable additional bad karma that having an abortion would bring her.

There have been many opinion polls taken on the issue of abortion in Thailand.[69] None of them asked questions relating directly to Buddhist beliefs, but indirectly all their results seem to reflect the marked dissonance between Thai religious theory, which judges abortion to be an unskilful violation of Buddhist principles, and Thai practical reality, which is that abortion is very common. In one study (1978), for example, the majority of the respondents believed that abortion is an immoral act, yet they also thought the law should be liberalised to allow it on socio-economic grounds and to broaden the medical reasons.[70] There is very little support for abortion on demand, no doubt in large part because Thais are very well aware of the precept against killing and the Buddhist idea that the fetus is a fully human being.

The most recent survey, published in 1998, basically confirms the earlier polls. The sample included 11 women who had been admitted to hospital for complications suffered after illegal abortions, 22 obstetricians, and 593 nursing staff and students.[71] All of the patients were Buddhists who were aware that abortion was both illegal and condemned by their religious tradition. Not surprisingly, most reported negative feelings after the procedure, including 36 per cent who feared for the bad karma they had accrued. As to the medical staff, nearly all supported abortions for women who had been raped, who were HIV positive, or who had contracted German measles in the first trimester of pregnancy. On the other hand, 70 per cent were opposed to abortions on socio-economic grounds. A very high proportion of the medical personnel surveyed believed that the availability of abortion was a threat to Thai cultural values. The questionnaire did not ask about Buddhism explicitly, but Thai culture is largely informed by Buddhist traditions. They also felt that sex education, family planning, and better family values should be encouraged and taught to eliminate the situations, which drive women to abortion decisions. In spite of their reservations about the negative effects of abortion on Thai society, 55 per cent of the medical personnel favoured a liberalisation of the abortion laws.[72]

Encouraged by the overwhelming support to widen the grounds for therapeutic abortions, reformers made several attempts in the 1970s and 1980s to have the law changed in Parliament.[73] The Buddhist community in Thailand is divided on the abortion issue. Major General Chamlong Srimuang, a leading figure in Thai democracy, one time political head of Bangkok, and a dedicated lay Buddhist who observes eight precepts, is firmly opposed to any liberalisation of the abortion law. He and his followers base their position on the absolute sanctity of life in the Buddhist tradition. It is perhaps worth noting that when General Chamlong was mayor of Bangkok, very little was done to suppress the illegal abortion clinics and quacks. Others, including some monastic leaders, take a much more liberal view, pointing out that in Buddhist morality the intent of the action has much to do with the karmic result of the act. They argue that, in some cases, for example when the mother's life is endangered by the pregnancy, abortion could, therefore, be a skilful act. At any rate Chamlong, when he was Governor of Bangkok, in alliance with Roman Catholics, led the fight against changing the law on abortion. Nothing got through Parliament. Delayed by religious opposition, various reform bills failed to work their way through the system before governments were dissolved, whether through parliamentary procedure or by military take-over.

After those attempts there was little interest in abortion law reform for several years. Former activists were worn out and, in fact, the law was essentially a dead letter. In 1987 a study showed that that therapeutic abortions were performed for social reasons in 77 per cent of the cases for single women and for socio-economic reasons for 70 per cent of the married women; 16 per cent of the married women gave contraceptive failure as the reason. All of these were illegal under the terms of the law. Only 14 per cent of the abortions performed for unmarried women and 5 per cent for married women were for the reasons allowed by law, rape and threats to maternal health.[74] Until 1994 no medical practitioner has ever been prosecuted under the current law,[75] so there was little incentive to change it.

As a result of the relatively recent prosecutions, convictions, and police raids against abortionists, the campaign to reform the abortion laws has been revived.[76] An important new factor is the plight of HIV positive mothers and babies,[77] a result of the country's HIV epidemic. Thousands of infected babies are simply left in hospital to be taken care of by the state or by charity, and all of them are destined for a short and painful life. Even those who are not infected will soon lose their mothers to AIDS as the disease progresses. No wonder, then, that many infected women choose to abort and that many medical people are willing to assist even though it is against both the law and Buddhist teachings. In 1996 the Public Health Ministry held public hearings, which indicated widespread support for a radical liberalisation of the law, with abortion on demand in the first twelve weeks, abortion for reasons of health of the mother or the child from 13–28 weeks, and a prohibition after 28 weeks of pregnancy. However, since then, there has been considerable opposition to 'free abortion,' that is abortion on demand, from a broad base of citizens. Abortion on demand is just too offensive to Thai traditional thought. The reform movement once again has stalled.

The crack-down against illegal abortions has been sporadic and has not fundamentally changed the situation. For the women who can afford it and who can find a co-operative doctor or a free clinic, Thailand essentially has therapeutic abortion on demand. From interviews I note that there is a wide range of personal responses by medical people to the question of abortions. Some have quite lucrative abortion businesses in private institutions. On the other extreme, I know practitioners who refuse to perform abortions, because of their firm Buddhist scruples; they also will not refer patients for abortions or even inform them that they are possible. Some physicians make it a rule not to charge for abortions, so they will not be tempted to profit from a morally dubious act, and strictly limit the number they will perform. It is all very personal. Hospital abortion policies, and the policies of departments within hospitals, depend on what the Director believes. If he or she is opposed to abortions altogether or for certain reasons, then they are banned. As usual in Thailand, the situation is not very simple, but of course, simple things are not so interesting.

It would seem that women in Thailand who have had abortions do not go to monks for direct consolation. Acharn Passano told me that in his twelve years as an abbot, he had never been approached for advice or solace in regards to abortion. He thought that this was because in northeastern Thailand, where his monastery is located, the traditional morality, family structure, and social safety nets are relatively intact, making abortion unthinkable. Unfortunately, he seems to be wrong; the studies mentioned earlier show abortions to be very frequent in his part of the Kingdom and to be well accepted as part of traditional rural life. My hypothesis is that he has never become aware of abortions in his congregation because they would not care to trouble a monk with such low matters.

Furthermore, I suspect that Thais would be very uncomfortable with the idea of having an open service to deal with the karma and feelings resulting from an abortion. Such things are much safer if kept secret for oneself. In fact, there are rituals within Thai Buddhism that women use to help them deal with their abortions.[78] The very common ceremonies of making money, flower, or incense offerings to Buddha images, and releasing birds, fish, or turtles at temples are frequently resorted to by women to assuage their feelings of guilt and to lessen the harm done to the aborted fetus. This would be achieved by transferring the merit of the ritual to the fetus. It is not at all surprising in cases like these, where religious theory condemns a prevalent practice, to find that there are ritual ways to deal with the ensuing psychological pressures.

Buddhist responses to abortion in Japan

Many of Japan's Buddhist temples have formal services called *mizuko kuyō*, or memorial services for dead children. *Mizuko* in Japanese literally means 'water babies,' and it refers to prenatal and very young children, both of which in Japan are understood to be fully alive and human in a sense, but not yet fully integrated into the human world.[79] The *mizuko kuyō* ceremony has generated considerable scholarly attention and controversy.

In fact, the only two monographs written to date on Buddhism and abortion[80] concern this ritual. On one side, a group of scholars with LaFleur as the most prominent, see the *mizuko kuyō* as a valid innovation which skilfully weaves together various strands of Buddhist and other Japanese traditional concepts to provide a compassionate aid for grieving women.[81] Those who see some good in the memorial service also recognise that it has some very distasteful aspects. Zwi Werblowsky's article, '*Mizuko Kuyō*,' one of the earliest and liveliest essays about this ceremony, while recognising good aspects of the rite, energetically reviews its abuses. The other side sees the rite as a modern aberration, a corruption of Buddhism, which greedily exploits women.[82] Helen Hardacre, who writes from a strong feminist position, can find no good at all in *mizuko kuyō* and is taken rather severely to task in a review article by LaFleur.[83]

My introduction to *mizuko kuyō* came in 1987 when I visited Kamakura, one of the great centres of Buddhist culture.[84] In the grounds of one Hasedera, a temple dedicated to Kannon and containing an exquisite monumental wooden statue of him, I came across an extraordinary sight. There were thousands of statues of Jizō Bosatsu lining the walkways and filling courtyards. Stone, porcelain, and plastic Jizōs of various sizes were grouped together. None of particular artistic merit, they came in about a half dozen varieties. The mass of these little statuettes was somehow very touching, and the pathetic effect was greatly intensified by the way many of them were decorated. Very often they were dressed with a red bib or a little red hand-knit cap. Some had soothers on a ribbon around their necks, some had pinwheels or rattles to play with.

What was going on here? My friend, an American who had been in Kamakura for several years as a Zen student, explained that the Hasedera temple was one of several around the country that specialised in memorialising miscarried and aborted fetuses – *mizukō* or water-babies – or very young children who had died. The vast majority of the statues are for aborted *mizuko*. At this particular temple, so many women commissioned statues that they continually were clearing away old ones to make room for the new. A major part of the income of the temple came from these services. The cheapest figurine cost the equivalent of $80 US, and memorial services, which many clients ordered, were extra. In the literature given out by Hasedera temple, the images of Jizō were explained as commemorating stillborn and miscarried children, but not aborted ones, even though it was noted that Jizō was the protector of aborted fetuses.

Not all temples display their votive Jizō figures in the casual mode of Hasedera, where they almost seem like mushrooms growing in profusion from the soil. In subsequent trips to Japan, I have seen a very different style, generally at newer temples, some of which are very recent and were founded only for the profitable business of *mizuko kuyō*,[85] where identical Jizōs are encased neatly in numbered rows in glass cases. To me this is rather depressing, bringing to mind sterile displays in a cut-rate department store. However, scattered amongst these dreary rows, were islands of pinwheels and racks of toys for the *mizuko* as well as occasional traditional images of Jizō.

Jizō Bosatsu's connection with aborted fetuses in Japan has a revealing history.[86] Originating in India as the Bodhisattva Kṣitigarbha ('womb of the earth,' or 'earth-store'), Jizō vowed to roam all six realms of existence in this dark time between Gautama, the historical Buddha, and Maitreya, the Buddha of the future. Because of this vow, in Japan his images sometimes appear in groups of six slightly different statues, each one representing his activities in one of the realms of reincarnation. In his wandering, Jizō aids all suffering creatures towards their ultimate salvation.

Introduced to China and Japan as one of the celestial Bodhisattvas of Vajrayāna or esoteric Buddhism, he became very popular in the folk religion due to his connection with the hells. In Japan he became connected with a folk belief concerning the fate of water-babies and very young children who die. Such youngsters are neither good enough to enter a paradise nor bad enough for a hell, so they find themselves on a deserted river bank called Sai-no-kawara in Meido, the ghostly realm of gloom. During the day there, they try to make the best of it and play with the pebbles they find, stacking them into the form of little pagodas. This play is more than it seems, as their building of pagodas, for the benefit of their surviving relatives, is a powerful act of merit. However, when night falls, they become cold and afraid of the dark, and to make things worse malicious demons come and destroy their little structures.

Jizō, who has vowed to help all creatures no matter how sad the circumstances, then appears. He is pictured as dressed in the robes of a monk and carrying a staff with six jingling rings on it, each ring representing one of the six realms that he constantly patrols. The jingling of the rings reassures the children; and by sheltering them in his robe, which gently glows dispelling the dark, the good bodhisattva comforts them. This scene is depicted on modern statuary and is the subject of traditional tales and hymns:

> Be not afraid, little dear ones,
> You were so little to come here,
> All the long journey to Meido!
> I will be Father and Mother,
> Father and Mother and Playmate
> To all the children in Meido!
>
> Then he caresses them kindly,
> Folding his shining robes round them,
> Lifting the smallest and frailest
> Into his bosom, and holding
> His staff for the stumblers to clutch.

To his long sleeves cling the infants,
Smile in response to his smiling,
Glad in his beauteous compassion.[87]

The contents and form of *mizuko kuyō* vary from temple to temple, but generally the service involves chanting a Jizō-Meido hymn similar to the one just quoted and the *Heart* or some other canonical *Sūtra* as well as the use of incense, gongs, and other customary ceremonial objects. The rite often provides a posthumous Buddhist name and memorial tablet, a Jizō image, and a grave marker for the *mizuko*.[88]

Japanese Buddhists are very well aware of the basic doctrines about the beginning of human life. 'According to Buddhist literature, especially the *Kusha-ron* (*Abhidharmakośa*) life is there from the moment of conception and it should not be disturbed for it has the right to live.'[89] Thus, one important reason to perform *mizuko kuyō* is to atone for the bad karma accrued in procuring an abortion, which is a violation of the first and most important Buddhist precept against taking life. Donations to temples and performing services are excellent ways to improve to compensate for unskilful acts.

One of the weakest parts of Helen Hardacre's *Marketing the Menacing Fetus in Japan* is her recurring claim that the *mizuko kuyō* reflects a 'fetocentric' distortion of Buddhist tradition. It is true, as Hardacre argues, that the fully developed concept of *mizuko* is not found in Buddhist scriptures and that the *kuyō* is quite a contemporary innovation. However, respect for fetal life is an authentic part of the tradition from the time of Buddha down to the present, and her dismissal of it as 'fetocentric rhetoric'[90] is simply wrong-headed. Furthermore, the practice of performing rites and dedicating gifts to temples to gain merit as well as the belief that spirits of the dead may need propitiation are both found in ancient and modern Buddhist traditions. For some reason, Hardacre completely ignores these very basic facts from Buddhist history that underlie the *mizuko kuyō*. Furthermore, her rather relentless focus on the fear of the vengeful aborted fetus as the primary motivation for *mizuko kuyō* oversimplifies the complex personal and theological reasons that lie behind the genesis of the rite and that bring men and women to sponsor it. It seems clear to me that Hardacre's tendency to reduce everything to 'fetocentric' fears is far too simple. It does not do justice to the complex stories and testimony of the subjects themselves in the case studies, interviews, and surveys presented in her book.

In fact, one of the major reasons for performing *mizuko kuyō* is compassion for the aborted fetus.[91] Two verses from a popular song about the ceremony capture some of the feelings involved.

This evening a lone shooting star,
what a wretched transient life;

The look-alike faces of the Mizuko Jizō;
what are the pinwheels beside them saying,
In this bitterly cold night wind?

The blessing of the child I had expected
vanished like a dream.
How bitter not to be able to cuddle my child.
As I secretly visit the *mizuko* resting-place
I offer this lotus flower from the last *kuyō*.
May it be a penitential proof of my love.[92]

Whether taken literally or metaphorically, the notion of Jizō protecting the lost *mizuko* would be very comforting to the mourning survivors. Also, by providing a posthumous name, the *kuyō* allows the aborted fetus to be bound into the family structure.

Jizō has a very large place in the hearts of the Japanese, and little shrines to him appear all over the country, often in unexpected sites, as one I saw in a display of pipes and fittings in a plumber's shop window. Often they have little stacks of pebbles before them, recalling the meritorious play of the departed water-babies. The traditional, outdoor votive images of Jizō tend to be very simple, stylised figures with him dressed as a Hīnayāna monk. Although it did not register on me the first time I saw Jizō images, these figures are undoubtedly phallic in appearance. Indeed, when the Japanese adopted Jizō, he partly supplanted the ancient indigenous Dosojin, 'Earth Ancestor Deity' or 'Road Ancestor Deity' a god of sexuality in the form of a husband-and-wife couple, who previously had the function of protecting children.[93] Jizōs images were often carved onto ancient phallic representations of Dosojin and, to my eye at least, his usual folk form reflects this origin. In this light, little images like those in the courtyard of the Hasedera temple, dedicated to so many *mizukos*, are even more poignant as a dual reminder of sexuality and reproduction gone wrong.

The tabloid press and some entrepreneurial temples promote the notion that an aborted fetus becomes a very dangerous spiritual being that is likely to take revenge on the mother, usually by undermining her health, unless propitiated by *mizuko kuyō*. Fear, then, is one of the major factors that have made the practice so popular. Hardacre's book is excellent in documenting this sordid aspect of the phenomenon. Unmarried young women, who have resorted to abortion, are particularly targeted by this sort of scare propaganda, which Hardacre interprets, correctly I think, as an attack on female sexuality. She is also right to insist that such frightening spiritualism has much more to do with the commercialisation and exploitation of new age thought than it does with any traditional Buddhist beliefs and practices.

The other major users of the ceremony are older women who have had abortions for socio-economic reasons. Since 1948 Japan has allowed abortion for 'eugenic' reasons and encouraged population stability. Accordingly, abortion became the major method of birth control in the country especially in the first few decades after the Second World War. Many women, perhaps the majority of Japanese women, in that period had one or more abortions, and most of them experienced a sense of loss or guilt in regard to the unborn *mizuko*. Reliable abortion rate statistics are difficult to come by for Japan, but Japan may have the highest abortion rate in the world.[94] Just as it was in the past, those married women who are forced by economic necessity to abort are pitied while those who do it to terminate a pregnancy caused by illicit sex are condemned.[95]

The precise history of the *mizuko kuyō* is much disputed, but it seems clear that it is quite a new innovation, which emerged in the 1960s and 1970s to help those post-war women and other family members as well cope with a number of unresolved traumas that accompanied abortions. In my view, it is largely a successful and compassionate weaving together of a number of themes from Buddhist and folk traditions in Japan, which may be directly descended from earlier practices that were used to memorialise infanticides, miscarriages and abortions. As Hardacre has amply documented, *mizuko kuyō*, even though very popular, is resorted to by a minority of women who have had abortions and miscarriages and is not endorsed by most Buddhist temples, clergy, and organisations. Many, in fact, discourage or oppose the practice as an inauthentic innovation based on a superstitious, non-Buddhist belief in vengeful fetal spirits and because it is all too often promoted as a moneymaking scheme. The Jodo Shinshu sect of Pure Land Buddhism, one of the largest Buddhist organisations in the country, actively opposes the rite for the above reasons and also points out that the real problem is the unskilful act of abortion, which cannot be undone by *kuyō*.[96]

It is noteworthy that the opposition of Jodo Shinshu to abortion has not led them to any political agitation at all to change Japanese law or the way they practice medicine. As LaFleur stressed in *Liquid Life*, it is customary for Japanese Buddhists not to take controversial stands on public issues. Organised religion in Japan has always been regulated by the state, and Buddhist organisations have rarely tried to impose their religious understanding on the majority. In general, Japanese society tries to preserve the appearance of civil tranquillity by coming to consensus through compromise. This very much works against extreme ethical posturing and seeing things simplistically as black and white. *Mizuko kuyō*, in this light, can be seen as a skilful example of Buddhist practical ethical problem-solving. It is true to the fundamental Buddhist teaching that abortion is the wrongful killing of a human being, recognises the complex, troubling human motivations and effects on those who find it necessary to obtain abortions, and provides a public ritual that helps repair the ensuing damage to individuals, families, and society.

The export of *mizuko kuyō*

In Honolulu, the Diamond Sangha, a Zen group led by the American Roshi, Robert Aitken, has instituted a service for aborted fetuses based on the Japanese model.[97] Roshi Aitken is a leading figure in the American wing of the 'engaged Buddhism' movement, an informal grouping of Buddhists who are trying to work out theories and practices to make Buddhism practical in the North American social context. Roshi Aitken's reflections on abortion are found in the context of a discussion of the first precept, to abstain from killing:

> Perhaps the woman considering abortion faces the most intimate and agonizing test. Over-simplified positions of pro-life and pro-choice do not touch the depths of dilemma. Usually she experiences distressing conflict between her sexual/reproductive drive and the realities of her life; ... and indeed, she faces such realities for any child she may bring to term.... I get the impression that when a woman is sensitive to her feelings, she is conscious that abortion is killing a part of herself and terminating the ancient process, begun anew within herself, of bringing life into being. Thus she is likely to feel acutely miserable after making a decision to have an abortion. This is time for compassion for the woman, and for her to be compassionate with herself and for her unborn child. If I am consulted, and we explore the options carefully and I learn that the decision is definite, I encourage her to go through the act with the consciousness of a mother who holds her dying child in her arms, lovingly nurturing it as it passes from life.... Once the decision is made, there is not blame, but rather acknowledgement that sadness pervades the whole universe, and this bit of life goes with our deepest love.[98]

The consequences of violating the first precept are fully recognised, and the persons involved are treated compassionately rather than judgementally. The Diamond Sangha service includes friends and family and gives a name to the unborn child to recognise the reality that life has been lost and to help the survivors mourn.[99]

In Thailand in 1992, I had the opportunity to address a class of student nurses about the Japanese approach to abortion, and they were very interested in the *mizuko kuyō* ceremony. After all, both Thailand and Japan are Buddhist and both have relatively high rates of abortion. The Thai student nurses, all females, thought that the ceremony had some value in terms of helping the women involved deal with their feelings. But they also had some misgivings that it perhaps was unseemly because ceremony might seem to condone abortion, which is so clearly against Buddhist first principles. One of the reasons for the difference in Thai and Japanese attitudes may be because the Thai *sangha* is very strict in its adherence to the traditional monk's code of conduct, which clearly condemns the clergy for having any positive connection with abortion. Furthermore, it strongly encourages the monks to remain aloof from anything sexual. In Japan, on the other hand, for some centuries, Buddhist priests have abandoned any attempt to regulate themselves closely by the *Vinaya*, to the point where most marry, and many priestly positions are in fact hereditary.

Buddhist responses to abortion in Korea[100]

Buddhism has the most adherents of any religion in Korea, but because of its long history of being repressed it has very little inclination to attempt to influence government or public morality. As in Thailand and Japan, although it is well known that the abortion rate in Korea is extremely high, reliable statistics are not available. Before 1973, abortion was illegal in Korea although the law was generally ignored. The abortion law was liberalised to allow the procedure only for health reasons.[101] In fact Korea is sometimes called an 'abortion paradise,'[102] because the operation is so easily obtained, on a cash and carry basis, with practically no questions asked. According to surveys, more than half of married women in Korea have had at least one abortion, with one third reporting two or more.[103] Opinion polls showed that in 1991, more than half of Korean women did not know abortion was illegal. Many who had procured an abortion expressed no feelings of sorrow or regret: indeed 49 per cent 'felt good to have it done,' while 26 per cent 'did not have any special feeling about it' at all.[104] It is very important to have sons in Korea, partly due to a very strong Confucian patriarchal way of thinking. So many female fetuses have been aborted since 1985; it is estimated that nearly 50 per cent of males aged five to nine in 1990 would be without wives when they reached marriageable age. The Korean Ministry of Health cracked down on doctors who performed sex-determination on fetuses, and the Korean Medical Association took steps to stop this practice in 1995.[105] Otherwise, nothing has changed in the wide-open although illegal practice of abortion.

When the abortion law was under review around 1973, there seems to have been no input at all from Buddhists, either on the individual or organisational level.[106] From this indifference and various surveys, which show that Buddhists have more abortions and more multiple abortions than the rest of the Korean population, one might conclude that abortion is not really an issue to Korean Buddhists.[107] However, in the last decade or so, a few Buddhists have recognised abortion as a serious problem. They were, in part, inspired by the *mizuko kuyō* practice in Japan. Koreans, and Korean Buddhists in particular, have a very ambivalent relationship with Japan, which occupied the peninsula for some forty years in the first half of this century. Japan showed very little respect for Korean customs or interests, and worked very hard to bring Korean institutions into line with Japan's, which is still very much resented. Korean Buddhist monks were forced to abandon the *Vinaya* and were encouraged to marry, and Buddhist orders were reorganised under Japanese supervision. All of this was very disruptive and caused problems, which still are not resolved. On the other hand, the scholarship, wealth, and prestige of Japanese Buddhists were and still are very impressive to Koreans.

In 1985, the Venerable Sŏk Myogak, a senior monk in the Chogye Order (a Zen school), published a book entitled *Aga-ya, yongsŏhaedo-o*, which Frank Tedesco translates as 'My Dear Baby, Please Forgive Me!'[108] This book has been very popular amongst lay women Buddhists. In part it is a translation of a popular Japanese *mizuko* text, which recounts 'the fears and suffering of the spirits of helpless, aborted children and their attempts to seize the attention of their parents through dreams'[109] and day to day misfortunes. The characters for *mizuko* are pronounced *suja* in Korean, which Ven Myogak uses in his book. Several monks, who were inspired by *Aga-ya*, began to perform rebirth ceremonies for aborted fetuses in some ten temples. These ceremonies are Korean innovations and not direct copies of *mizuko kuyō* and have given comfort to thousands of Korean women.

Ven Myogak's book also includes discussions of basic Buddhist principles and relates them to the Korean context of how abortion, miscarriage, and the death of very young children have generally been ignored.

> For example, when children die in Korea they are usually cremated or buried without any funeral ritual. Those little lives which are aborted or miscarried without seeing the light of the world are treated as if they were vestigial organs ... And, since many babies were conceived through immoral behaviour, they are dispatched even more mechanically to avoid discovery ... I believe something is wrong here when we are so indifferent to the lives which grow in our own bodies. Babies who have been aborted through artificial means should be guided to a better rebirth. At the same time, we should consider the condition of many women who suffer in so many ways ... and try to alleviate their anguish if even only slightly.[110]

The solution to these problems, according to Ven Myogak, is to perform a ceremony for the spirit of the deceased baby. It seems clear that the motivation is respect for the first precept to abstain from taking life and compassion for the victims – both the child who died and the mother whom suffered from the loss.

Another Korean Buddhist leader, the nun Venerable Sŏngdŏk, has developed her own form of ceremony for aborted fetuses, which she began performing in 1991.[111] She opposes the use of the term *suja*, or water baby, as it is not traditional, and calls her ceremony an 'auspicious rebirth offering ceremony for an aborted fetus,' using the traditional Korean word rather than the transliteration of *mizuko*.[112] Her ceremony lasts for forty-nine days, the traditional period between death and rebirth, and the length of time for funeral rites for adults in Korean Buddhism. Her writings note that Buddhists have always considered human life as a repetitious continuum with each particular existence beginning at the moment of conception. Therefore, killing a fetus is a major unskilful act with severe karmic consequences.

> The spirits of aborted fetuses ... refers to the spirits of the fetuses who were intentionally, artificially aborted. All living beings including humans have Buddha nature created by the noble energy (*ki*) of the universe. To abort the precious life of the fetus conceived in the womb is against nature, undesirable morally, and very harmful to its mother medically. Besides, the life which is about to be born disappears from darkness to darkness without witnessing the light. It will become resentful and can cause harm and misfortune to the living who are related to the fetus.[113]

It is interesting to note the Mahāyāna emphasis on universal Buddha nature as well as the belief that the aborted fetus is a vengeful spirit. Her general emphasis is on compassion for the dead babies through providing them a ceremony to insure a successful rebirth and the necessity of the mother who procured the abortion to repent sincerely.

It should be noted that the Korean Buddhists who advocate and provide services for aborted fetuses are quite a small minority. The vast majority of temples, monks, and nuns are not involved in such rites. Furthermore, most Korean Buddhist lay women, who have had abortions, do not see any need for the service, as they do not feel that they have done anything culpable at all. Finally, those Koreans who do believe that there is a place for rebirth ceremonies for aborted children in their religious life are very keen to avoid the commercial exploitative excesses of the Japanese practice. Accordingly, prices are kept low and hard-sell advertising is not used.[114]

Notes

1 See also Damien Keown, *Buddhism and Bioethics*, (London: Macmillan and New York: St. Martin's Press, 1995), Chapter Two; Robert Florida, 'Abortion in Buddhist Thailand' in Damien Keown, ed. *Buddhism and Abortion* (1999), and James P. McDermott, 'Abortion in the Pali Canon and Early Buddhist Thought' in Keown, *Buddhism and Abortion*.

2 Although this characterisation of Buddhist thought is primarily Mahāyāna, I believe it is also essentially true to the Theravāda view.

3 Hema Goonatilake, 'Women and Family in Buddhism,' in Sulak Sivaraksa, ed., *Buddhist Perception for Desirable Societies in the Future* (Bangkok: The Inter-Religious Commission for Development, 1992), p. 235.
4 See Damien Keown, *Buddhism and Bioethics*, chapter 2, for the most complete discussion of this topic.
5 Keown, *Buddhism and Bioethics*, pp. 69ff.
6 Etienne Lamotte, *Histoire du Bouddhisme Indien* (Louvain-La-Neuve: Université de Louvain, 1976), pp. 38ff.
7 Louis de La Vallée Poussin, tr., *l'Abhidharmakośa de Vasubandhu* (Bruxelles: l'Institut belge des hautes études chinoises, 1971), 6 vols., ii. 62–63.
8 Taniguchi, 'A Study of Biomedical Ethics from a Buddhist Perspective' (Berkeley: Graduate Theological Union and the Institute of Buddhist Studies, MA Thesis, 1987), p. 19.
9 R.H.B. Exell, 'Science, Technology and Buddhism,' in Sulak Sivaraksa, *Buddhist Perception*, p. 220.
10 Keown, *Buddhism and Bioethics*, p. 71.
11 K.L. Moore, *The Developing Human: Clinically Oriented Embryology* (Philadelphia: Saunders, 1973), p. 1.
12 Keown, *Buddhism and Bioethics*, p. 68.
13 Frank E. Reynolds and Mani B. Reynolds, trs and eds, *Three Worlds According to King Ruang: A Thai Buddhist Cosmology* (Berkeley: University of California, 1982), pp. 5–45.
14 Reynolds and Reynolds, *Three Worlds*, pp. 118–119.
15 Wasin Indasara, *Theravada Buddhist Principles: Book II* (Bangkok: Mahakut Buddhist University, 1988), p. 90.
16 Alex Kennedy (Dharmachari Subhuti*)*, *The Buddhist Vision: An Introduction to the Theory and Practice* (London: Rider, 1985), pp. 139–140.
17 Edward Conze, *Buddhist Scriptures* (Harmondsworth, Middlesex: Penguin, 1959), p. 70. See also Alex Kennedy (Dharmachari Subhuti), *Buddhist Vision* (London: Rider, 1985), p. 78.
18 Keown, *Buddhism and Bioethics*, p. 93.
19 See Keown, *Buddhism and Bioethics*, pp. 95ff, and McDermott, 'Abortion,' pp. 164ff, for a careful analysis of the cases.
20 Cited in Keown, *Buddhism and Bioethics*, p. 96.
21 David Stott, 'Buddhadharma and Contemporary Ethics: Some Notes on the Attitude of Tibetan Buddhism to Abortion and Related Procedures,' in *Religion* (1992), vol. 22, p. 173–174.
22 The Venerable Rechung Rinpoche, presenter and translator, *Tibetan Medicine: Illustrated in Original Texts* (London: Wellcome Institute of the History of Medicine, 1973), p. 33. See also Tom Dummer, *Tibetan Medicine and Other Holistic Health-Care Systems* (London and New York: Routledge, 1988), pp. 45–46. Ven. Rechung Rinpoche, *Tibetan Medicine*, pp. 32–37, and Nawang Dakpa, 'Certain Problems of Embryology According to the Tibetan Medical Tradition' in *Bulletin of Tibetology: Aspects of Classical Tibetan Medicine* (Gangkok, Sikkim: Sikkim Research Institute of Tibetology, Special Volume of 1993), pp. 83–95, review Tibetan Buddhist embryology. It would seem that the Tibetan view of the state of the fetus is somewhat less harrowing than the Theravādin picture presented above.
23 For examples see Stott, 'Buddhadharma,' and Keown, *Buddhism and Bioethics*, p. 103.
24 Michael G. Barnhart, 'Buddhism and the Morality of Abortion,' *Journal of Buddhist Ethics* 5 1998:276–297, p. 5.
25 Keown, *Buddhism and Bioethics*, p. 88.
26 Keown, *Buddhism and Bioethics*, p. 96.

27 Florida, 'Abortion in Buddhist Thailand,' p. 18. My position has changed significantly from that paper and from an earlier one: R.E. Florida, 'Buddhist Approaches to Abortion,' *Asian Philosophy* (1991, Vol. 1, No. 1).

28 Conze, *Buddhist Scriptures*, pp. 70–71.

29 Keown, *Buddhism and Bioethics*, pp. 97ff. McDermott, 'Abortion,' pp. 160–161, reviews this issue and comes down strongly on the side of Keown.

30 Stott, 'Buddhadharma,' p. 176.

31 Exell, 'Science,' p. 220. On pp. 220–221, he has an interesting discussion of several different aspects of the morality of abortion from the Buddhist view. His paper has no scholarly citations at all, and it is not clear that he is familiar with the usual commentators. In any case, it is an open ended, sensitive consideration of the issues.

32 Pinit Ratanakul, 'Socio-Medical Aspects of Abortion in Thailand,' in Damien Keown, *Buddhism and Abortion*, pp. 56–57.

33 Keown, *Buddhism and Bioethics*, p. 92.

34 Keown, *Buddhism and Bioethics*, p. 92.

35 The analysis that follows is loosely based on Taniguchi, 'Study,' chs. 4–5.

36 Kennedy, *Buddhist Vision*, pp. 96–97.

37 Reynolds, *Three Worlds*, p. 98.

38 This Thai story is very similar to two found in the ancient and authoritative although non-canonical Pali *Petavatthu* texts. See McDermott, 'abortion,' pp. 159–161. It is likely that the *Three Worlds* version is derived from the Pali prototype.

39 Phra Nyavorotama, *Plan of Life* (Bangkok: Mahmakua Educational Council, 1992).

40 Conze, *Scriptures*, pp. 72–73.

41 Phra Nyanavorotama, *Plan*, p. 78.

42 Pinit Ratanakul, 'Community and Compassion: A Theravada Buddhist Look at Principlism,' in E. DuBose, Ronald P. Hamel, and Laurence J. O'Connell, *A Matter of Principles: Ferment in U.S. Bioethics* (Valley Forge, PA: Trinity Press International, 1994), p. 128.

43 Stott, 'Buddhadharma,' p. 179.

44 Rita M. Gross, *Buddhism After Patriarchy: A Feminist History, Analysis, and Reconstruction of Buddhism* (Albany: State University of New York Press, 1993).

45 Stott, 'Buddhadharma,' p. 174.

46 This section is a heavily revised version of my chapter, 'Abortion in Buddhist Thailand' in Keown, *Buddhism and Abortion* (1999). Much of the research for this section was done from 1989 to the present in Thailand. I am grateful to the generosity of my colleagues in the Department of Humanities of Mahidol University where I spent a year's sabbatical leave. Suporn Koetsawang, M.D., Siriraj Hospital, Department of Obstetrics and Gynaecology, Faculty of Medicine, and Institute for Population and Social Research, Mahidol University, who has been very active in abortion reform in Thailand, was also very generous with his time (1993). Finally, Acharn Passano, Abbot of Wat Pah Nanachat in Isan province graciously discussed the issue of abortion with me in May 1993. Some of this was presented in my address entitled 'Buddhist Attitudes towards Abortion: Thailand and Japan Contrasted' in The Public Lecture Series of the National Museum Volunteers in Bangkok, delivered on 8 June 1993.

47 'Special squad to track illicit abortion clinics,' *The Nation* (Bangkok, Jan. 24, 1994), p. A5.

48 *Bangkok Post* (Bangkok, May 2, 1996 and August 4, 1996).

49 Sanitsuda Ekachai, 'Women Must Have Abortion Choice,' *Bangkok Post* (Bangkok: June 11, 1997.)

50 Bencha Yoddumnern-Attig et al, *Changing Roles and Statuses of Women in Thailand: A Documentary Assessment* (Bangkok: Mahidol University Institute for Population and Social Research, 1992), p. 30.

51 Phra Nyavorotama, *Plan*.

52 Somdetch Phra Mah Samaa Chao Krom Phray Vajiraṭavarorasa, *The Entrance to the Vinaya (Vinayamukha)*, (Bangkok: Mahmakuarjavidyalaya, 1969, first published in Thai in 1913), vol. 1, p. 45.

53 Siralee Sirilai, 'An Analytical Study of Buddhist Ethics, Ethical Rules, and Criteria for Judgement of Ethical Problems in Medicine at the Present Time' (Bangkok: Abstract presented to the National Research Council of Thailand, 1986), p. 4.

54 The relevant sections of the Penal Code are translated in The Population Council, *Abortion in Thailand: A Review of the Literature* (Bangkok: The Population Council, Regional Office for South and East Asia, 1981), Appendix II, pp. 101ff and Institute of Population Studies, Chulalongkorn University, *Knowledge and Attitudes Concerning Abortion Practice in Urban and Rural Areas of Thailand: Paper Number 43* (Bangkok: Institute of Population Studies, Chulalongkorn University, 1982), pp. 2–4.

55 This includes intercourse against the will of the woman, intercourse with any woman under thirteen years of age, intercourse with any woman under eighteen in the sex trade, or intercourse with any woman over eighteen who is in the sex trade against her will (ibid).

56 Ruth Roemer, 'Laws of the World' in R. Hall, ed., *Abortion in a Changing World*, 2 vols, (New York: Columbia University Press, 1970), p. 122.

57 The Population Council, *Abortion in Thailand: A Review of the Literature* (Bangkok: The Population Council Regional Office for South and East Asia, May 1981) in addition to considerable original interpretative work, has useful summaries of the work done up to the date of publication, including English summaries of Thai publications. Two later studies are also important: Institute of Population Studies Chulalongkorn University, *Knowledge and Attitudes Concerning Abortion Practice in Urban and Rural Areas of Thailand: Paper Number 43* (Bangkok: Institute of Population Studies, Chulalongkorn University, July 1982) and Amorn Koetsawang, M.D. and Suporn Koetsawang M.D., *Nation-Wide Study on Health Hazard of Illegally Induced Abortion* (Bangkok: Mahidol University/United Nation Fund for Population Activities), 1987.

58 Estimated for 1981 in Christopher Tietze and Stanley K. Henshaw, *Induced Abortion A World Review 1986*, 6th edn (New York: Allan Guttmacher Institute, 1986), p. 50. See Malee Lerdmaleewong and Caroline Francis, 'Abortion in Thailand: A Feminist Perspective,' *Journal of Buddhist Ethics* 5 1998:22–48, p. 2, for other, lower, estimates.

59 Adapted from Tietze and Henshaw, *Induced Abortion*, table 2, pp. 28–42.

60 Koetsawang, *Study*, pp. 1–4.

61 Koetsawang, *Study*, p. 7.

62 Koetsawang, *Study*, p. 6.

63 Koetsawang, *Study*, p. 6.

64 Koetsawang, *Study*, pp. 2 and 4.

65 Population Council, *Abortion*, p. 90.

66 Population Council, *Abortion*, p. 81.

67 Cleo Odzer, 'Abortion and Prostitution in Bangkok,' in Damien Keown (ed.), *Buddhism and Abortion*, pp. 42ff. Odzer notes that a study done on prostitutes who worked in massage parlours, thus less well paid than Patpong workers, showed that 19 per cent of them had had abortions (p. 44).

68 Odzer, 'Abortion,' p. 38.

69 Reviewed in Population Council, *Abortion*, pp. 88–99.

70 Population Council, *Abortion*, p. 91.

71 Lerdmaleewong and Francis, 'Abortion in Thailand,' p. 8.

72 Lerdmaleewong and Francis, 'Abortion in Thailand,' pp. 8–9.

73 Population Council, *Abortion*, pp. 48–51.

74 Suporn, 'Study,' tables 10 and 11, rounded off to the nearest whole per cent, p. 11.

75 Population Council, *Abortion*, p. 4.

76 Kulcharee Tansubhapol, 'Abortion: The Right to Choose' (*Bangkok Post*, September 20, 1997) provides a long and careful review of the renewal of the campaign.

77 Pinit Ratanakul, pp. 58ff, also discusses HIV and abortion.

78 Personal communications; see also Pinit Ratanakul, 'Socio-Medical,' pp. 56ff.

79 Zwi Werblowsky, '*Mizuko Kuyō*, Notulae on the Most Important "New Religion" of Japan,' *Japanese Journal of Religious Studies* (Vol. 18, 1991), p. 296.

80 William R. LaFleur, *Liquid Life: Abortion and Buddhism in Japan* (Princeton, N.J.: Princeton University Press, 1992) and Helen Hardacre, *Marketing the Menacing Fetus in Japan* (Berkeley: The University of California Press, 1997).

81 See Anne Page Brooks, '*Mizuko Kuyō* and Japanese Buddhism' *Japanese Journal of Religious Studies* (Vol. 8, 1981), pp. 119–147; R.E. Florida, 'Buddhist Approaches to Abortion' *Asian Philosophy*, Vol. 1, No. 1, 1991; LaFleur, *Liquid Life* (1992), and Elizabeth G. Harrison, 'Mizuko Kuyo: The Re-production of the Dead in Contemporary Japan,' in P.F. Kornicki and I.J. McMullen, eds, *Religion in Japan: Arrows to Heaven and Earth* (Cambridge: Cambridge University Press, 1996), and 'I can only move my feet toward *mizuko kuyō*: memorial services for dead children in Japan' in Keown (ed.), *Buddhism and Abortion*.

82 George Tanabe's review of LaFleur's book in the *Japanese Journal of Religious Studies* (Vol. 21, 1994), pp. 437–440, leans towards the negative view of *mizuko kuyō*. This review led to a response and a counter-response, both of which are useful additions to the discussion. See LaFleur, 'Silences and Censures: Abortion, History, and Buddhism in Japan: A Rejoinder to George Tanabe,' *Japanese Journal of Religious Studies* (Vol. 22, 1995), pp. 189–196 and Tanabe, 'Sounds and Silences: A Counterresponse' (*Japanese Journal of Religious Studies* (Vol. 22, 1995), pp. 197–200.

83 William R. LaFleur, 'Abortion, Ambiguity, and Exorcism,' *Journal of Buddhist Ethics* (Vol. 5 1998), pp. 384–400. This article is also scheduled to appear in the *Journal of the American Academy of Religion*.

84 Parts of this are adapted from Florida, 'Approaches' (1991).

85 Hardacre, *Marketing*, pp. 91–100, concludes that the popularity and profitability of the practice is declining and that some of the temples have gone out of the business.

86 Miriam Levering, 'Kṣitigarbha' in Mircea Eliade, ed., *The Encyclopedia of Religion* (New York: Macmillan, 1987) and Pierre Grimal, ed., *Larousse World Mythology* (London: Hamlyn, 1965), pp. 318–323; Anne Page Brooks, 'Mizuko Kuyo,' pp. 127–131.

87 Masaharu Anesaki, *The Mythology of All Races*, J.A. MacCulloch, et al, eds (New York: Cooper Square, 1964, 13 vols.), vol. viii, p. 240.

88 Brooks, '*Mizuko Kuyō*,' pp. 123 ff. Werblowsky, '*Mizuko Kuyō* provides an example of a hymn used in a Shinto temple which also practices *mizuko kuyō*.

89 Japanese Buddhist Federation, *Understanding Japanese Buddhism* (Tokyo: Kyodo Obun Center Co. Ltd., 1978), p. 162, as cited in Brooks, '*Mizuko Kuyō*,' p. 133–134.

90 Hardacre, *Marketing*, p. 2 and passim.

91 All of the sources cited in note 81 above would agree.

92 Werblowsky, '*Mizuko Kuyō*,' pp. 319–320.

93 Michael Czaja, *Gods of Myth and Stone: Phallicism in Japanese Folk Religion* (New York: Weatherhill, 1974, pp. 169 and p. 265f; Werblowsky, '*Mizuko Kuyō*'), p. 308.

94 For a scathing discussion of this issue, see Werblowsky, pp. 310 ff.

95 Hardacre, *Marketing*, p. 20.

96 Harrison, 'I Can Only,' in Keown (ed.), *Buddhism and Abortion*, p. 98.

97 The service is included in Robert Aitken, *The Mind of Clover: Essays in Zen Buddhist Ethics* (San Francisco: North Point, 1984), pp. 175–176.

98 Aitken, *Mind*, pp. 21–22.

99 For the complete service see Aitken, *Mind*, pp. 175–76, also reproduced in Florida, 'Approaches,' pp. 47–48.

100 Frank Tedesco, 'Abortion in Korea,' in Keown (ed.) *Buddhism and Abortion* is the only extensive treatment of this topic.
101 Tedesco, 'Abortion,' pp. 128–129.
102 Tedesco, 'Abortion,' p. 130.
103 Tedesco, 'Abortion,' p. 131.
104 Tedesco, 'Abortion,' p. 129.
105 Tedesco, 'Abortion,' pp. 131–132.
106 Tedesco, 'Abortion,' p. 129.
107 Tedesco, 'Abortion,' p. 133.
108 The material on Ven Myogak is summarised from Tedesco, 'Abortion,' pp. 134–139.
109 Tedesco, 'Abortion,' p. 34.
110 Tedesco, 'Abortion,' pp. 137–138.
111 The material on Ven Sŏngdŏk is summarised from Tedesco, 'Abortion,' pp. 139–145.
112 Tedesco, 'Abortion,' p. 139.
113 Tedesco, 'Abortion,' p. 142.
114 In Taiwan, which had an oppressive Japanese occupation very like that in Korea and which has a very high abortion rate, Buddhists have also been very slow and cautious in adopting anything like *mizuko kuyō*. See Werblowsky, '*Mizuko kuyō*,' p. 332f.

CHAPTER SEVEN

To Save or Let Go: Thai Buddhist Perspectives on Euthanasia

Pinit Ratanakul

In few areas have the advances in scientific knowledge and the new medical technologies raised more basic questions about the very nature, meaning and value of human life than in the whole area of death and dying. That health-care professionals find themselves in conflict over ethical dilemmas in this area is not surprising, since there is a lack of public consensus on what is morally acceptable. Already in the West, there has begun a groundswell of cultural change in which traditional attitudes and ideas about death and the dying process are being modified or rejected by many, and the same development is occurring now in Thai society. In this society, undergirded by the teachings of Theravāda Buddhism, the replacement of traditional medicine with high technological medicine has raised new ethical issues that traditional Thai morality and accepted practices cannot adequately deal with. The new life-support technologies have blurred the line between prolongation of life and prolongation of the dying process, and have raised questions about the adequacy of the traditional definition of death as the cessation of all vital signs. At what moment in the dying process should we declare that 'death' has occurred? Shall we continue the traditional definition of 'death' or declare 'death' when the new measuring devices detect the cessation of higher brain activity, or when both the higher and lower brain activities cease to function spontaneously, unassisted by machines or procedures like hyperalimentation? There are also other questions such as: Is the refusal of life-preserving treatment by artificial means a morally acceptable option or does it constitute a kind of suicide prohibited by Buddhist teachings? Is it morally wrong for doctors, nurses and families to withdraw life-preserving treatments or to stop such treatment, once these have begun? Are such actions the same as 'killing' patients or are there important ethical distinctions to be made between 'letting-go-of-life' by withholding or stopping treatment, and actual 'killing' or causing death?

The lack of public and professional consensus on these questions creates the possibility for emotionally laden moral conflicts within the general public, between families and their doctors and even among medical professionals themselves. Therefore it is necessary for Thai Buddhists to make a systematic review of Buddhist morality and traditionally accepted practices concerning death and dying, and to rethink or reinterpret Buddhist ethics in its application to these new issues that are not so far clearly defined in Buddhism. Such a need, and the moral conflicts involved, were brought to the attention of Thai Buddhists by the case of eighty-six year old Venerable Buddhadāsa, a leading Buddhist scholar-monk and teacher of this century.[1]

Living wills: should they be recognized?

Venerable Buddhadāsa Bhikku who had suffered a stroke was flown from his forest hermitage in Southern Thailand to Bangkok and was admitted to Siriraj Hospital shortly after 1 a.m. on 29 May 1993. He was in a comatose state most of the time during his stay at the hospital. A conflict arose there between the attending doctors and his monk-disciples who had followed him to Bangkok to care for him.[2] While still fully rationally competent, and long before the stroke, this reverend monk had written a 'living will' indicating that in case of an irreversible coma he did not want to prolong his life by extraordinary means using sophisticated devices such as respirators, heart-lung machines, and intravenous feeding to maintain simple bodily functions. He wanted to die naturally.

Before his illness in 1991 he had confided these wishes to his disciples, and in his writings he had consistentently emphasized the important role of Nature or Dhamma in healing.[3] He reminded his disciples that controlling the body by the use of chemical and mechanical means is 'unnatural,' and that it interferes with the body's own self-healing. He had suffered previously from minor strokes but each time had been restored to health through natural means such as meditation practice, use of herbal concoctions, dieting and plain and simple living in accordance with Dhamma. When this last stroke occurred, there was a debate among his disciples – lay and monastic – whether he should be taken to a hospital against his expressed wishes, or kept at the temple. One of his lay disciples, a leading neurologist at the technologically equipped Siriraj Hospital, believed that the monk could be successfully treated if taken to this hospital and successfully persuaded the other disciples to take their *ajarn* or spiritual teacher there with the promise that the monk would not be intubated. If no improvement in the patient's condition occurred within seven days he would be taken back to his forest temple.

In the past, after his previous strokes, Venerable Buddhadāsa had refused to go to a hospital. When he was ill doctors had been brought to the temple to treat him without high-tech devices. He had a strong belief in the power of nature and natural surroundings to effect a cure and a belief that high-tech modern medicine has its limitations in dealing with natural life processes. He also found the atmosphere of modern hospitals alienating and not conducive to humane care, and especially not a suitable place for dying. He had been admitted earlier to a hospital in a southern city for treatment of another illness and had found the experience so deeply unsatisfactory that he hurried back to his temple, trusting in the power of self-healing through cooperative work of the body and the mind.

The concept of a 'living will' is still new to Thai society. It has been discussed for decades and in some Western societies recognized and enforced. Its underlying premise is 'informed consent,' namely that a competent individual has the right to select or reject medical treatments according to his own beliefs and values. In Thai society the notion of the autonomy of the individual to choose or refuse medical treatment has not been a focal issue.[4] In a sense it is an expansion of democratic thinking into the medical field, an expansion which only began in the West after World War II. Before this, how patients were to be treated was the doctor's decision alone and the rights of patients were not recognized.

The case involving Venerable Buddhadāsa has raised the issue of the right to refuse treatment, and of the doctor's obligation to honor such right. In the case of Venerable Buddhadāsa it specifically raised the issue as to whether doctors should or should not respect his expressed wishes both verbally and in writing. Though a 'living will' is not a usual practice in Thailand, the case of Venerable Buddhadāsa is specially worthy of serious consideration for it was expressed by an eighty-six year old monk who had dedicated his life to understanding, practicing, and disseminating Buddhist teachings, and who was ready to let go of life.[5] It is much different from the 'living will' written while a person is still young, healthy and unaware of possible future medical developments in treatment and cures. The young person may change his mind when he is actually facing death and, if he could, might express the desire that everything possible be done to sustain and prolong life.

At Siriraj Hospital during his final stroke, the attending doctors found it necessary to use artificial means such as tubes for feeding and drainage to save Venerable Buddhadāsa's life. Without this equipment, the haemorrhage in his brain would not drain rapidly enough to prolong life. It would take months for the body to deal with the hemorrhage naturally. But these procedures were against the wishes of Venerable Buddhadāsa. The treatment was also contrary to what the disciples had been formerly promised. Some of the disciples, who believed that the 'living will' morally obligated the doctors to allow their *ajarn* to die, were unhappy with such treatment, but they had to accept the doctors' decision as the only way to save the monk's life. When, however, by this treatment the monk still remained in coma for a month with no improvement, they began to doubt the wisdom of the doctors' decisions and wanted the doctors to stop such futile treatment and allow them to bring the monk back to his temple to die a natural death in peace. The doctors, however, insisted on continuing the treatment, believing that through this modern medical technology the patient's life could be saved. Their underlying belief was that it was a doctor's duty to save lives when there was some spark of hope and that prolonging life for even hours was worthwhile. Saving the life of this particular monk was of great importance because of his reputation as a prominent scholar and teacher, and his inspiration as a modern saint of Buddhism.

Moral conflicts: who is right?

We have here, then, a conflict of values and moral perceptions between, on the one hand, the doctors who have faith in the healing powers of modern technological medicine and who have the obligation to save lives as part of their professional ethics; and on the other hand, the monk's and his disciples' belief in the limitations of modern medicine particularly in its interference with the processes of natural dying. As evident in his 'living will' this famous monk who accepted natural death had wanted to set an example of facing it without fear or anxiety, in keeping with the tenets of Buddhism. These teachings emphasize non-clinging to life, and the non-craving for the prolongation of life, that is, the acceptance of death as part of the human condition.

Over sixty years Venerable Buddhadāsa had devoted his life to the propagation of these teachings, and through his meditation practices had prepared himself to be faithful to them, so that the egoistic self would not be in command of either his life or his dying, but be dissolved. The model for him was that of the Buddha's dying, a peaceful letting go of life in the presence of his disciples. The image of the Buddha hooked to machines or sustained at a meaningless level of human existence could have given an entirely different meaning and impact on Buddhist adherents. This was what inspired the well-know monk to write a 'living will,' to request that no extraordinary means, no hi-tech equipment be used on him when the state of irreversible coma occurred. At the age of eighty-six he accepted the natural deterioration of his body and the decline of its functions, and was ready to let go of life to accept timely death (*kālamaraṇa*). He did not want people to cling to him nor to his physical life as refuge, but wanted them to practice Dhamma to which he had dedicated his life.

Venerable Buddhadāsa did not object to the use of modern high-tech medicine when it could clearly save lives and was the only available resource. But he rejected its use to prolong the dying process and for him, as for all Buddhists, the last conscious moments of life are precious. For some

Buddhists these dying moments could be the occasion for final liberation from the wheel of life (*saṃsāra*).[6] For others these are the occasions to fill their minds with remembrance of their good deeds (good kamma) and thus ensure a better rebirth. Even a recollection, with true remorse, of previous bad deeds can mitigate bad consequences in the next life. According to Buddhist teachings these last moments should be accompanied by rituals (such as listening to the chanting of passages from Buddhist Scriptures or bestowing gifts for the monks) that could assist the dying to achieve a tranquil state of mind.

In his writings Venerable Buddhadāsa underlined the Buddhist belief in the preciousness of human life. But he made a distinction between a life that is truly viable, in which the individual has full command of his faculties, is responsive, responsible and interrelated; and a life merely existing on the biological level without human awareness and human interactions, such as a vegetative life totally dependent on artificial means. This is another important reason why he wrote a living will requesting that he must not be kept artificially alive on solely a biological plane. This does not mean that Venerable Buddhadāsa, or Buddhism in general, support euthanasia – that is, the taking of life either by the self or others.

Euthanasia: who decides?

Venerable Buddhdāsa's case has started a debate among Thai Buddhists on the issue of euthanasia in Buddhism. Out of their care and respect for their *ajarn*, and seeing that the treatment was futile and dehumanizing, the disciples wanted the doctors to remove the feeding tubes and the respirator which was keeping his vital signs going and thereby allow the monk to die according to his wishes. In other words, they wanted the doctors to perform 'passive euthanasia,' which in western bioethics has come to mean 'pulling the plug' or ceasing the use of artificial means to keep a patient alive. But the doctors, seeing that the monk's condition was stable though not improved (sometimes he even could wiggle a toe), refused their request. The doctors acted according to their conscience, which prevented them stopping this kind of treatment once it had begun. Again what we have here is a clear case of conflict between two sets of values and obligations. The problem is how to decide which of these sets in this circumstance represents the meaning of Buddhist compassion. Both sides wanted to do what is best for Venerable Buddhadāsa. The disciples on one hand wanted to respect his beliefs and wishes by removing the respirator and allowing him to die naturally at his forest temple, while the doctors on the other hand wanted to save his life by using whatever means are necessary, even against his wishes as expressed in a living will. For the disciples the continuation of the futile treatment showed the lack of respect for their *ajarn's* personhood. In the eyes of the disciples this continuing treatment implied that the doctors saw him only as a body to be mechanically controlled, and not as the embodiment of Buddhist teachings for which he had lived.

A further implication of his case became part of the on-going debate as to whether a doctor should place and maintain a patient on a life-support system without the 'informed consent' of a competent patient or a patient's chosen surrogate. Whatever the decision, it would have to be regulated by law to ensure realistically that it becomes standard practice to protect the doctor, the patient and the family involved. In Thai society doctors have the trust of the public because modern medicine with its new technologies has produced apparent 'medical miracles,' saving lives which in the past would have been lost. It has given doctors the aura of power over life and death and inflated the sense of self-importance of some doctors. A doctor's decisions have usually been accepted by the Thai public, without question or quarrel, because they simply believe that doctors know best.

Can reason dissolve moral conflicts?

The objections raised by the monk-disciples of the famous patient in this case was a sign of a new perspective on modern medicine and the decisions of doctors who utilize modern technologies fully to save lives. Given the fact that sufficient ethical thinking has not been done on this new issue by Buddhist ethicists or by doctors, and given their different values, the conflicting claims of the doctors and the disciples could not be mediated through arguments alone. At this juncture, both sides practiced compassion, patience and tolerance as Buddhists and accepted a compromise. Finally, realizing that their life-support treatment could not restore health or a meaningful human existence for Venerable Buddhadāsa, the attending doctors were willing to let their patient be taken back to his temple but with the respirator on and feeding tubes in place. None of them wanted to be blamed for causing the death of such a saintly monk as it would have very grave kammic consequences for them.

Does euthanasia interfere with the law of kamma?

To find a Buddhist solution for the issue of euthanasia in all its complexity, it has to be considered within the framework of the doctrine of kamma, Buddhist psychology, and the teaching of compassion. According to the doctrine of kamma the disease the patient is suffering from may have a physical cause such as bacterial infection and/or a kammic cause due to past bad kamma. When the suffering has a kammic cause it will have to run its course until the kammic potency is exhausted. Even if the patient seeks to end his suffering by taking his own life he is only interrupting the course of kamma since the suffering will arise again in his life until that bad kamma is completely expended. Within this framework the doctor ought not to interfere with the working of kamma through the means of euthanasia either by actively taking the patient's life or by withdrawing life-support systems. If the bad kamma is allowed to run its full course here and now, the patient might be reborn into a higher state when the present life has come to its end. But that could not happen if the patient's life were to be cut short while the bad kamma was still to be undergone.

The Buddhist understanding of health and disease in terms of kamma does not lead to a fatalistic attitude of not seeking any care at all or giving up treatment out of despair. Buddhism advises us that for practical purposes we have to look upon all diseases as though they are produced by mere physical causes, for no ordinary person can definitely know which disease is caused by kamma. And even if the disease has a kammic cause it should be treated. As no condition is permanent, and as the causal relation between deed and its correlated consequence is more conditional than deterministic, there is the possibility for the disease to be cured so long as life continues. On the other hand, we need to take advantage of whatever means of curing and treatment are available. Such treatment, even if it cannot produce the cure, is still useful because appropriate physical and psychological conditions are needed for the kammic effect to take place. The presence of the predisposition to certain disease through past kamma and the physical condition to produce the disease will provide the opportunity for the disease to arise. But having certain treatment will prevent bad kammic results from manifesting fully. This kind of treatment does not interfere with the working of the individual's kamma but reduces its severity instead. The advice of Buddhism to a person with an incurable disease is to be patient and to perform good deeds to mitigate the effects of the past bad kamma.[7]

Is mercy-killing really merciful?

In Buddhist psychology, 'mercy killing' or active euthanasia cannot be carried out without the ill-will or feeling of repugnance (*dosa*) of the perpetrator toward the fact of the patient's suffering. Even though the motivation behind this action may have been good, namely to prevent further suffering for the patient, as soon as such thought becomes action to terminate life it becomes an act of aversion. So when a doctor performs what, he believes is 'mercy-killing,' actually it is due to his repugnance of the patient's pain and suffering which disturb his mind. Subsequently, the doctor experiences negative emotions toward this disburbance and projects it on the suffering of the patient. But he disguises his real feeling (i.e. repugnance) as a morally praiseworthy deed to justify to himself 'mercy-killing.' If he understood this psychological process he would recognize the hidden hatred that arises in his mind at the time of performing the lethal deed, and would not deceive himself with the belief that this deed was motivated by benevolence alone. Therefore from the view of Buddhist psychology 'mercy-killing' is not really a benevolent act. It is done from ill will and thus has bad kammic effects both for the doctor and the patient.

However, the Buddhist teaching of compasion complicates the issue, for to end the suffering of others is the goal of this Buddhist ethical value. In health care, compassion implies two obligations doctors have towards their patient, namely to do all they can in their power to enhance the well-being and health of their patients, and to do no further harm to the patients by preventing and alleviating their harm and suffering. Accordingly, doctors and nurses are obligated not to expose their patients to further harm and suffering because of their lack of knowledge, inadequate skills or negligence. In the case of terminal patients compassion is limited to giving drugs in sufficient quantities to relieve intense pain, as that experienced by cancer patients, as a last resort when no hope of recovery is possible and the patient is dying. This is the farthest that compassion can go. Beyond this point the precept against taking of life is violated.[8]

Is letting-go-of-life a form of killing?

The case of 'passive euthanasia' is more difficult to resolve in Buddhist terms. In this case the ethical waters become more muddy. Because of its complexity involving scarce medical resources, the high costs of treatment, and medical uncertainty, the majority of lay Thai Buddhists are more cautious in their approach to 'passive euthanasia.' Despite their belief in the law of kamma, for some of them withdrawing life support systems can be justified in a case when, by the best medical wisdom and through rigid testing, there has occurred in the patient total brain death which means irreversible coma and no hope for recovery. Some Thai Buddhists recognize that there is a real moral distinction between 'letting-go-of-life' or allowing a patient to die, and directly and intentionally taking life. For them, allowing a patient to die does not violate the precept and is considered an altruistic action for those involved.[9]

In Buddhist ethics intention is crucial in determining actions as right or wrong, but with regard to passive euthanasia other factors are also important. In real life there can be mixed motivations behind the intention to act in seemingly good ways. The intention of family members and the doctor to let the patient die may be motivated by selfish as well as altruistic desires. For example, for family members there may be the desire to relieve the suffering of a patient and the desire to inherit his fortune. In the case of the doctor, there may be the desire to end the pain and suffering of one patient and the desire to have a viable organ for transplantation into another. A hospital can have a policy of accepting passive euthanasia with both a desire to relieve the suffering of patients and families and to contain medical costs. For these reasons lay Thai Buddhists are cautious about extending the grounds for 'letting-go-of-life' by the withdrawal of medical technologies beyond the strict and narrow grounds in the case just mentioned above. And because of many factors entering into decisions about withdrawing life-support treatments such decisions have to be made on a case-by-case basis. Sometimes in real life human choices are only between two evils. Yet even in this tragic situation one still has responsibility to choose the lesser evil. But for such agonizing decisions there has been little guidance culled so far from Buddhist sources to help Buddhists and to ease their conscience. As generally known, Buddhism encourages each person to face the troubles by relying on oneself alone, without expecting any divine power to intercede and help. Choosing among evils requires wisdom (*paññā*) or insight arising from a regulated mind (*samādhi*), right understanding (*sammādhiṭṭhi*) of the real nature of existence characterized by conditionality (*paṭiccasamuppāda*) imperma-nence (*anicca*), suffering (*dukkha*) and unsubstantiality (*anattā*), and from continuing learning (*sikkhā*). With *samādhi* and *sammādiṭṭhi* one is able to make a realistic evaluation of a given situation and to act thoughtfully and unselfishly. *Sikkhā* enriches *paññā* diminishing the number of mistakes made. Since there have been cases especially with younger people where remarkable recoveries have occurred even after doctors pronounced them terminally ill or as being in irreversible coma, Thai lay Buddhists also are unwilling to see general policies adopted accepting passive euthanasia for fear of possible abuses that are detrimental to patients and existing moral norms of society. As there are always risks and uncertainties, they would prefer to err in favour of life and not against it.

What criteria should influence euthanasia decisions?

The problems surrounding the euthanasia issue are complex. They involve the expanded use of high-tech medicine, doctor's traditional values, patient's autonomy, medical costs, family's desires and religious teachings. There are also many cases of moral conflicts between doctors and families over the continued life or death of patients and between nurses and doctors. The fact of medical costs for serious illnesses weighs differently on the rich and the poor. Distribution of scarce and expensive high-tech medical treatments follows no rule of justice. Lay Thai Buddhists in general are opposed to euthanasia, considering it to be against the Buddhist precept of taking life. At the same time they have become aware of the many aspects of the issue which make it not that clear-cut. For example, through the newspapers they have become aware of cases such as that of a niney-four year old woman, kept alive by artificial means for over a year at the cost of the bankruptcy of her family. Another case was that of an eleven year old girl in irreversible coma for years, again at high cost to the family. These lay

Buddhists are faced with questions as to whether economic factors, the age of the patient and the quality of life would make any important difference in their decisions regarding the use of life-support systems. None could give a definite Buddhist answer. Some say yes and some no, but they could not find grounds in Buddhism to support their answers.

The reality is that though euthanasia is a criminal act, some forms of it are being currently practiced in some Thai hospitals by doctors who make life and death and decisions alone without any directives, whether these be ethical, religious, moral or legal. If such practice is allowed to continue unchecked, public suspicions and therefore mistrust of medical professionals will increase to the detriment of all, patient, families and doctors. At stake will be the primary social role and image of doctors who have traditionally been conceived of as 'preservers of life.' What will happen to the public when the doctors become 'death advocates'? Central Buddhist teachings must be reinterpreted to deal with the issue of euthanasia, which is a new challenge arisen as a result of the discovery and expanded use of modern technological medicine.

Is there a Buddhist principle for euthanasia decisions?

Perhaps the Buddhist concept of mutual dependency and interrelatedness (*paṭiccasamuppāda*) should be applied to the field of medicine.[10] This concept affirms the interdependence of all beings. When all beings depend on other beings, none of them is primary, and concern for others, co-operation and harmony are crucial human values in social relationships. Choices regarding suicide, assisted suicide, or a 'right to die' cannot be completely autonomous because people do not live alone but are members of communities who might be injured by their death or by a social policy that encourages such death. With regard to life and death decisions, doctors and other medical personnel should not decide and act by themselves but in partnership with patients, their families and/or surrogates when making decisions on treatment, including the use of life-sustaining technologies. Accordingly, doctors ought to include in their professional ethics the need to have the consent of their patients or surrogates for any treatment. When conflicts between doctors and patients or surrogates arise, some form or structure of mediation is needed. As in the case of Venerable Buddhadāsa described above, lacking such meditational means, resolution of conflicts depended upon the good will of the two sides to find a compromise. Such good will or possible compromise may not always be present and a law might be enacted to regulate decision-making in cases of conflict. But the law tends to be a blunt instrument, unable to deal with the individual differences and nuances that mark human interactions especially in matters of life and death. Rather, the public must be more educated about what is involved in such decisions.

Similarly doctors and nurses must be educated to change their roles to be more of a partner and facilitator in helping patients and surrogates make decisions. Apart from this, while keeping their primary image as healers, dedicated to preserving and prolonging the life of all patients under their care, they have to develop a new approach to death and dying, so that when death becomes imminent they would become graceful acceptors of the inevitable, without considering the hopeless condition of the dying patient as representing the failure of their skills and knowledge. They should instead turn their full attention now to the compassionate care of the dying. Their main concern, of course, is to relieve the suffering of patients and families and ensure a 'good death.' To make these changes a long process is required but it is a necessary one if conflicts, and pitfalls are to be minimized.

Is hospice care a Buddhist alternative?

Especially in regard to euthanasia, there are grounds in Buddhism for supporting hospice care. This is because in the Buddhist tradition death is accepted as the natural end of life and one is not encouraged to either hasten it or to save life at all costs. Buddhism is also known for its holistic approach to health care focussing on the entire person, for its emphasis on the last stage of life as being of great importance, and on the practice of compassion on the part of doctors and nurses to provide a special care for the dying. The ideal is to help them to die in a calm, conscious state, so that a good rebirth is obtained.

Hospice care provides humane treatment, comfort, consolation and companionship to the dying either in their own homes or in special units at hospitals staffed by specialists specially trained to deal with all kinds of suffering that people and families endure at the end of life, involving physical, mental, emotional, moral and spiritual. These hospice specialists have successfully demonstrated not only that no one needs to suffer from unbearable pain toward the end of life, but that most people can be maintained at a level of pain-relief which does not impair their faculties or cloud consciousness, but permits them to have meaningful lives at the end. Such care obviates much of the concern that underlies support for euthanasia and is in conformity with the Buddhist teaching about life and death and the practice of compassion. The success in pain-relief and the atmosphere and policies of the hospice movement indicate that no one needs to die neglected, alone, shunted aside by doctors and nurses, busy with the living-yet-unconscious, and hooked to machines and kept from their families. The hospice movement shows that death with dignity and humane treatment is still possible in our time. The question of the use of artificial means to keep a patient alive does not arise in hospice care, for the acceptance of death is one of the main tenets of the hospice movement when dying is the only option. If hospice care had been a possibility the case of Venerable Buddhadāsa described above would not have occurred and the suffering of all concerned would have been avoided.

Conclusion

Euthanasia is an agonizing problem for Thai society as more and more high-tech treatments are being used by doctors. It has raised many unresolved ethical problems as witnessed by the case of Venerable Buddhadāsa. The issue is further complicated because of the increase in the practice of organ transplantation. The question being raised now is whether Buddhist compassion as practiced by doctors should go beyond their concern for their own immediate patients to those patients whose lives could be saved by their own dying patients' organs, as Buddhist compassion is impartial and is directed to all involved in a given situation. There should be extensive dialogue between members of the public and medical profession about this issue. Doctors, patients and the public alike will be benefitted by this discussion of the reality and possibility of organ transplantation.

It is clear that active euthanasia, including assisted suicide, is against Buddhist teachings. But passive euthanasia presents a complex ethical challenge to Buddhist morality. Doctors cannot prolong the use of life-support systems indefinitely because of the complicated factors involved such as medical cost for family members, scarce medical resources, medical uncertainty, and the resulting quality of patients' lives saved or sustained. Contemporary emphasis upon patients' autonomy, that patient should have the right to choose and refuse treatment and the possibility of conflicts between patients and doctors, and doctors and family members, are the other factors that complicate the issue. But the situation is even more aggrevated when cases involving incompetent patients such as seriously defective infants (e.g. spina bifida babies, and anencephalics) who may be spared the agony of a short and futile life by stopping life-sustaining treatments. In this case it is not the length of life that is really significant in making life and death decision but the infant's own agony and the futility of treatment that matter.

The suggestion made by some Thai Buddhists that one can draw a distinction between 'killing' and 'letting-go-of-life' is worthy of serious consideration because in Buddhist ethics the motivation and intention behind actions are morally significant factors, not simply the end result. If there really is such a distinction Thai Buddhists may feel that letting-go-of-life does not constitute a breach of the Buddhist first precept, and Buddhism can offer a 'middle way' between the two extremes of active euthanasia including assisted suicide, and the position of sustaining life at all costs and under all circumstances. However, for the general public there is still uncertainty about distinguishing between 'killing' and 'letting-go-of-life,' and passive euthanasia remains problematic for them. It is even more problematic for the doctors who strongly believe that sustaining the lives of their patients is their primary duty and obligation. Therefore the question of whether to save or let-go-of-life is a continuing ethical issue as Thai Buddhists grapple with the reality of existence in the modern world and the need to be faithful to Buddhist teachings. Like Venerable Buddhadāsa, more and more elderly Buddhists, monks and lay people alike, express their wishes to be allowed to die in the last stage of their lives accepting death as a natural end simply because, they believe, this is the Buddhist way of facing the inevitability of death.

Notes

1 Many of his works were translated into English, French, and German. Some of the English/French books and articles on his life and work are Donald Swearer, *Thai Buddhism: Two Responses* (Leiden: E.J. Brill, 1973); Louis Gabaude, *Une Hermeneutique Buddhique Contemporaine de Thailande: Buddhadāsa Bikkhu* (Paris: École Franraise d'Extrême Orient, 1988); Peter A. Jackson, *Buddhadāsa: A Buddhist Thinker for the Modern World* (Bangkok: Siam Society, 1988); Grant A. Alson, 'From Buddhadāsa Bhikkhu to Phra Debvedi: Two Monks of Wisdom,' and Donald Swearer, 'Buddha, Buddhism and Bhikkhu Buddhadāsa,' in S. Sivaraksa (ed), *Radical Conservatism: Buddhism in the Contemporary World* (Bangkok: Thai Inter-Religious Commission for Development, 1990).

2 Data concerning the last days of Venerable Buddhadāsa at Siriraj Hospital was compiled from the author's interviews with some attending doctors and his disciples.

3 In his writing Dhamma is used as equivalent to Nature, the ways things really are, and 'natural law,' 'natural duty,' and 'natural fruit' are conceived of as the essential dimension of Dhamma. Cf. Damien Keown, *Buddhism & Bioethics* (New York: St. Martin's Press, 1995), pp. 18–20.

4 I have discussed the concept of individual autonomy in Thai culture in an article entitled 'Community and Compassion: A Theravada Buddhist Look at Principlism' in Edwin R. Du Bose et al (eds), *A Matter of Principles: Ferments in U.S. Bioethics* (Pennsylvania: Trinity Press International, 1994), pp. 121–130.

5 Letting-go-of-life means letting nature take its course i.e. the disintegration of the five aggregates (*khandha*), or the psycho-physical elements (i.e. form, *rūpa*, feeling or sensation, *vedandā*, perception, *saññā*, volition, *saṅkhāra*, and consciousness, *viññāna*) of which the self consists.

6 The term *saṃsāra* refers to the round of life and death in which the whole range of sentient beings, from the tiniest insect to man, exists. Only the human being, however, has the potential to terminate this endless cycle. Final emancipation is referred to as *nibbāna*. *Saṃsāra* is usually represented in Buddhist art by the Wheel of Life (*bhavacakra*).

7 The belief in kamma in relation to health and disease does not lead to fatalism nor pessimism, as often wrongly understood. The law of kamma does not entail complete determinism. It only stresses the causal relation between the preceding 'cause' and the following 'effect' understood in terms of mutually conditioning factors. The emphasis on the kammic cause of health and disease implies individual responsibility for health and disease. It, however, does not mean that Buddhism assigns personal responsibility for *all* illness. In Buddhist thinking kamma has both the individual and social dimensions. This

latter component may be termed *social kamma* which, for example, refers to the environmental factors that could aggravate or mitigate an individual kamma. For further discussion on this issue, see Pinit Ratanakul and Kyaw Than (eds), *Health, Healing and Religion* (Bangkok: Mahidol University, 1997), pp. 29–33.

8 For a discussion on different Buddhist perspectives on euthanasia, see Damien Keown, *Buddhism & Bioethics*, pp. 168–173.

9 Based on a survey of the perspectives of practicing Thai Buddhists on euthanasia. The survey was conducted by the Center of Human Resources Development, Mahidol University, and consisted of interviews with 200 practicing Buddhist teachers in high schools and universities in Bangkok and its neighboring provinces from February– December 1996.

10 This concept is also referred as 'dependent origination' and is stated as 'this being so, that is; this not being so, that is not.'

CHAPTER EIGHT

Buddhism Returns to the Market-place

David Bubna-Litic

For me, however the belief in the meaning of making dollars crumbled; the proposition that the more money you earn, the better the life you are leading was refuted by too much hard evidence to the contrary.

Michael Lewis, *Liar's Poker*

Introduction

In the famous series of Ox-herding pictures the culmination of Buddhist[1] practice is symbolised by the return to the world. The world in this period of history is one that is dominated by commercial activities. The sheer ubiquity of commerce means that returning to the world inevitably requires an integration of practice with the sphere of commerce. In essence this final ox-herding picture is about the integration of the practice with *every* aspect of life. Since much of the Buddhist cannon was written in times when commerce played a limited role in secular life, Buddhists must now seek new ways in which the Dharma can continue and thrive in an era when as Korten[2] suggests 'Corporations rule the World.'

When Buddhism encounters a new culture it transforms and is transformed by that culture. The split in Buddhism between the northern Mahāyāna schools and southern Hīnayāna schools also reflects the impact of the different cultures Buddhism encountered in its paths of migration out of India. Now Buddhism has taken root in the 'West' (European and New World countries) and as it encounters these great cultures it too will be transformed. Buddhism so far has attracted a small, but committed group of what can best be described as 'innovators,'[3] to use marketing jargon. Innovators generally experience most of the bugs which come with the introduction of a major new product or technology (remember the

183

very first computers). This has been the case with Buddhism in the West with *Saṅghas* experiencing a range of problems including violations of trust by teachers, permanent body damage from sitting too long in meditation postures, financial abuse and problems associated with lack of management skills.[4] However Buddhism is rapidly evolving to meet the challenges of its new environments and in doing so may revive itself in the old ones.

Already Buddhism's evolution is beginning to create new forms of practice. Although presently strongly influenced by Asian tradition, interesting Western variations are developing. If there is a theme to what is arising, according to Rick Fields,[5] it has 'an emphasis on householder instead of monk, community instead of monastery, and a practice that integrates and makes use of all aspects of life, for all people, women as well as men.' These values are deeply embedded logistically and culturally in Western society. This shift away from its monastic heritage means that Buddhism must find a new way to relate to the societies in which its practitioners are engaged. It is inevitable that this new branch of Buddhism will encounter the world of commerce as part of its metamorphosis, as this is an epoch in which commerce holds a central place in Western societies.

Commerce has not always held its present position and is, historically, relatively new to the West and even newer in the old heartlands of Buddhism in Asia. In the two hundred or so years since the Industrial Revolution began, the world has seen a period of unprecedented change. Our capacity to transform raw materials into products has grown exponentially. For example, total global economic output has expanded by more in *each* of the past four decades than from prehistory to the middle of this century. It would have been inconceivable to the people of Renaissance Europe that mercantile and commercial organisations would control budgets of trillions of dollars,[6] larger than that of entire nations. The benefits of the Industrial Revolution can not be denied – in no other period of history have ordinary people been able to obtain such material surplus. The corresponding accumulation of technical knowledge and organisational skills have granted people freedom from sickness and the ability to do things that, in previous eras, were thought reserved for the gods.

Many Westerners virtually live like the gods in material and sensual abundance, collectively conspiring to pretend immortality through medical intervention, and having miraculous powers, by virtue of technology. The games and rivalries that are lived out in Greek, Nordic and Celtic mythologies seem to be reflected in recent history. Bernie Neville[7] explores the notion that we are in an era archetypally dominated by the myth of Hermes. Hermes (Mercury) seems most clearly manifested in post-industrial workers, such as the paper entrepreneurs and advertising executives who, like Hermes, are revered as movers and shakers, and although creating nothing of substance make things happen. We applaud successful risk-takers, who are able to play the market with breathless temerity and adroitness, although, like Hermes, they have no consideration of the ethics nor the implications of their actions in terms of human costs.

From a Buddhist perspective the life of the Gods has its dark-side. This abundance and the sheer enormity of the collective activity of commerce creates shadows. The shadows of commerce are the partially hidden and unacknowledged activities that lurk outside the awareness of our collective consciousness. Most pressing is the real threat caused by commercial activities to the future of life on this planet. There are huge divisions between the rich and the poor, both within and between nations. Full employment is rare and for vast numbers of people the quality of their work life is low – arguably worse than if industrialisation had not taken place. Even in wealthy nations a culture of consumerism keeps people bonded to a cycle of work and spending. The dominance of work in our lives leaves gaps in our humanity and important soul-work unattended.

The traditional Buddhist view is that it is preferable to be born as a human rather than a god because gods are blinded to the inherent suffering of *saṃsāra* and hence do not practice the Way. The affluence of Western societies seems to blind us to the inherent suffering of the human condition and to the effects our actions have on others. This blindness seems to be an ongoing theme in most cultures. The example of Scrooge in Dicken's classic *A Christmas Carol* is symbolic of the consistent failure of wealthy people to recognise the consequences of their greed, even after facing one painful reality after another. This tale rings as true today as it did when it was written. We only need to observe the recent inquiry into the tobacco industry in the US to see how painfully obvious this denial process is.

Buddhist cosmology includes both hell realms and god realms. If the affluent live like gods, the plight of the poor nations in the global economy seems more akin to that of hell realms with burgeoning over-population, environmental poisoning by industry, sweat-shop industries, corruption, mass-prostitution, political violence and repression.

In taking a path of engaged action Buddhists must ultimately encounter both the virtue and shadow of commerce. Yet Buddhist theology was written in an era in which work was predominantly agricultural. Buddhist thought on commerce needs to be interpreted within this historical context and hence little direct guidance is available to the modern practitioner. The upheavals of Western society during and after the Renaissance have opened up great freedom for critical and reflective inquiry, which appear to have rarely been available in Buddhist history. As part of this, the role of the Buddha as a supra-human authority figure is being revised. This freedom has allowed Western *Saṅghas* to introduce major innovations to Buddhist practice, for example, a re-evaluation of the role of women and discussion of sex and inter-tradition dialogues. Using this freedom Buddhism can experiment with new ways to integrate its practices so as to have a broader appeal to secular society.

The world of commerce in the post-industrial era has expanded to pervade almost every aspect of our lives. Commercial activities provide the products, services and information for almost everything we do including our most intimate activities. Industrialisation has not only touched all aspects of our existence, but also the deepest levels of our thinking. An important issue at stake here is how is Buddhism going to *use* rather than *be used* by the world of commerce?

The Ox-herding pictures of Zen Buddhism are one source from which Buddhists can find some guidance to achieve this. In the final Ox-herding picture the seeker returns to the market place dishevelled, carrying a wine-gourd in hand and remains untainted by the muddy visicitudes of worldly life. This last picture represents the final point in the long journey of Buddhist training. The student is completely at home in the world and caring little for her/himself sets about a life of helping others. It is a useful archetype to which we can aspire. It may appear to many lay Buddhists that to fully live this is a long way off, but if skills for entering the marketplace were already part of their practice, much of the ocean would already be crossed. As Jack Kornfield points out Buddhism is a process – enlightenment is not something one gets and thereafter retires.[8] Instead, we need to explore ways in which ordinary people can combine a Buddhist practice with their work life and find how Buddhist morality may best inform them about how to act in connection with commerce. It is also important to go beyond the individual level of analysis and look at ways in which Buddhists can organise and transform the economic system recognising that these two levels are not separate, but interlinked.

Buddha's rejection of materialism and sensuality

There are strong parallels between the life of the Buddha and that of modern Western living. The Buddha was not a poor uneducated peasant, but was born into wealthy Indian nobility. Like in most Western societies, amongst the nobility of the Śākya the dominant values embraced a path of materialism and sensuality. The Buddha's father, it seems, was mainly concerned about position, status and material achievement, and his desire for his son to be 'successful' is not unlike that of many Western parents. The life of the Buddha has strong archetypal resonance for many contemporary Western men and women who have all the earmarks of nobility: education, wealth and surrounded by sophisticated sensual pleasures. We too are presented with the dominant worldview that explicitly and implicitly values status and material success. The view of measuring life using the yardstick of money and implicitly the status and material and sensual satisfaction it can purchase, underpins the greater body of economic theory currently taught in Business Schools. Yet as there is a growing sense of having 'arrived' we too are facing the same dissatisfaction which the Buddha experienced in his life. This appears to be supported by the increased interest in inner-life related activities and products of the ageing baby-boomers population.

What makes the myth of the Buddha's life such a powerful instruction is the clarity with which the Buddha encounters the suffering inherent in life. It is the folly of the Buddha's father, in the thoroughness of his conspiracy to hide the realities of sickness, old age and death, which provided the Buddha with his powerful insight into the human condition. The luminosity of seeing a sick person, an old person and a dying person for the first time in his life, as an adult, clearly shocked the Buddha deeply. For many of us, like gods, we can either cushion or avoid these shocks for the greater part of our lives, often till old age. The modern Western experience of these realities is clouded by softening explanations, euphemism and denial. Medical intervention through drugs, medical technology and specialised personnel with their paternal values means that when we do encounter death it is often mediated. In this way our connection to our friends and family in their final hours is distant. Their pain and anguish can be hidden by visiting hours and a vacant narcotic smile. Yet encountering these basic truths can bring about important learning. This learning is part of our maturity as people and when the reality of the human condition eventually sets in, it may not be until mid-life. Old age and death are the central preoccupations in a mid-life crisis.

But of equal importance as this series of shocks was to the Buddha, was his meeting a saint or holy person. This was significant because he was able to confront the possibility of enlightenment or a way out of suffering. This is the unique contribution of Buddhism to the West. As more Westerners gain deep insight into Buddhism and bear witness to this as a genuine personal experience, an alternative path to materialism can develop credence. The alternative path to materialism is the path of spirituality. The impact of Buddhism is also bringing into greater focus the mystic traditions of Christianity and Judaism.

Yet the distinction between materialism and spirituality is not as the Buddha first thought when he chose to wholly reject sensual materialism. Implicit in leaving his palace, family, royal status and lifestyle and trading his equivalent of an expensive Italian suit for rags was a rejection of his former lifestyle. In leading the life of an ascetic the Buddha assumed that the spiritual path was the opposite of sensual materialism. As one Zen teacher told me – the Buddha was a royal dropout!

Yet the myth of the Buddha does not finish there. He found that the spiritual path is not denial of sensual materialism, nor is it the opposite of it. Joanna Macy[9] examines four paths commonly characterised as being spiritual. The first two of these paths split the world into the spiritual and the profane. These views resemble the Buddha's worldview when he left the palace. It is likely, according to Misra,[10] that the Buddha's worldview reflected that of the Śrāmaṇa movement of around 500 BC, which essentially denounced sensual materialism as the root of suffering. These first two views see the sensual-material world either as something bad to be overcome or a trap to be avoided. The first position, which has parallels in many religions (including some forms of Buddhism), is that *the world is a battlefield* between good and evil. The simplicity of this view has strong popular appeal in countries that have suffered transition crises in their encounter with the world economy and Western cultures. This view grants a sense of security in the certainty of being right. In religions based on a written tradition the appeal of this has massively empowered fundamentalist movements in many countries and similar movements revolving around non-theistic and a-theistic world-views, such as free-market capitalism and communism. The world as a battlefield is a powerful metaphor; however, it is an oversimplification of the spiritual path.

The second position is that *the world is a trap* from which we must avoid entanglement. In renouncing the confusing material world the Buddha sought the tranquillity of the forest to escape from the suffering of *saṃsāra*. Macy[11] shows how systems theory can explain how this desire to become detached from the world creates a negative spiral that does not lead to transcendence. The Buddha too became caught in a circle of increasing physical self-abuse and denial, ultimately reaching a crisis point in which he almost perished. The greatness of the Buddha was that he did not give up at that point, slipping back into a cynical and wounded life, but creatively ventured out to the middle path – a harmonious balance between the two.

Having found this balance the Buddha was able to go beyond his peers and realised his Self-nature through the dissolution of his egoistic delusions. It was this middle path that the Buddha followed which lead to his insight into Macy's last two views which are the 'World as Lover, World as Self.' The view of the 'World as Lover, World as Self' is the recognition of our close intimacy with the world, like lovers we seek union with the universe and 'fall into oneness.'[12] The mysteries of love continue after enlightenment and as Macy observes, the detachment that the Buddha taught was from the ego, not from the world

The Buddha did not teach that lay people could not attain high spiritual states. Layman Pang is a famous example in Zen. Walpola Rahula[13] points out that 'if some one lives an entire life in solitude thinking of only his or her happiness and salvation, without caring for fellow beings, this is surely not in keeping with the Buddha's teaching which is based on love compassion, and service to others.'

The Bodhisattva in business

The return to the market place can also be seen in the story of the Buddha who, after sitting for a week or so after his great realisation enjoying his insight into the forms and emptiness of the universe, comes back to teach his five companion ascetics. The reason for this, according to Robert Aitken, is that 'Nirvana all alone by itself is not enough.' The Buddha under the tree in his state of absolute emptiness was still not complete, he lacked fulfilment: 'The Buddha's karma, like yours and mine, is to save all beings – thus we find completion in our lives and fulfilment of the Dharma.'[14] Kenneth Kraft[15] points out that 'spiritual maturity includes the ability to actualise transcendent insight in daily life.' It is this relationship to the world that is expressed in Mahāyāna Buddhism through the archetype of the 'Bodhisattva.' Saving all beings is the work of the Bodhisattva.

The Bodhisattva, free of self-preoccupation, understands the interpenetration of all things, and as Robert Aitken[16] explains: 'if you can see that all phenomena are transparent, ephemeral, and indeed altogether void, then the thrush will sing in your heart, and you can show compassion ...' It is through this intertwining of compassion and insight that the Bodhisattva makes his or her way through the world. But what exactly does it mean to save all the many beings? How do we live unselfishly? These are fundamental issues in Mahāyāna Buddhist practice, matters that are made clear over a lifetime of practice.

Work is recognised in many spiritual traditions both as a powerful tool to penetrate into the depth of daily life and as an expression of deep insight. Thomas Moore[17] recognises this deeper function of work: ... 'all work is a vocation, a calling from a place that is the source of meaning and identity, the roots of which lie beyond human intention and interpretation.' In Ch'an and Zen Buddhism, work was an essential part of monastic life and considered as important as other aspects of practice such as meditation and chanting *sūtras*. Work in a monastic community was mainly based around the simple life of subsistence agriculture. Although many monasteries had busy public schedules, most monastic work roles involved relatively simple tasks. This was further contained by the monastic structure that carefully selected senior positions and ritualised jobs to maintain work as an extension of meditation. Work is a powerful way of confronting a student's attachments and delusions, in the mindful carrying of refuse, organising a public funeral and the cleaning of toilets. It connects us with our bodies, our feeling life, our intellect and provides a structure for the development of community relationships. Work under these circumstances is deeply enriching.

Western lay practitioners are, however, often confronted with very different work environments. Unlike the monastery, commercial work organisations are designed for completely different outcomes. Firstly, it is extremely difficult to maintain that seamless movement from meditation, to work, to meditation, in the rough and tumble of modern organisational life. Contrasting with the simplicity of monastic life, in which work was generally less than eight hours a day, modern work dominates the larger part of many peoples' lives. The fast moving, complex and uncertain world of the modern business creates high levels of stress and it is full of subtle seductions that have deeper consequences in people's lives. Collectively, the weight of this experience is so great that many authors perceive that society has become a victim exhibiting a vague malaise. De Foore and Renesch[18] call it 'soullessness.' Needleham[19] calls this 'the new poverty,' where, despite a society's affluence, there is an undercurrent of fear, apprehension and loneliness. Buddhists see these as children of the first noble truth – that life is suffering.

Suffering is not a surprising consequence in the chaos and upheavals of the seemingly endless transitions characterising this century. New technologies are constantly re-arranging the furniture of our lives. The present transitions from industrial to post-industrial and inter-nation-based economies to a global economy have brought yet another series of bewildering changes. Carried by the promise of a golden age of wondrous new technology and new competition these changes bring further social and environmental restructuring and discontinuity. We find major corporations 'down-sizing,' increasing disparities in wealth, a weakening labour movement, and the rise of a class of permanently unemployed who are unable to compete in a global economy without advanced education. As businesses move from the small creeks and ponds of local industry to the oceans of the global economy they too find themselves becoming subjected to waves and currents of a new magnitude.

Secondly, most modern business organisations have little or no interest in the sacred and so, for the Buddhist employee, conditions are not ideal. The assumption that Buddhists can maintain a separate belief system and still function with harmony in such organisations is one that has to be questioned. There is substantial evidence to suggest that we are highly influenced by the values and assumptions of those around us. Organisations can be seen as comprising a range of shared meanings and taken-for-granted assumptions which structure and influence the way things happen in them. In order to survive at work Buddhists may find that they must either subordinate their values or become peripheral to the organisation. Where there is a fundamental conflict of values this may result in resignation or dismissal. To participate in the world of commerce we need to find ways of negotiating modern organisational life without abdicating our values. This may be difficult but it is not impossible.

Many contemporary Buddhist teachers have written on the art of navigating the rough seas of modern life using techniques based on meditation and mindfulness. Mindfulness is the foundation of work practice according to John Daido Loori.[20] Although working in business organisations creates difficulties, mindfulness can be practiced wherever one is, as true mindfulness is the practice of being in this moment. It is a practice which, as John Kabot-Zinn[21] explains, 'may be simple to practice … it is not necessarily easy.' Through mindfulness we get in touch with ourselves and with our real work in life. In this way work can become the vehicle for insight as well as the development of character – the embodiment of insight.

Mindfulness has multiple dimensions. As we become open to the moment and we become aware of ourselves, this awareness brings new and hidden aspects of ourselves into consciousness. Richard Strozzi Heckler[22] describes three steps when working with awareness in the body and this strongly parallels how mindfulness works with our complete psyche over time. The first is bringing attention to what is, that is, what is in the foreground of our experience. The second step is becoming aware of feelings, memories, or images of the past that arise. These are the background of our experience. The background should not be a diversion from what is presently being lived, but seen in relation to the moment. The final step is to become aware of what *'wants to come to life,'* that is, changes which will open up new growth. This is the dynamic nature of our experience and our awareness develops as we come into contact with what is happening on deeper levels. It is the very essence of healing.

Thomas Moore draws on Jung when he recognises these deeper levels of awareness and how important work is in dealing with the material of what he calls 'soul.' Moore[23] explains how work can become the cauldron in which the raw materials of ordinary life are alchemically turned into gold. The deepness of the connection we have with our work provides us with that which satisfies us at the very root of our being. It is a source for deep character development that reflects spiritual maturity and is the embodi-ment of insight. The value of work from a Buddhist perspective also lies in its process. From this perspective we do good work when we engage in it fully and feel good about it. Moore is careful to separate the pride we have in our own process from the relative or narcissistic pride we gain through achievement outside ourselves. Work becomes a true act of love when we see the world as our lover and our self. The Narcissus myth, according to Moore,[24] 'suggests that we will never achieve the flowering of our own natures until we find that piece of ourselves, that lovable twin, which lives in the world and as the world. Therefore, finding the right work is like discovering your own soul in the world.'

There is a strong parallel here with Jacob Needleham's[25] exploration of the legend of Solomon, in which Solomon loses everything he has to Asmodeus the king of the demons in order to learn the nature of his power. At Asmodeus's request, Solomon first lets him free and gives Asmodeus his sacred ring. On receipt of the ring, Asmodeus immediately grows to an enormous size, hurls King Solomon to a distant country, and tosses King Solomon's power ring into the depths of the sea. After, Asmodeus steals into the royal chambers and by changing his face into the face of King Solomon assumes the role of the king. Needleham points out that allegorically Solomon has lost his true self. This loss of self is the most powerful of demons. In the same way as Narcissus failed to recognise himself as his lover when he mistook the reflection of himself for another, when our work no longer reflects our true self we seek satisfaction outside the work itself through secondary rewards such as money status and symbols of success. According to Needleham this is the danger of materialism. It blinds us from seeing who we really are.

In a similar vein, Marx[26] described the alienation that he saw when 'work is external to the worker, that it is not part of his nature; and that, consequently, he does not fulfil himself in his work but denies himself, has a feeling of misery rather than well-being...' Christopher Titmus[27] sees a parallel between the views of the Buddha and Marx's concepts of alienation noting that they are both concerned about humankind's alienation from itself and the world. The key difference is that the Buddha stressed spiritual change whereas Marx sought relief through political and social action.

When we are free from alienation, work becomes like play. From this perspective, as Fran Peavy[28] puts, it 'good work is all about love.' This is not to say that work is devoid of sweat and grind. No matter what our calling is, work usually consists both of mundane activities as well as acts of imagination. Even in highly technical areas of science there are repetitive and mundane tasks such as data recording and analysis. Suffering is part of the human condition. At the same time, even in the most simple tasks there are, as Japanese production workers have shown through continuous improvement, opportunities for imagination and innovation. Imagination, according to Jung, is integral to our inner lives or the soul life. It is through deep reflection on a task that we allow our imagination to work. This deep reflection is mindfulness.

The interrelationship between practice, insight and character work has long been recognised in Buddhism. According to Thich Nhat Hanh[29] the Threefold Training: *Śīla*, the practice of the precepts, *Samādhi*, the practice of concentration and *Prajñā*, the practice of insight are co-requisite to each other. Mindfulness through meditation and awareness is the base upon which *Samādhi*, or concentration, develops in order to gain insight. The second aspect of training, *Śīla* consists of the precepts which facilitate concentration, but are also the marks of character development and act as a container in which we can alchemically develop insight. The precepts are both a means and expression of Buddhist practice. They provide a guide to practitioners at all levels to the work of the Bodhisattva. It is important to the understanding of Buddhist morality that these three elements cannot be separated. As Thich Nhat Hanh[30] says 'The three are intertwined; each helps the other two, and all three bring us closer to final liberation.'

Although Buddhist morality encompasses the entire thrust of the religion, historically there are formally expressed 'precepts' or general rules that govern the *Saṅgha*. In Mahāyāna Buddhism these are derived from the rules for monastic life set out in the Vinaya, which was collated in the centuries following Śākyamuni Buddha's death. These rules prescribed a very simple and restricted life with a collective aim of understanding the Dharma.

Although the various strands in Mahāyāna Buddhism have different variations on the precepts, the 'Three Vows of Refuge' are central to almost all:

I take refuge in the Buddha;
I take refuge in the Dharma;
I take refuge in the Saṅgha.

This simple set of vows is repeated in initiation ceremonies and in daily *sūtra* recitations. They are a sign of trust in the realisation-experience of the Buddha, the truth of the Dharma and the importance of harmony in relationships within the *Saṅgha*. They also set out simply the essential aspects of the Buddhist experience: the attainment of insight through practice, the expression of insight into the Dharma, and the context of these relationship in the world and among other beings. In Mahāyāna schools these are elaborated at length through further monastic vows or precepts. Fundamentally, however, the emphasis on ethics in Mahāyāna schools has been organic: as an understanding of the Dharma develops through practice, this insight naturally allows the practitioner to develop an unaffected compassion beyond any mechanistic following of a set of rules of conduct (precepts).

Aitken[31] discusses at length contemporary applications of the 'Sixteen Bodhisattva Precepts,' a set of vows that are studied and followed as part of Zen Buddhist practice. These sixteen precepts consist of the 'Three Vows of Refuge' discussed above, the 'Three Pure Precepts' and the 'Ten Grave Precepts.' The 'Three Pure Precepts' are an adaptation from the *Dhammapada*:

Renounce all evil;
Practice all good;
Save the many beings.

The 'Ten Grave Precepts' are:

1 Not killing
2 Not stealing
3 Not misusing sex

4 Not lying
5 Not giving or taking drugs
6 Not discussing the faults of others
7 Not praising yourself while abusing others
8 Not sparing the Dharma assets
9 Not indulging in anger
10 Not defaming the Three Treasures.

The precepts are the formal expression of the social contract which characterised early Buddhist communities setting out the rights and obligations of members in a monastic community. The social contract that characterises a community, however, goes beyond mere codification and can be found, informally, in the web of understandings and commitments that develop overtime between the members of the community. These understandings and commitments and their symbolic manifestation in the architecture, art, music, literature and ritual of Buddhist monastic life incorporate, to a large degree, the technology of Buddhist practice and ultimately express the Dharma.

The understanding and values which reflect the Dharma represent a paradigmatic contrast to current commerce. Gregory Bateson[32] summarises the ideas that dominate our civilisation as follows:

A. It's us *against* the environment.
B. It's us *against* others [humans].
C. It's the individual (or the individual company, or the individual nation) that matters.
D. We *can* have unilateral control over the environment and must strive for that control.
E. We live within an infinitely expanding 'frontier.'
F. Economic determinism is common sense.
G. Technology will do it for us.

The idea that economic wealth leads to happiness can be added to this list.

These values are reflected in the actions of commercial organisations. They differ from the Buddhist view of the world in that they represent the perspective of egoistic delusion and attachment. Furthermore, many commercial organisations act in ways that perpetuate these values and so too, attachment and delusion. The cynicism of the advertising industry is most salient. For example, a common advertising ploy is to associate a product targeted at lower income groups with 'the good life' (of the rich) using sports stars, or beautiful people in salubrious settings. To follow the precepts in a commercial organisation a Buddhist employee is constantly presented with a range of moral difficulties. These difficulties are not just peculiar to commercial organisations, but to all aspects of human life. As

Thich Nhat Hanh[33] recognises, 'practicing right livelihood has ceased to be a personal matter.' The actions of commercial businesses depend on the actions of others. A breakfast cereal maker that doesn't use salt, sugar or flavour enhancers could easily go out of business in favour of one that does. Restaurants which don't kill rodents and insects will be shut down by health authorities. Business make many decisions on the basis of 'what the customers want' rather than what they think is good for the customer in order to survive.

A commonly held Buddhist perspective is that we are part of a society which is caught up in a cycle of pernicious delusion in which almost every aspect of the society participates. Christopher Titmus's work[34] exemplifies this view. We do not need to look far to find examples of the proliferation of weapons of violence, alienating and destructive occupations, social and personal degradation and ecological destruction. Yet as members of society how can we not participate? This is the point of Joanna Macy[35] – we are not separate from the world. John Kabat-Zinn[36] develops his ideas on mindfulness from the ground point of the human condition which he feels is best described as the 'the full catastrophe!' The first step to mindfulness according to Kabat-Zinn[37] is finding and coming to terms with the 'poignant enormity of our life experience.' The full catastrophe of our lives is everything we experience including thoughts, fantasies, opinions, material possessions, and bodies. For many the full catastrophe seems overwhelming, but as Joanna Macy[38] suggests: 'if we not open to feel the anxiety and despair brought about by the sheer weight of magnitude of life and world problems – we are cutting off important parts of ourselves.' The process of opening oneself to the bits and pieces of one's life that one has repressed, separated or split off from oneself has strong parallels to the Jungian idea of individuation. Several Buddhist teachers including John Tarrant and Jack Kornfield[39] recognise the important contribution that the psychotherapies offer to Buddhism in working through this process. As we open ourselves to the ground of our life's experience we can begin to walk the Bodhisattva path. One of the most popular archetypal Bodhisattvas is Kuan Yin, the Bodhisattva of compassion. Kuan Yin is the Chinese name for Avalokiteśvara: 'The one who looks down in compassion.' She/he represents the experience of *Prajñāpāramitā* (Perfection of Wisdom) witnessing the suffering of the world.

Although we are part of a world full of problems we do not have to act in ways that exacerbate them. The key to maintaining the precepts lies in how we navigate the myriads of moment-by-moment choices that arise in our working lives. John Tarrant[40] has explored the concept of integrity as a container for Zen practice. The root of the word integrity is *integ* which means *not touched*. Put into a Buddhist context it is that part of us which is untouched – our essential Self. According to John Beebe,[41] *integer* has the meaning of intact, whole, complete, perfect, and honest – which also characterises the essential Self. Integrity can be seen as an expression of our essential Buddha nature.

Integrity is the wellspring through which we develop a sense of connectedness, coherence, wholeness, and adaptive vitality. Using this definition as a base, Julian Gresser[42] has developed a methodology for negotiation that can be used in virtually any circumstance. The key to Gresser's method is mindfulness or openness to the moment which he calls presence. By entering each activity with a sense of having a 'beginners mind,' that is, being willing to see everything as if for the first time, people can be receptive to new possibilities and see things as they are. In negotiating their work lives people characteristically make assumptions about what is and what is not possible. These assumptions and ideas get in the way of being open to the world and pre-empt the attainment of integrity with themselves and their work.

A deep commitment to the cultivation of integrity encompasses the precepts and brings them together with mindfulness. According to John Tarrant,[43] spiritual practice involves true integration of both spiritual and soul dimensions. As mindfulness links us with deeper levels of ourselves we gain greater sense of our intuitive side. Deep integrity in this context reflects both these elements of who we are: our insight and our character. It links these two together.

By approaching each encounter at work with the stance of open awareness we can use these moments as opportunities to develop our integrity. This stance was valued in Japan by the Samurai, who knew the subtle power of having a mind free of expectations. The true mind of 'not knowing' takes this a further step, so we can meet our fellow workers not as opponents, but as ourselves with the compassion and freedom to respond to their actions just as they are, without expectations, prejudice or predisposing assumptions. From this point we can integrate the precepts with our work, making decisions on the basis of what is right for the circumstances based on logic and intuition.

Genuine integrity is not easily achieved and it requires that we let go of our conditioned ways of holding onto things. Through the cultivation of mindfulness we can free ourselves from delusory needs and attachments. One of the fundamental steps in Gresser's approach to negotiation is to come to grips with what we actually need in life. This too requires integrity since we live by more than bread alone. Part of our soul work is understanding what is true to ourselves, what our soul life needs. This may appear to be in opposition to spiritual work.

Moore[44] warns against the 'puer' attitude that is so prevalent in religion and in spiritual practice. The puer image of the soul is that of a boy or young man. It is a relationship to the soul that is completely unattached to things worldly. The famous puer myth is that of Icarus, the young man who, after escaping from the labyrinth, puts on waxen wings made by his father and despite warnings, flies too close to the sun, which melts his wings, so that he falls to his death. The tale of Icarus warns of the perils of using religion as an escape to rise above the mundane and worldly. This trap is also recognised in Buddhism and there are plenty of admonitions about this in the Rinzai koan curriculum. According to Yamada Koun Roshi[45] 'the truly great Zen person ... should be indistinguishable from the ordinary person, at least in externals.' The ordinary great person is the Bodhisattva, one who has not forsaken the muddy world of suffering and desire, but remains with the loose ends, the difficulties, the material that is in darkness and mystery. The work of the Bodhisattva is, according to John Tarrant,[46] 'to live and understand, and not to worry too much what fate brings.'

As we develop integrity and understand our true needs, we can begin to negotiate our work lives. Although the precepts are instructive guides to integrity, they sit uncomfortably with it and can become burdensome. The spirit is quickly lost in the clouds of good and evil and the soul can easily be suffocated by rules. The precepts, in a world of ambiguity and contradictions, are also easy prey to the solipsistic manoeuvres of a clever mind, justifying acts that poison the heart. Integrity development encompasses all aspects of a person. Integrity, as John Tarrant[47] observes, '... comes from the heart, not just the head, and we have to feel our way into it.'

The process leading to integrity is a spiral pathway of learning in which we encounter the ordinary and unclear in life. There will be times when decisions will be clear, at other dark times we will need to agonise and hold the pain of deep conflicts. Out of all the events in the life of Jesus why does the Cross remain the most powerful symbol of Christianity? According to Rene Guenon[48] the cross is a symbol of union of opposites (or complements). Perhaps the spirit is being represented by the vertical and the soul represented by the horizontal. According to Robert Johnson,[49] when we are confronted with powerfully opposing forces in our lives, movement in either direction is not appropriate; rather we need to hold the questions so that over time inner work can be done and then life will present us, as of miraculously, with a solution.

Despite the tendency in the management literature to focus on short-term success stories,[50] a long-term view shows the life of most commercial organisations as generally short and significantly dependent on the ebb and flow of broad economic, natural and societal forces.[51] Life in organisations is correspondingly chaotic, uncertain and full of conflict. This experience is often painful. Buddhist practice is to cultivate the capacity to hold one's integrity in the face of pain. As we develop the capacity to be open to the 'full catastrophe' we learn to get a very firm grip on the inner forces that drive the creation of false needs. It is these mentally fabricated needs that seduce us into greed, materialism and over-work. The purpose of Buddhism is to realise the delusory nature of needs and yearnings. Murray Stein[52] believes that because people get caught up and identify with their plans, successes and failures they are likely to experience organisations as painful. When these projections and identifications are contained, they begin to see things as they are and can act according to their needs.

The letting-go of attachments is basic to Buddhist practice. Historically, monks gave up all material possessions before joining the monastery. Traditional Buddhist lay practice emphasised frugality, right occupation, and sharing wealth – particularly in the form of *dāna*. The *Sigalovāda Sutta*[53] suggests four specific ways in which accumulated wealth should be divided; however, the key theme is simple and frugal living. Is it possible to live simply surrounded by wealth? This is an important question of practice and the answer depends on each person. It can equally be argued that attachment to poverty is the same attachment to wealth. Wealth may come to us in a variety of different ways, by birth, as a consequence of our work or as an unexpected windfall. However it comes, we need to create a life style that maintains our integrity. What we do with this wealth depends on our own integrity.

Wealth and success have subtle seductions, which come in many guises and affect us in invisible ways. For example, we hear it in a subtle reverence for someone who has wealth or success and, more obviously, in name-dropping. This does not mean that wealth should be avoided. Monks were not without wealth. Although traditional monastic life was simple and monks had little private property, the community as a whole was often well provided for. Wealth existed in other forms, such as, monastery buildings themselves, which are among the most beautiful places in Asia. Lay Buddhists need material possessions to function in the world. The difficulty arises when we accumulate wealth beyond our needs. Awareness of the traps of material wealth requires mindfulness. An important part of the process of understanding our true needs is to pare down from what want to what we need. It is not necessary to 'act-out' this understanding by getting rid of everything we own, although from time-to-time it could be valuable to find ways to test our detachment. There are many myths and stories, for example, of the rich finding new wisdom after changing places with the less fortunate.

The power and integrity of being in a position of few needs is the theme of the *Tao Te Ching*. Herman Hesse[54] showed the virtue of just being able to think, to wait and to fast in the story of Siddhartha. Gresser[55] discovered how we lose this power in negotiation when we lapse into thinking wants are needs. To maintain our integrity we need to be free of unnecessary commitments and attachments, so that we are free to do our work.

Some attachments and commitments have a real basis, since many people owe money and have a family to support. Joe Dominguez and Vicki Robin[56] see one of the biggest drawbacks to integrity as lack of financial independence. To have financial independence is to be in a position in which we are free from being dependent on money in making life choices. Many people place themselves in precarious financial positions in order to have the things they want. They then pay for them with interest both in the credit charges and in the financial insecurity that ensues. Financial integrity is 'knowing what is enough money and material goods to keep you at the peak of fulfilment – and what is just excess and clutter.'[57] We lose our integrity because we fear the high price of losing our income. This is because, as Dominguez and Robin[58] point out, most people 'owe their soul to the company store.' The curious reality is that most people earn far in excess of their basic needs. Western culture not only encourages consumption through commercial marketing, but increasingly we are obliged to buy things out of social conventions – a round of drinks, restaurant dinners with friends, farewell presents, flowers, gratuities and so on. Consumerism is rampant.

Economically developed societies are typically navigating their lives using what Dominguez and Robin call 'old road maps' designed at a time when the new availability of material possession enabled many to fulfil previously unmet, but real, needs. The benefits of production at least seemed to balance the moral and ethical, and environmental and social costs. Over time the commercial world has changed exponentially and what once fulfilled the population's needs now facilitates luxury and excess. Furthermore, old maps saw the world as an unlimited resource, which it is not.

Based on the work of Dominguez and Robin, Gresser and others, it is possible to develop an alternative framework for navigating work life that resonates well with Buddhist precepts and may shed new light on 'right livelihood.' There are two important and inter-related elements to this alternative framework. The first is the development of detachment through Buddhist practices of mindfulness and meditation. Through this process we become aware of what our true needs are in life. As we become free of attachments and by being fully mindful and open to the myriads of decisions which make up the maze of dilemmas which we encounter at work – including the difficult tasks, the politics, environmental con-sequences, competition, selfishness, successes and failures – we can navigate with integrity. Complementary to this is a lifestyle that reduces a substantial proportion of the costs of living through living simply, healthily and frugally. Learning to consume less is fundamental to the long-term survival of life on the planet. Buddhists who live such a lifestyle should also find financial independence achievable. Financial independence allows freedom to follow right livelihood with the virtue of not being a burden to others.

The second element is to live life with integrity. Through the development of deep integrity we can learn to trust our insight and intuition, and our actions are informed by our integrity with each moment. In this way we can integrate our work with the Tao. This is following our calling. By being aware of our soul needs and how these inform our life priorities we can define our work in relation to integrity. Through re-visioning our work, as separate from that which gives us income, paid work then becomes just one activity among many in which we can save all beings.

Acting with integrity in work cannot be separated from how we act in other aspects of our lives. Financial independence does not pre-empt the accumulation of wealth. Buddhists who accumulate large amounts of money, however, should be mindful of how they came to it and be aware of the responsibilities that go with the power that money brings. Reyong of Baoneug said, 'Use the property and possessions of the community as carefully as if they were your own eyes.'

Buddhist organisation

Whilst it is possible for Buddhists to individually navigate the world of commerce with integrity, it must be recognised that many will find that the wind is against them. Commercial organisations are driven by a different belief system, and they are part of a broader political and economic system which confronts Buddhist ethics and its sense of harmony with the world and ourselves. On the one hand we wish to cross the ocean through negotiating a path full of mindfulness and integrity, and on the other hand we are confronted with a world in which pathos and shadow material have set many traps for the unwary. The demands of work often conflict with the demands of Buddhist practice, family life and community. Negotiating to maintain integrity as an individual is therefore likely to involve sacrifices. The competitive work-place already confronts us with values of self-sacrifice and conformity to the Corporation as proof of our commitment. Buddhists who maintain integrity by working less or by confronting organisational shadows may find themselves surfing dangerous waves at the periphery of organisations.

As Buddhism grows however, it will become increasingly possible for Buddhists to organise themselves and work together. Historically, Buddhists organised themselves into monastic communities separated from the seductions and confusions of worldly life. The different cultural values in China meant that monasteries had to be self-sufficient and subsequently, in Mahāyāna Buddhism, work became an central part of monastic life and practice. So much so that, according to D T. Suzuki,[59] the first rule of monastic life was that 'A day of no work is a day of no eating.' Eventually it may be possible for Buddhists to collectively organise work in such a way that they can maintain integrity at an organisational level.

Over the centuries, Asian monastic communities developed sophisticated and complex organisational cultures which embody the Dharma. The monastic model, however, cannot be simply transposed to the commercial sector. Western Buddhists have no clear organisational models that may facilitate integration practice and work in a commercial context.

The lack of models has been evident in some of the attempts by Western Buddhists groups to organise Dharma-related businesses. The most salient group is the San Francisco Zen Centre under Roshi Baker. In terms of the content (the *what*) of their actions, many of the business of the San Francisco Zen Centre reflected important steps towards the values of integrity. The food businesses were truly pioneering in quality vegetarian food. There was a rejection of pre-processed ingredients which was standard practice in the industry at that time and employment policies were extremely liberal. On the other hand, the process (the *how*) by which the businesses were managed reflected lack of business experience and integrity. Since there were none or few advanced Buddhist students with management experience around at the time, it is not surprising that some ventures became unstuck. It is difficult to reconstruct these events, but many things seemed awry. From a business perspective, a comparatively low return on investment was achieved when low pay rates, voluntary labour, financial and material donations and tax breaks for religious organisations were taken into account. In the end, the San Francisco Zen Centres' enterprises became a major source of resentment towards Baker Roshi as Saṅgha members perceived that the benefits of their hard work had been squandered on ill-conceived ventures or had gone to subsidising their Teacher's lifestyle. In terms of integrity, accounts of former members of San Francisco Zen Centre suggest that some of these commercial ventures also failed to distinguish themselves from other non-Buddhist businesses and in some instances compared poorly.

Other Buddhist groups have mixed Dharma-related commercial ventures with general community projects. The results of such ventures are hard to evaluate. An example of this is the Nyingma organisation, which has, according to its own publications, managed a string of important projects over its eighteen years of existence.[60] Another example of a reportedly[61] successful project is the Greyston Bakery in Yonkers, NY founded by the Zen Community of New York thirteen years ago. The Bakery, I am told, is profitable and is a $3 million enterprise that employs about 40 local, low-income, 'hard-to-employ' residents, providing life and job skills as well as jobs (with decent wages and benefits). It is regarded as a success because it has found a balance between economic imperatives and yet has an intense commitment to a core set of values and to the low-income residents of the neighbourhood.

Commercial organisations, whether they are Buddhist or not, are embedded in a market-economy. The activities of the organisation are the result of a complex set of decisions which must be responsive to the actions of other organisations in its environment. In the modern global economy this means competition. Survival in a competitive market-place generally requires that organisations make a profit. Profit[62] in a market transaction is made by selling something (either a service or product) for more than it cost. The market price of a good or service is determined by a complex set of factors. Of these, three are usually considered as most important. The first is the degree of information and knowledge buyers and sellers have about the market. What sort of understanding do they have regarding the nature of the product and what is the prevailing price? The second is the availability of alternative sellers, or the amount of competition in the market. The final one is the value that the buyer places on the product.

Buddhism is not fundamentally against the market as a mechanism for exchange.[63] On the contrary, any exchange can be made on the basis of integrity. It is the unethical behaviour that can occur in market relationships that is of concern from a Buddhist perspective. The somewhat arbitrary nature of price-setting in real (as opposed to theoretical) markets creates a degree of uncertainty. It is this uncertainty that is the basis for ethical dilemmas in the market place. Taking advantage of another's lack of market information for one's own gain would seem to contradict integrity. On the other hand, the rules of the game are pretty clear and it up to the buyer to decide what price they are prepared to pay. It is foolish, if not arrogant, to impugn another's motives. Historically, markets in many countries have operated on the principle 'let the buyer beware,' yet there are boundaries to what the buyer should be wary of, both legally and ethically. Practices that involve deliberate deception are illegal in most countries. There is a difference between a buyer who pays a premium for a product because he or she did not do their homework or bought on impulse, and the buyer who finds the product does not do what the seller said it would. The key to understanding appropriate market transactions from a Buddhist perspective lies in the precepts, especially not harming, not lying and not selling drugs.

Market transactions should not harm others. This does not mean not harming egos or pride, but not placing others in the position of genuine hardship. For example, when an opportunity arises to make an extraordinary profit the buyer or seller should act as would a Bodhisattva – listening to the sounds of the world. In being mindful of the situation, one might inquire as to why the person is selling or wants to buy so urgently. If the sale appears likely to have harmful effects on the person, then it may be appropriate to change or withdraw the offer. To do this, is to act with integrity.

Market transactions should embrace the way of not lying. Lying in market transaction operates in subtle ways. Sales people quickly learn to highlight the benefits of a product rather than discuss the faults. There is something awry here, and Gresser points out the need to encounter every transaction empty handed not clinging to winning or losing. Many salespeople fall into the trap of pushing their customers into a sale.

According to Gresser, the final presentation in a negotiation[64] should be 'simple, clear, without wobbling, exaggeration or adornment.'[65]

In developing detachment and grounding in our real needs, Buddhists can rise above their fear of losing a sale. It is this fear that is the source of falsely building up customer's expectations, manipulating their weaknesses and failing to be mindful of their needs. Often salespeople are trained to act in ways that potentially manipulate customers. Much of their training is based around the need to 'close the sale.' This ranges from asking for the sale to pushing people into making a decision. Sales courses are full of subtle ways to do this – 'can I wrap it up for you?' or 'if you buy today we will throw in a radio for free.' There is a fine line between dealing with indecision in human nature and subtle trickery. If we are open to others and include them by acting with integrity we may find we can negotiate in the market-place without resorting to deception and lying.

Many salespeople fail to address fully the needs of their customers because they have assumptions of independence. This is encouraged by the impersonal and distant relationship firms create to deal with the mass society in which they operate. Axelrod[66] found that opportunistic behaviour is related to the likelihood of further interaction. The less likelihood there is of a further interaction the higher the chance of opportunism. When we do business on the assumption that we are completely separate and will never see a person again, we are subtly splitting them off from ourselves.

Fundamentally, a market exchange is a cooperative relationship – two parties work together. It is when one party in such a relationship lacks integrity and abuses the relationship for 'excessive' profit that problems arise. Some recent studies[67] have highlighted the importance and value of relationship and trust. Such theories suggest that by exploring a trust relationship more deeply, more cooperative approaches may be more efficient economic mechanisms. Interestingly, trust develops out of honesty and open communication, which are encouraged by Buddhist precepts.

Trust and cooperation allow for a variety of different economic relationships in which suppliers, buyers or sellers work together, such as partnerships, networks, alliances and joint ventures. These relationships are born out of a recognition of interdependence and mutual gain.[68] An increasing number of firms are finding that collaborative strategies and joint ventures can unlock new resources. These are allowing for faster product development, better quality, and improved distribution. The conception that simple competition leads to economic efficiency has to be questioned.

The precept of not selling drugs applies to the self-centred delusions that cloud and darken the mind. It is the encouragement of these delusions and the egoist value that buyers place on products and services that is a source of Buddhist concern. We are now in a symbolic economy. What people are buying is as much a construction of marketing technology as a construction of manufacturing technology. We are being sold dreams and ego extensions for use as props in the drama of life. The power of modern media to twist our perception of reality is not recognised by the general public. Anyone with children will know how difficult it is for them to separate reality from the fiction that appears on the television screen. The contemporary parent is confronted with questions such as: 'Dad, are you as strong as Batman?' Behind these dreams is the manufacture of a false consciousness in which happiness and freedom from suffering are obtainable through the purchase of material goods and inevitably a life-style. This false consciousness pervades the entire spectrum of marketing which portrays others enjoying lives that are free from suffering or at least living happily ever after. This is not wrong in itself, yet in the context of such powerful media, and with little contradiction, many lose sight of what Buddhist call the first noble truth.

Organisations lack integrity when they present their products as being more than they really are. Yet in a society in which the dominant ideology is the false promise of escape from suffering, the supplying of egoist dreams is what the customers want. The success of Rupert Murdoch's press reflects this dilemma. On the one hand he shows integrity by his callous honesty about the wants of the news and magazine purchasing public. There is a certain sort of humility in acknowledging that a newspaper that leaves out the salacious and sordid does not sell. It is painful to acknowledge the shadow of public mores. It is a reflection of a social fascination with such shadow events as murder, rape, incest, scandal and corruption. On the other hand, deep integrity can avoid being cynical by seeking ways to work with such material so that there is progress. Without growth based on integrity the power of the press becomes a stagnant force, reinforcing delusion and corrupting society.

Yet the assumption that drives our current economic system is that the accumulation of wealth brings about cessation of suffering. This is a contradiction of the fourth noble truth – that freedom from suffering is cultivated by practicing the Eight-fold Path of the Middle Way.

The awareness of the possibilities for integrity in each market transaction needs to be carried to the collective level. Paul Hawken[69] notes that whilst markets are efficient at setting prices they are incapable of recognising external costs. Hawken[70] argues that markets could operate beneficially to humankind when they reflect real costs to the environment. Our very existence comes at a 'cost.' Gary Snyder[71] eloquently points out how we are part of a food web where beings live by eating other beings. 'Our bodies – or the energy they represent – are thus continually being passed around.' The issue is holistic, as it is the collective cost that counts. Human consumption has increased astronomically in the last two hundred years. Individual consumption in Western countries is currently over a hundred times of what it was two hundred years ago. This combined with the world increase in population means that humans have radically altered their position in this food web. We are consuming the rest!

The collective costs of modern commerce are not only environmental. Ever since the beginning of industrialisation the human costs of the mechanisation of work and the mass market economy have been the subject of many writers. One does not have to dig deep to find some variant of Malthusian economics concerning the role of commerce in helping third world countries. When political barriers to economic activities develop in these countries, firms are known to interfere with the political system, financing supportive regimes regardless of their human rights records.

The collective actions of commerce can not be separated from the societies in which they operate. That the purpose of our economic system is to maximise the accumulation of wealth is enshrined in legislation. Company and corporate directors have a legal duty in most countries to maximise the wealth of their shareholders. In most OECD countries, as Kenneth Galbraith[72] observed, even the major shareholders have very little direct role in the day-to-day operation of corporations. Rather, it is professional management who, in the role of agents of the shareholders, make the strategic decisions of the firm. There has been considerable debate as to in whose interests professional managers actually make decisions. Shareholders are often unaware of the full extent of the operations of the business and even when they are, few mechanisms exist to facilitate collective or democratic action. Institutions make investment decisions on behalf of their depositors, or insurance policy holders, of which these investors have no awareness. When we shop around for the best interest rate on our savings we may be providing capital to armament factories, abattoirs, feedlot farms and companies which support governments notorious for human rights abuses. Contrary to the popular image of shareholders, as being a monolithic bloc of like-minded people all holding similar values regarding what they want managers to do with their funds, they are highly heterogeneous. The imperative of optimisation of shareholders' wealth seems to be greatly abstracted from what the actual people who supply the money really want. A fascinating example of this was the outrage of ordinary Exxon shareholders when they found out about the causal role Exxon had played in the Exxon Valdez oil spill disaster.

The advent of the global economy has created a system that is almost beyond the control of nation-states. The history of international trade has been of no or little compassion for local suppliers of materials and labour forces that can not compete. There has developed an international business culture that has much in common with the colonial past that many large global corporations share.

Global corporations have found a new power in the global economy in their ability to play one national government off against another. This shift in power from the nation-state will take on a new significance for the middle-classes of previously 'developed' nations. The widening of the world's education base and the introduction of high-technology capital-intensive manufacturing will mean a global rationalisation of employment. Not since early industrial times have employers had the power to pick and choose labour. The increasing availability of low cost 'brain' workers means that this erosion of labour power is spreading to all occupation groups. Nations, especially small nations like Australia, are confronted with a potential capital exodus unless they can provide competitive packages in terms of infra-structure, tax advantages, stable and low wages, and an educated and 'trouble-free' workforce. As nations begin to compete with each other the resultant transfer of government expenditure to the commercial sector will lead to further disparities in wealth. Korten[73] describes how these forces have resulted in a deterioration of social relations in Sweden.

As the power of professional labour weakens, many Westerners will be shocked to find their quality of work life eroded by employers with expectations of increased performance. These changes are the echoes of a dark history of exploitation, in which Western imperialist powers scarred and humiliated the lives of millions of workers in under-developed countries around the world. Ironically, several generations later, they must compete with the now educated workforces of previously exploited nations whose hard earned industriousness stems from the deep psychological and social significance that material and economic success has as a path to freedom and security. The present work ethic in such countries casts a long shadow because economic success has a symbolic value, far beyond the material wealth that is generated. The result is work-obsessive cultures in which the heroes are the economically successful, with many of the attributes of Hermes.

These work-obsessive cultures are experiencing strong growth in the competitive world economy. Their success lies in a hard-working and educated workforce prepared to subordinate personal lives to work lives. In subordinating the personal to the corporate something important is lost. World-wide we are seeing relationships, health and other interests being sacrificed through working long hours in order to achieve economic success. Whilst the value of these attributes may be questioned from a holistic perspective they are certainly resulting in the desired goal – the seductive life of the gods. Perhaps the greatest barrier to Buddhist practice lies not in the long hours that support this life-style, but in the values that underpin the work culture of modern business organisations. Many of these values run counter to the Buddhist path. The model of who we are is based on a mixture of economic rationalism, scientific management assumptions and social Darwinism in which humans are portrayed as mechanistic, self-interested, opportunistic and competitive, attributes which characterise us as both distinct from nature and each other.

Strategic business decisions are those which could significantly impact on the long-term survival of the business. It is well understood that the fundamental assumptions about the world held by executives and other key stakeholders mediate a wide range of strategic decisions.[74] These assumptions, about the environment in which the firm operates, and ways in which the firm can be organised, ultimately guide the types of strategic decisions that are made. Recently research has been reflecting a shift to an interpretive perspective which highlights how managers, like other people, construct their view of the world. The implications of this are, as Weick[75] points out, that 'people invent organisations and their environments and these inventions reside in ideas that participants have superimposed on any stream of experience.' This process of construction is not a random or frivolous act, but is the result of one's lifetime cultural experience including the dominant ideas and explanations of reality prevailing in any society at one time.

Buddhism presents an alternative worldview, in which economic motivation as an end in itself is seen as delusory. In formulating and constructing strategic decisions from a Buddhist perspective managers can extend the ideas of integrity to the organisation as a whole. As Beebe notes: 'Of the qualities we seek in ourselves and in each other, surely integrity is among the most important.[76] If integrity drives our world-view and bleaches our values then strategic activities will slowly reflect this. Integrity may lead us collectively to a new social and economic order, it may even create revolution, but it does not, in itself, suggest a particular structure. Integrity like DNA is probably capable of forming many different structures depending on the environment. Integrity is not against making profit per se, but rather how one makes a profit and what one does with the earnings one makes. Buddhist-oriented managers can make competitively sustainable business decisions and may still act on the basis of integrity.

Acknowledging the real costs of what we are doing to others, including the environment, and being mindful of how any profit came to us, guards against ethical wrong doing. In seeking integrity, Buddhists can be realistic about the competitive realities of commerce yet still have a bias towards strategic alternatives that help others and reflect a view of interconnection. Integrity should be a value in itself. It may not make any difference in terms of corporate financial performance one way or the other, although casual observance suggests that the most common mistakes in commerce are due to greed. By maintaining a strategic poise of mindfulness and 'just integrity,' holding no assumptions and relinquishing all attachments, Buddhists in the market place may find the threefold path an advantage rather than an impediment. At times their practice is likely to run counter to the values of the rational economic world-view which currently dominates the commercial sector. Buddhists should be prepared to be flexible in how they continue their work of integrity and one way is to seek financial independence through simple and frugal living.

Conclusion

Buddhism has reached a turning point. The crossing of the great divide between East and West has begun in earnest. The potential significance of this event can be imagined if we reflect on how historically central religion has been to both civilizations. And although religion no longer is a dominant force in both worlds, this historically legacy is still deeply rooted in their psyches. Each time there has been an interchange in some aspect of cultural understanding such as technology, cuisine, the arts, or architecture there is a small wave of change that runs through each. The spiritual experience of enlightenment, the pearl of Buddhism, lies at the very heart of our being. What sort of wave would that make? At a time when both great cultures have experienced a decline in the value of spiritual pursuits, a new Buddhism is taking root. This Buddhism is not growing out of the old soil of dusty *sūtras* and ritual, but from the living experience and insight of acknowledged Western-born adepts who bring to it the treasures of a Western civilisation. The west offers a new freedom of thought and critical reflection to Buddhist scholars, and a new opportunity to redress errors of the past.

The encounter with the west will also bring new challenges. One is the integration of Buddhist practice and commerce. Commerce holds a central role in Western societies and is a primary means of survival. Even public service organisations are being organised on pseudo-commercial guidelines. The world of commerce is driven by a loose collection of assumptions about reality. These are, at base, the assumptions of egoism and sensual materialism, which are fundamentally different from the perspective of the Dharma. The view of Buddhism is that everything is essentially empty and that human development is the realisation of this. It is this emptiness that gives rise to interpenetration and oneness. The path of Buddhism is to realise the emptiness of ourself and our oneness with all beings. The way to this is not egotism or sensual materialism nor the opposite of it.

The complete attainment of the way is depicted in the final ox-herding picture: return to the market-place.

> Barechested, barefooted, he comes into the market place.
> Muddied and dust-covered, how broadly he grins!
> Without recourse to mystic powers,
> withered trees he swiftly brings to bloom.[77]

We can use this image as an archetype for the Buddhist practitioner in the world of commerce. The image of the barechested, barefooted master represents detachment, which is achieved through the Buddhist practices of mindfulness and meditation. This is not the simple detachment of one immersed in the spirit, separated from the concerns of the world, but the result of a deep awareness of our true ecology. Free of attachments and by being fully mindful we can be open to the thousands of decisions that we encounter at work and we can act on these with integrity. Yet we also need to develop a complementary lifestyle which reduces our exposure to manipulation and seduction, as well real financial attachments which may affect our integrity. We can do this through living simply, healthily and frugally. This also helps us meet our responsibilities to the long-term survival of life on the planet.

The image of being muddied and dust-covered suggests the converse of an 'untainted gem in the mud.'[78] This is the symbol of a life lived with integrity. Through the development of integrity we can negotiate each moment without losing sight of our true nature. In this way we can integrate our work with the Tao. We can follow our soul needs with wisdom and intuition, knowing that these can inform our life priorities with loving-kindness. Our integrity is the *bodhicitta* arising from our self-nature, which interpenetrates all beings. We can embody this in our work as a natural expression of the precepts, *samādhi* and *prajñā*.

The final line speaks to the wider impact of Buddhist practice. Almost unnoticed, and without doing anything special the returning sage has a healing effect. From the great depths of her integrity, through every action, the sage benefits others – for every action is an expression of his true nature. As more Buddhists join the commercial world and negotiate their work lives with integrity, changes will naturally emerge at the collective level. These cannot be prescribed. What will emerge from this new growth of Buddhism in the West hopefully will express itself with the grace and beauty of nature in the market place.

Notes

1 Buddhism is described mainly from a Mahāyāna perspective and hopefully extends beyond this.

2 D. C. Korten *When Corporations Rule the World* (San Francisco: Kumarian Press & Berret-Koehler Publishers, 1995).

3 The typical profile of early adopters is young, educated, affluent, and enthusiastic.

4 Rick Fields *How the Swans Came to the Lake* (Boston: Shambala, 1986) and Stephen Batchelor *The Awakening of the West: The Encounter of Buddhism and Western Culture* (Berkely: Parallax Press, 1994) have written informative accounts of this experience in the US.

5 Fields (1986).

6 Trillions of dollars are amounts of such great magnitude that it is difficult to comprehend them. We can get some insight into the real meaning of a trillion dollars if we ask ourselves the question of how long it will take to spend a million dollars if we spent a dollar every second? The answer is 11.5 days. If we extend this to a billion dollars and the answer is about 32 years. If we then ask how long it would take to spend a trillion dollars? Since a trillion is a thousand billion it would take us 32,000 years

7   Bernie Neville 'Seeing Through the Postmodern Organisation' *Temenos*, 2, 1995, pp. 49–55.
8   Public talk, Cotati Synagogue, California, 1995.
9   J. Macy *World as Lover, World as Self* (Berkeley, Ca.: Parallax Press, 1991).
10 N. Misra *Development of Buddhist Ethics* (New Dehli: Munshiram Manoharlal Publishers, 1984).
11 Macy (1991).
12 Ibid. p11.
13 W. Rahula *What the Buddha Taught* (London: Grove Press, 1959), p. 23.
14 R. Aitken *A Zen Wave: Basho's Haiku & Zen* (New York: Weatherhill, 1978), p. 58.
15 K. Kraft 'Meditation in Action: The Emergence of Engaged Buddhism' *Tricycle* Spring 1993, p. 43.
16 R. Aitken *The Mind of Clover: Essays in Zen Buddhist Ethics* (San Francisco: North Point Press, 1984).
17 T. Moore *Care of the soul: A guide for cultivating depth and sacredness in everyday life* (New York: Harper Collins, 1992), p. 181.
18 B. DeFoore and J. Renesch 'Spiritual Insolvency: Insufficient Soulfulness in the Workplace' in DeFoore and Renesch (eds) *Rediscovering the Soul of Business* (San Francisco: New Leaders Press, 1995).
19 J. Needleham *Money and the Meaning of Life* (New York: Currency Doubleday, 1994).
20 J. Daido Loori 'The Sacredness of Work' *in Mindfulness and Meaningful Work: Explorations in Right Livelihood* Claude Whitmyer (ed.) (Berkeley, Ca.: Parallax Press, 1995).
21 J. Kabot-Zinn *Wherever You Go There You Are: Mindfulness Meditation in Everyday Life* (New York: Hyperion Press, 1994), p. 8.
22 R. Strozzi Heckler *The Anatomy of Change: A way to move through life's transitions* (Berkeley, Ca.: North Atlantic Books, 1993).
23 Moore (1992).
24 Ibid. p. 186.
25 Needleham (1994).
26 Karl Marx 'Alienated Labor' in R. Schmitt and T. Moody (eds) *Alienation and Social Criticism: Key Concepts in Critical Theory* (New Jersey: Humanities Press, 1994), p. 24.
27 C. Titmus *The Green Buddha* (Denbury, Totnes: Insight Books, 1995).
28 F. Peavy 'Love of Work' *in Mindfulness and Meaningful Work: Explorations in Right Livelihood* Claude Whitmyer (ed.) (Berkeley, Ca.: Parallax Press, 1994), p. 68.
29 Thich Nhat Hanh 'The Art of Living' *in Mindfulness and Meaningful Work: Explorations in Right Livelihood* Claude Whitmyer (ed.) (Berkeley, Ca.: Parallax Press, 1995).
30 Ibid. p. 8.
31 Aitken (1984).
32 G. Bateson *Steps to an Ecology of Mind: A revolutionary approach to man's understanding of himself* (New York: Chandler Publishing House, 1972), p. 492.
33 Thich Nhat Hanh (1995:245).
34 Titmus (1995).
35 Macy (1991).
36 Kabat-Zinn (1990).
37 Ibid. p. 6.
38 Macy (1990: 24).
39 J. Tarrant 'Mestizo Buddhism' *Blind Donkey*, Vol.14 (1), 2–4, 1994; and Jack Kornfield *A Path with Heart,* (New York: Bantam Books,1993).
40 J. Tarrant 'Soul in Zen' *Mind Moon Circle*, Summer, 3–19, 1992.
41 J. Beebe *Integrity in Depth* (New York: Fromm International Publishing Corporation, 1995).

42 J. Gresser *Piloting Through Chaos* (Sausalito: Five Rings Press, 1995).

43 Tarrant (1992).

44 Moore (1992).

45 K. Yamada 'Gateless Gate: Newly Translated with Commentary' (Los Angeles: Center Publications, 1979), cited in R. Aitken *The Gateless Barrier: The Wu-Men Kuan (Mumonkan)* (San Francisco: North Point Press. 1990), p. 57.

46 Tarrant (1992: 18).

47 Tarrant (1995: 5).

48 R. Guenon 'Symbolism of the Cross' excerpted from *Symbolism of the Cross* (London: Luzac & Company, 1958) in *Parabola*, 18(3), pp. 80–82, 1993.

49 Robert Johnson, public talk, Sydney.

50 For a review see A. Pettigrew *The Awakening Giant Continuity and Change in ICI*, (Oxford: Basil Blackwell, 1983).

51 H. Aldrich *Organisations and Environments* (Englewood Cliffs, NJ: Prentice Hall, 1979).

52 M. Stein 'Organizational Life as Spiritual Practice' in Stein and Hollwitz (eds) *Psyche at Work* (Wilmette, Illinois: Chiron Publications, 1992).

53 Rahula (1959).

54 H. Hesse *Siddhartha* transl. by H. Rosner (London: Pan Books, 1973).

55 Gresser (1995).

56 J. Dominguez and V. Robin *Your Money or Your Life: Transforming your relationship with money and achieving financial independence* (New York: Penguin Books, 1992).

57 Ibid. p. xxvi.

58 Ibid. p. xix.

59 D.T. Suzuki *The Training of The Zen Buddhist Monk* (Berkeley: Wingbow Press, 1974).

60 Nyingma Organization (Collective work) *Ways of Work: Dynamic Action* (California: Dharma Publishing, 1987).

61 Personal correspondence with Judith Shapiro Jobs & Environment Campaign, Cambridge, MA.

62 Profit is, however, a particularly confusing concept mainly because it is relative, depending on the amount of money invested and the amount of risk involved. Many large corporations appear to make extremely large profits, yet when compared to the amount of money invested in the company, the profit per dollar invested may be less than if the money had been put in a bank. Furthermore, profitability varies over time and some firms may make high profits in boom times and low profits in recessions. Average profitability is therefore a better indicator of performance. Profit may appear higher or lower depending on the accounting conventions used, and it may also vary according to the amount invested in future profits. Risk is a further complication. For example, some firms, such as mineral exploration firms, operate in high-risk areas in which failure is common. The high profitability of surviving companies is related to the high chance of failure.

63 see Rahula (1959).

64 It could be argued a market transaction is a negotiated outcome.

65 Gresser (1995: 51).

66 R. Axelrod *The Evolution of Cooperation* (Penguin: London, 1984).

67 P. Lorange and J. Roos *Strategic Alliances: Formation, Implementation, and Evolution* (Oxford: Blackwell, 1992).

68 D. Bubna-Litic *Managing Cooperative Relationships: A Case Study* Unpublished Masters Dissertation, University of New South Wales, 1995.

69 P. Hawken *The Ecology of Commerce: How Business can Save the Planet* (London:Wieidenfeld and Nicolson, 1993).

70 Ibid. p. xi.

71 G. Snyder *A Place in Space: Ethics, Aesthetics and Watersheds.* (Washington: Counterpoint, 1995), p. 76.

72 K. Galbraith *The Industrial State* (New York: Signet, 1967).

73 Korten (1995).

74 see G. Johnson, *Strategic change and the management process* (London: Basil Blackwell, 1987).

75 E. Weick 'Enactment Processes in Organisations.' In B. Staw and G. Salancik, G. *New Directions in Organisational Behaviour* (Illinios: St Clair, 1977), p. 288.

76 Beebe, (1995: 5).

77 P. Kapleau *The Three Pillars of Zen: Teaching Practice and Enlightenment* (Tokyo: Beacon Press, 1965), p. 311.

78 Z. Shibayama *A Flower Does Not Talk: Zen Essays* (Tokyo: Charles E. Tuttle Company, 1972), p. 199.

Index

213